# The Big Con

David W. Maurer

# The Big

## The Story of the Confidence Man

Introduction by Luc Sante

Anchor Books
Doubleday
New York London Toronto Sydney Auckland

Affectionately Dedicated
to the Countess, the Emir, and the Egge

An Anchor Book
PUBLISHED BY DOUBLEDAY
a division of Random House, Inc.
1540 Broadway, New York, New York, 10036



*The Big Con* was originally published by the Bobbs-Merrill Company in 1940.

Library of Congress Cataloging-in-Publication Data

Maurer, David W.
The big con: the story of the confidence man / by David W. Maurer.
p. cm.
Originally published: Indianapolis: Bobbs-Merrill, [c1940].
1. Swindlers and swindling. I. Title.
HV6691.M3 1999
364.16′3—dc21 99-25494
CIP

ISBN 0-385-49538-2

Printed in the United States of America
First Anchor Books Edition: August 1999

1 2 3 4 5 6 7 8 9 10

# Contents

Luc Sante

# Introduction to the Anchor Edition

The book you are holding in your hands, now reprinted after a shamefully long hiatus, is, like its subjects, crowned with many hats. Its origins are in linguistics; it is nominally a work of criminology; it has blood ties to folklore; it falls within the scope of Americana; it serves up a parcel of social history; and of course it is a robust and spring-heeled piece of literature. Swindling is a literary subject that must go back to Egyptian and Mesopotamian antecedents, certainly to Reynard the Fox by way of the Elizabethan coney-catchers and the Spanish picaresque. In American culture it looms as one of the major themes, along with self-invention and going on the lam, which are not unrelated. Edgar Allan Poe put it conclusively:

> A crow thieves; a fox cheats; a weasel outwits; a man diddles. To diddle is his destiny. "Man was made to mourn," says the poet. But not so:—he was made to

diddle. This is his aim—his object—his *end.* And for this reason when a man's diddled we say he's *"done."*

*The Big Con* can also be considered a piece of art criticism, since it is not just any taxonomy of styles in diddling, but a refined appreciation of the high swindle, the confidence game in its Augustan Age.

David Maurer was a linguist, eventually professor emeritus of linguistics at the University of Louisville. He began his publishing career in 1930 with *Speech Peculiarities of the North American Fisherman* and not long after began his lifelong study of criminal and demimonde dialects. His other books include *Whiz Mob: A Correlation of the Technical Argot of Pickpockets with Their Behavior Pattern* (1955), *Narcotics and Narcotic Addiction* (1973), *The American Confidence Man* (a more scientific enlargement of the present book; 1974), *Kentucky Moonshine* (1974), and the posthumously published omnibus volume *Language of the Underworld* (1981). He was one of the editors of H. L. Mencken's *The American Language* in its single-volume format, and he contributed the entry on "Slang" to at least one edition of the *Encyclopaedia Britannica.* His correspondents included fellow language addicts such as S. J. Perelman, and an enormous number of denizens of the underworld, both behind bars and at large. When Prudence Crowther, editor of Perelman's letters, sought out his end of their exchange, she discovered that Maurer had requested in his will that his entire archive be destroyed upon his death, for fear of compromising his pen pals pursued by the law. Maurer, as this book will amply demonstrate, earned the intimate confidence of many vulnerable and close-mouthed miscreants, people who would not have opened up to journalists. The kind of fieldwork he engaged in, as the linguist Stuart Berg Flexner, a former student of Maurer's, pointed out, "takes a great deal of physical stamina and a strong personality, as well as mental ability." It didn't hurt that "Maurer is big, with large shoulders and strong arms and hands, a man who can help pull in a heavy fishing net in freezing weather or push a car out of a muddy backroad on the way to an illegal still." He was also, quite evidently, blessed with a considerable sense of humor.

Maurer studied the lingo of—among others—carnies, junkies, safe-crackers, forgers, pot smokers, faro-bank players, shell-game hustlers, race-track touts, pickpockets, moonshiners, prostitutes, and pimps, but his interest in the language of the confidence men was a case apart. More than any other of the dialects of the American underworld, it approached the comprehensiveness of French argot or Australian rhyming slang. It is one of the peculiarities of all American subcultural lingos that they focus solely on technical terms or other weighted topics—there are invariably words for sex, death, and money, but not for table, door, or window. Grifter slang is more complex by virtue of covering a more complex subject, with an enormous range of situations, nuances, and subtleties that find no equivalent in the language of circuses or dice games or heroin traffic. To study the lingo of the con is inevitably to study the con itself, since a term such as "cackle-bladder" or "shut-out" cannot be properly defined without giving a full account of its use, and such an account cannot be illustrated with stick figures. That is why this book stands alone in Maurer's oeuvre: Whereas it is possible to map out the generic behavior of pickpockets, tracing patterns and supplying copious examples without necessarily referring to individuals, confidence men are after all artists, laden with idiosyncrasies that distinguish their work. There are styles, schools, trends, evolutions, innovations, reactions, triumphs, failures. And it takes much more than cupidity and unscrupulousness to make a con artist. The best possess a combination of superior intelligence, broad general knowledge, acting ability, resourcefulness, physical vigor, and improvisational skills that would have propelled them to the top of any profession. The big con would be poorly served by entomology; it demands narrative.

Poe, in "Diddling," provides a list of necessary characteristics of the swindler: "minuteness, interest, perseverance, ingenuity, audacity, *nonchalance,* originality, impertinence, and *grin.*" They are items needed for the short con as well as the long or big. But while any practitioner of the big con can play the smack, the tat, or the wipe, the reverse does not obtain. The big con is the game of an elite; to Poe's list must be added ambition, endurance, rigor, concentration, organization, compartmentalization, persuasiveness, and ironclad self-confidence. If the short con is an anecdote, the long con is a novel. Essentially, a short con involves taking the pigeon for all the money he has on his person, while the big con sends him home to get more. What all confidence games have in common is that they employ the victim's greed as a lever. The most primitive—the gold brick, which is supposed to be literal, or the green goods, which is a machine alleged to crank out banknotes—operate on the same basic principle as the most elaborate rigs involving intercontinental travel, multiple furnished sets, and dozens of carefully rehearsed extras. In all of them the mark is induced to participate in an extralegal moneymaking scheme that requires an investment. The cruder mechanisms are simple bait-and-switch devices—the wipe, for example, in which a rustic or an immigrant is invited to pool his resources with the sharper and deposit the total as security against a lost-wallet rakeoff or something similar, continues to figure in the press at intervals to this very day. In the most sophisticated cons, however, the doe may ever after remain unaware that he has been bilked, merely registering the affair as a gambit that failed.

That last, Cheshire-cat item in Poe's list merits attention. Humor is never very far from the heart of the con. After all, garden-variety swindles from shortchanging to fortune-telling to patent-medicine manufacture are merely theft without a weapon. The con, however, which hoists the victim by his own petard, combines formal elegance, careful imitation of legitimate enterprise, and rough justice into what can only be called parody. The subgenre called the rag, for example, involving as it does a pretense of stock manipulation, attracts the sorts of birds who would be drawn to actual stock manipulation and skins them alone, thus producing a far lesser loss to society than the swindles engaged in by ostensibly respectable sorts. The big con can also be considered as a form of theater, very nearly a *Gesamtkunstwerk,* staged with minute naturalistic illusionism for an audience of one, who is moreover enlisted as part of the cast. The con game always has at least two principals, the roper and the inside man, whose roles are as archetypal as Punch and Judy, or Mr. Tambo and Mr. Bones in minstrelsy. They bounce the victim between them the way cops in a Mutt-and-Jeff torture team manipulate a suspect; it is a kind of three-man tango. Then there are two sorts of settings: available real-life items, such as restaurants and hotel rooms, which might verbally be given imaginary properties but are otherwise unaltered, and outfits completely rigged up, empty offices or storefronts made over into bookie joints, brokers' suites, or high-end gambling clubs. A scheme might require one or more of these, furnished down to carpets, ashtrays, and spittoons, with crowds of several dozen currently unemployed con men acting as shills, fronts, or mere bodies, at the center of it a manager who is both acting the part of a manager and actually managing the outfit. And such a production must be called into being on very short notice.

I'm referring to all these matters in the present tense,

but while there is undoubtedly some surviving form of the big con in operation, these days perhaps being staged on the Internet (aspects of the late savings-and-loan boondoggle had notably big-con-like appurtenances), the high and elegant style described by Maurer was already in eclipse by the time he wrote the book. Its decline, like its rise, was occasioned by changing technology. The reader will note, of course, that all dollar values quoted must be multiplied by at least ten to achieve their equivalent in current sums. Even so, the big con's Golden Age, which is usually agreed to have run from the turn of the century to the Depression, with its peak occurring roughly between 1914 and 1923, was a period of unprecedented prosperity for the American upper middle class. Provincial dentists and wholesale grocers, whose fathers had been blacksmiths or coopers, were making fortunes apparently without effort in a stock market that appeared to have permanently defeated the law of gravity. Often enough, such types were persuaded that their success was owed to their perspicacity, rather than to luck or general trends. And while a lack of material advantages is customarily cited as defeating moral strictures and preparing the ground for criminal activity, there is at least as much to be said for the exact opposite circumstance: Good fortune can lead to the sense that one stands above the common clutter, that one can't lose, that one's prosperity can't help but benefit the rest of society. Does any of this sound familiar from more recent times?

In that period, however, communication was slower and more haphazard, making possible the payoff, for example, which depends on an interval between the end of a horse race and the broadcasting of its results. And there were just fewer people in the world, so that business was more personal and intimate, and casual trust in others—especially within the apparent bounds of one's own class—was greater. It was, after all, a world in which it was actually possible to get in on the ground floor of something big just by striking up a conversation in a Pullman smoker. Some of those bilked by Limehouse Chappie or Yellow Kid Weil may have known others for whom an apparently equivalent setup actually led to a timely investment in Oldsmobile or Goodyear. And it was possible, at least in second-rank towns, to grease the entire municipal apparatus with only one or two convenient handoffs. By 1940, when *The Big Con* was originally published, the big con had already retreated into a kind of music-hall nostalgia. Before George Roy Hill's *The Sting* (1973), which was inspired by the present volume, the most memorable representation of the topic in a Hollywood film was probably in Preston Sturges's *The Lady Eve* (1941). Barbara Stanwyck plays an ingenue grifter traveling with her elderly relatives, all of whom are veteran confidence men; they are preserved in Edwardian amber. Stanwyck's character is a parody of a stock type, the good girl who hews to family tradition in the face of modernity. If you ever see a photograph of Yellow Kid Weil, you will note he could pass for one of her uncles.

*The Big Con* may be the only one of Maurer's books that can be read for purely literary value, but whether or not this is owed to a natural ability otherwise repressed in the interest of science, it flies along as if it had written itself. The language on display certainly must have had something to do with it—available vocabulary can lubricate a subject (or, alternatively, tie weights to its shoes and throw it into the river). But the jovial demeanor, linguistic invention, and casual hyperbole of the grift establish a natural rhythm that ties together accounts by retired con men, by police detectives, and by a linguist like Maurer all together into a common barstool chorus. And the slang is only part of it, although it's hard to see how anyone could resist the joy of typing a sentence such as: " 'It's a lot easier to just plug the roper and watch the mark light a rag,' he laughed." Maurer's informants can also sound a mythic note, straight from the frontier of Mike Fink: " 'At that time marks were so thick in Florida that you had to kick them out of your way.' " Of course the names themselves suggest an origin on the flatboats and in the lumber camps and along the railroad lines of an earlier America: The Square-Faced Kid, Slobbering Bob, The Hashhouse Kid, The High Ass Kid, The Indiana Wonder, Wildfire John, The Christ Kid. Throughout the narrative it is necessary to remind oneself that these various "kids" were distinguished-looking gentlemen in frock coats and homburgs and Vandyke beards. The Narrow-Gage Kid was so called because his "height was just the distance between the rails of a narrow-gage railway," the Yenshee Kid because he chewed gum opium. (Maurer is wrong about Yellow Kid Weil, however, who derived his moniker not from the fact that he had peddled cheap watches but, according to his autobiography, from his fondness for the comic strip of the same name by R. F. Outcault.)

These grifters do emerge from American tradition, combining in their persons aspects of both the Yankee peddler and the backwoods trickster. The genre, furthermore, had been given its epic nearly a century earlier in Herman Melville's famously "unreadable" novel *The Confidence Man: His Masquerade* (1857), apparently a parody of Plato's *Republic,* in which the con artist keeps reappearing in different guises—land agent, herb doctor, charity supplicant, snake-oil butcher, etc.—aboard a Mississippi steamer. He later appears aboard other boats in the works of Mark Twain, notably as The King and The Duke in *Huckleberry Finn,* and continues making episodic appearances, as deathless as the Comte de Saint-Germain, throughout the course of American letters up to the present day. That *The Big Con* is nominally a work of popular sociology should not prevent it from numbering among the landmarks of this serpentine traditional path. After all, a look around present-day American institutions should suffice to demonstrate that the character in question has now fully emerged from the underworld and entered the mainstream, where he may be far less colorful and imaginative, but no less on the grift.

# Introduction

This bit of journalism came into being in a rather curious fashion. It is really a by-product of linguistic research, in the course of which I have had to examine the backgrounds of many rackets. The impetus for it came from the half-humorous suggestion of a confidence man who was going through my files; the execution of it was made possible only by the co-operation of competent professionals.

The methods by which I collected my material were not in any way bizarre or unusual. I did not resort to false whiskers. I did not, like the author of a recent "exposé" of the arts of the professional gambler, feel it necessary to palm myself off as a detective. I did not try to join any mobs incognito. I simply talked to confidence men, who, little by little, supplied the necessary facts, facts which were not available in libraries or in police records, facts which could come only from the criminals themselves.

In the course of preparing the manuscript, it has

seemed advisable to suppress some material which might damage confidence men now operating and prominent individuals who have been victimized. Also, upon advice of attorney, I have omitted the names of some high police officials and politicians who act as fixers for criminals, and have attributed pseudonyms to others in order to avoid the repercussions which might result from linking ostensibly respectable citizens with the underworld. Often it has seemed better to generalize upon certain sensational material, retaining the essential facts but omitting or altering the specific circumstances. Some underworld folk and police officials who read this will observe that occasional episodes are here attributed to persons who did not actually figure in them, that, for very obvious reasons, the names of dead con men have sometimes been substituted for ones now operating; this has been done, not to reflect unfavorably upon anyone, but rather, in a few instances, to avoid embarrassing persons whom the exact truth might damage. To this extent it has seemed necessary to fictionize. But these changes are only superficial; they do not in any way vitiate the truth of the general principles which they illustrate.

This book is not intended as an exposé; it does not purport to reveal "forbidden" secrets of a dark and sinister underworld; it is not artificially colored or flavored. I have not attempted to appear as an apologist for the criminal. On the other hand, I have scrupulously refrained from passing any judgments with a moral bias. I have only attempted to tell, for the general reader, the story of American confidence men and confidence games, stripped of the romantic aura which commonly hovers over the literature of the modern big-time criminal.

# The Names Used in This Book

Most of the names and "monickers" for confidence men appearing in this book are genuine. However, in some cases it has been desirable to disguise the identity of certain men under synthetic underworld nicknames. When this has been done, the monicker has been so composed that underworld figures may, without too much difficulty, discern the true identity underneath. For instance, 102nd St. George is so called because his first name is George and his swindling establishment is located in the 200 block on W. 102nd St., New York City. The Hashhouse Kid conceals the identity of a very successful modern big-con man who was a waiter before he turned out on the rackets. The Clinic Kid has made a fortune swindling wealthy patients who visited a famous mid-western clinic. However, there are relatively few of these counterfeit names and the lay reader will probably not be conscious of them.

# 1

# A Word About Confidence Men

The *grift* has a gentle touch. It takes its toll from the verdant sucker by means of the skilled hand or the sharp wit. In this, it differs from all other forms of crime, and especially from the *heavy-rackets.* It never employs violence to separate the mark from his money. Of all the *grifters,* the confidence man is the aristocrat.

Although the confidence man is sometimes classed with professional thieves, pickpockets, and gamblers, he is really not a thief at all because he does no actual stealing. The trusting victim literally thrusts a fat bank roll into his hands. It is a point of pride with him that he does not have to steal.

Confidence men are not "crooks" in the ordinary sense of the word. They are suave, slick, and capable. Their depredations are very much on the genteel side. Because of their high intelligence, their solid organization, the widespread connivance of the law, and the fact that the victim must virtually admit criminal intentions himself if he wishes to prosecute, society has been neither willing nor able to avenge itself effectively. Relatively few good con men are ever brought to trial; of those who are tried, few are convicted; of those who are convicted, even fewer ever serve out their full sentences. Many successful operators have never a day in prison to pay for their merry and lucrative lives spent in fleecing willing marks on the big-con games.

A confidence man prospers only because of the fundamental dishonesty of his victim. First, he inspires a firm belief in his own integrity. Second, he brings into play powerful and well-nigh irresistible forces to excite the cupidity of the mark. Then he allows the victim to make large sums of money by means of dealings which are explained to him as being dishonest—and hence a "sure thing." As the lust for large and easy profits is fanned into a hot flame, the mark puts all his scruples behind him. He closes out his bank account, liquidates his property, borrows from his friends, embezzles from his employer or his clients. In the mad frenzy of cheating someone else, he is unaware of the fact that he is the real victim, carefully selected and fatted for the kill. Thus arises the trite but none the less sage maxim: "You can't cheat an honest man."

This fine old principle rules all confidence games, big and little, from a simple three-card monte or shell game in a shady corner of a country fair grounds to the intricate *pay-off* or *rag,* played against a *big store* replete with expensive props and manned by suave experts. The three-card-monte grifter takes a few dollars from a willing farmer here and there; the big-con men take thousands or hundreds of thousands from those who have it. But the principle is always the same.

This accounts for the fact that it has been found very difficult to prosecute confidence men successfully. At the same time it explains why so little of the true nature of confidence games is known to the public, for once a victim is fleeced he often proves to be a most reluctant and untruthful witness against the men who have taken his money. By the same token, confidence men are hardly criminals in the usual sense of the word, for they prosper through a superb knowledge of human nature; they are set apart from those who employ the machine-gun, the blackjack, or the acetylene torch. Their methods differ more in degree than in kind from those employed by more legitimate forms of business.

Modern con men use at present only three *big-con* games, and only two of these are now used extensively. In addition, there are scores of *short-con* games which seem to enjoy periodic bursts of activity, followed by alternate periods of obsolescence. Some of these short-con games, when played by big-time professionals who apply the principles of the big con to them, attain very respectable status as devices to separate the mark from his money.

The three big-con games, the *wire,* the *rag,* and the *pay-off,* have in some forty years of their existence taken a staggering toll from a gullible public. No one knows just how much the total is because many touches, especially large ones, never come to light; both con men and police officials agree that roughly ninety per cent of the victims never complain to the police. Some professionals estimate that these three games alone have produced more illicit profit for the operators and for the law than *all other forms of professional crime* (excepting violations of the prohibition law) over the same period of time. However that may be, it is very certain that they have been immensely profitable.

All confidence games, big and little, have certain similar underlying principles; all of them progress through certain fundamental stages to an inevitable conclusion; while these stages or steps may vary widely in detail from type to type of game, the principles upon which they are based remain the same and are immediately recognizable. In the big-con games the steps are these:

1. Locating and investigating a well-to-do victim. *(Putting the mark up.)*
2. Gaining the victim's confidence. *(Playing the con for him.)*
3. Steering him to meet the insideman. *(Roping the mark.)*
4. Permitting the insideman to show him how he can make a large amount of money dishonestly. *(Telling him the tale.)*
5. Allowing the victim to make a substantial profit. *(Giving him the convincer.)*
6. Determining exactly how much he will invest. *(Giving him the breakdown.)*
7. Sending him home for this amount of money. *(Putting him on the send.)*
8. Playing him against a *big store* and fleecing him. *(Taking off the touch.)*
9. Getting him out of the way as quietly as possible. *(Blowing him off.)*
10. Forestalling action by the law. *(Putting in the fix.)*

The big-con games did not spring full-fledged into existence. The principles on which they operate are as old as civilization. But their immediate evolution is closely knit with the invention and development of the *big store,* a fake gambling club or broker's office, in which the victim is swindled. And within the twentieth century they have, from the criminal's point of view, reached a very high state of perfection.

# 2

# The Big Store

## I

In the fall of 1867 the Union Pacific Railway reached Cheyenne, Wyoming, and that hurly-burly outpost became the spearhead of a frenzied effort which thrust its way relentlessly up the canyons, through the passes, and over the badlands ever toward the West. Its population increased many fold. It swelled until the frontier town became a teeming little city, sprawling on the plateau like a heavily muscled giant in a suit too small, threatening momentarily to burst every seam. Close-packed frame buildings lined the mud streets, ridiculous in their raw elegance, while around the outskirts clustered the shacks and tents of the myriads of adventurers who sought they knew not what in this new country. In the dust-swirled streets cattlemen, miners, laborers, engineers, land speculators, soldiers and gamblers surged in a tangle of men, horses and material; the gunman elbowed the itinerant evangelist and the Oriental jostled the American Indian. Over the odor of horses and men and raw whisky and wood smoke there hung a more elusive smell, one which emanated from the fevered blood of the men and tainted the air with an electric quality. It was the odor of an ancient lust, the lust for easy money.

Ben Marks understood all about easy money, for his business was sure-thing gambling. Ever since he had left his home in Council Bluffs, Iowa, he had roamed the country from the Mississippi on west. His youthful, stocky figure and red whiskers, bristling in friendly fashion, were a familiar sight on river steamboats, at land-openings, and on the streets of frontier towns. Suspended from his broad shoulders he carried a board upon which he played a most popular frontier gambling game which had come up from Mexico—three-card monte. It was a simple little game in which the players bet against the operator, whose deft manipulation of the cards and amusing spiel drew a crowd about him on the street. He threw three cards, face down, upon the board in plain view of the spectators, then invited them to pick out the queen, first for fun, then for money. They knew it was easy, for they could see the queen flash as he threw the cards. Then he offered to bet upon the ability of anyone to find the queen. One of his accomplices (a *shill*) bet a dollar and picked out the queen. The crowd grew interested. More and larger bets were taken; meanwhile, another accomplice had located a fat sucker and connived with him to examine the cards, surreptitiously bend the corner of the queen slightly, and beat the operator. When the bet had been run up high enough, the trick was tried, but Ben deftly removed the "ear" from the marked card and put it on another as he manipulated the cards. The player was dumfounded when the queen evaded him.

Ben ground away at this little grifting game, picking up bets of five and ten dollars, occasionally one as large as twenty-five. It made a living for him and his shills, but that was about all. He had too much competition on the streets of Cheyenne, where catering to the vices of lusty men had become one of the chief enterprises. The fat suckers paid little attention to a monte-player who plied his trade on the street.

Then Ben had an idea, an idea which was eventually to revolutionize the grift, an idea which was to become the backbone of all big-time confidence games. Why not set up a place of business of his own? Why not operate from a permanent base, let the players come to him? But how would he get trade? He would have to compete with numerous saloons where gambling was carried on amid other forms of red-blooded entertainment.

He turned the idea over in his mind for some time and finally opened, in a shack of a building, what he called The Dollar Store. In the windows he exhibited all kinds of colorful, useful, and even valuable merchandise—with all items priced at one dollar—and he soon had customers a-plenty. Inside there were several monte games going, replete with shills and "sticks" to keep the play going at a lively pace. Once a gullible customer was lured in by the bargains he saw displayed, Ben "switched" his interest from the sale to the three-card monte, which was being expertly played on barrelheads. The merchandise never changed hands. It remained always the same. But the customers were different, and each one left some cash in Ben Marks' money belt. Like most pioneers Ben did not realize the importance of his innovation.

Thus, in a very crude form, developed what we know today as the "big store"—the swanky gambling club or fake brokerage establishment in which the modern pay-off or rag is played. It became the device which enables competent modern operators to take, say, $75,000 from a victim and at the same time conceal from him the fact that he has been swindled. Although today there are several types of stores used, they all operate on the same principle and appear as legitimate places doing a large volume of business. So realistically are they manned and furnished that the victim does not suspect that everything about them—including the patronage—is fake. In short, the modern big store is a carefully set up and skillfully managed theater where the victim acts out an unwitting role in the most exciting of all underworld dramas. It is a triumph of the ingenuity of the criminal mind.

The use of a store against which to play the victims of a confidence game developed gradually. Previous to the very end of the nineteenth century there were no big-con games, although the country was overrun with what were then called "confidence games" but which are today known as *short-con* games. They were played on the street, on passenger trains, in saloons and gambling houses, on passenger ships, with fairs and circuses—in short, any place where short-con workers could find people with a little money. During the last quarter of the nineteenth century there were thousands upon thousands of these short-con workers plying the country; they liked to follow the boom-towns connected with mining and the land-openings on the westward-sweeping frontier, for there people had money and were speculation-bound. The feverish atmosphere west of the Mississippi River was a healthy one in which con games could flourish and grow. It was quite natural that the principle of the store should have been discovered in Cheyenne. But as yet the mobs were not organized, the fix did not extend beyond the occasional bribing of a sheriff or constable, and the grifters made a small income at best.

The idea of a store caught on among grifters and they began to organize, raise enough capital to open stores, and profit by Ben's simple invention. It spread over the West, then to the East, where it housed *green-goods* games and the *gold-brick*. Other forms of the short-con, largely some form of gambling games, copied the idea, and little Dollar Stores sprang up all over the United States—one of them, incidentally, in Chicago, growing into a great modern department store owing to the fact that the founder, who originally leased the building for a monte store, found that he could unload cheap and flashy merchandise at a dollar and make more money than he could at monte. But the idea of a store was well established and was to be forever afterward associated with confidence games. Ropers and steerers (long used by gambling dives) were adopted, which of course increased the volume of business tremendously, and eventually made the display of merchandise unnecessary.

Gamblers took up the idea, and the *mitt store* succeeded the Dollar Store. The mitt store masqueraded behind the front of a legitimate business—for instance a sample-room where cloth was sold wholesale, or, in the South and Southwest, under the guise of an institute where farmers were to be instructed in the control of the boll weevil or some other agricultural pest. Old Farmer Brown sometimes used exhibits of cotton bolls in various stages of destruction, together with bottle specimens of the weevil showing its development from egg to maturity. A lecture which compensated in color for what it lacked in scientific value was used as a stall for the farmers from the cotton states and served to lure unsuspecting farmers into his monte game. The steerer for a mitt store brought the victim in on some equally legitimate pretense, invited him to sit down until the proprietor arrived, and pushed him into a chair at a table. Other strangers were seated there, too. A newspaper covered the top of the table. Finally the newspaper was raised to reveal a little game of poker which was going on to pass the time. The mark was "mitted in" whether he wanted to be or not, was cold-decked on his own deal, and fleeced. This type of store, housing both mitt and monte games, flourished prosperously well into the first quarter of the twentieth century, and is still occasionally used by some short-con workers.

Before 1900 crime had not become a big business. Confidence men did not realize that they were destined to become the aristocrats of crime. They had not visualized a smoothly working machine, its political cogs well greased with bribe-money and its essential parts composed of slick, expert professionals. While even in those days the police were frequently paid off, the "fix" as we know it today was still to be developed. The operators of mitt and monte stores simply gave the cop on the beat an occasional five- or ten-dollar bill to avoid being run in, and their game went merrily on. The idea of inducing the victim to try to beat the store had not yet germinated; he was pitted against the players, and the store was only a center for the game, a device to facilitate getting the sucker to play. The grifters had to content themselves with the money which the sucker had on his person. If they took off scores of from twenty-five dollars to two hundred dollars, they were satisfied. Some of the better monte-mobs made fairly good money, but nothing to compare with the consistently large scores taken off by modern con mobs. On the whole, they lived a hand-to-mouth existence, with only the best ones making much of a profit over and above their operating expenses.

From 1880 to 1900 thousands of these small-con games appeared, played in crude stores which offered little more than shelter to the players. The fix was a simple transaction between con men and officers, with influential saloon-keepers or politicians occasionally acting as intermediaries in difficult cases. In New York and especially in Chicago, there were hordes of gamblers, thieves, grifters and short-con workers. These men naturally made saloons their headquarters, came to know the proprietors, and the machinery of the fix was established. From 1893 for some ten or fifteen years, the famous proprietor of two of these saloons was unquestionably the best fixer for all kinds of criminals, but especially for grifters; his saloons were a veritable rogues' gallery most of the time. He still wields a powerful influence in Chicago. There were, of course, many others, some of whom still operate prosperously. The situation in Chicago was typical of the rest of the country, except that both grifting and fixing went on on a larger scale there than anywhere else, with the possible exception of New York.

But bigger things were ahead. Times were to change, and the days of the small score were to end. After 1900, when the big-con games began to develop, the mitt and monte stores gradually dwindled away. With the advent of the big-time games, the simple fix for a small fee was no longer sufficient. Con games were to pass into the realm of big business.

Meanwhile, other types of short-con workers realized the advantage of playing their marks against a store, with ropers to bring the victims in and an insideman to do the playing. The sporting proclivities of the American public were exploited and thus arose the *fight store,* the *wrestle store,* and the *foot-race store,* immediate ancestors of the big store as we know it today. Ben Marks had not stopped with his original Dollar Store, but continued to contribute liberally to the development of confidence games, and had quite an extensive layout at Council Bluffs, Iowa, his home town, where marks taken off the railroad trains or roped at their homes were brought in for the slaughter. He built a large clubhouse where he had a faro-layout, dealt one-handed with great dexterity by his partner, Stebbins, who had lost an arm while blowing a safe. Also, Marks had a prize-ring where he played marks against the fight store, and a circular cinder track for the foot race.

These early stores are important because they not only developed the principles later applied to the big-con games, but also trained a host of both inside and outside workers who brought the benefit of their experience to the big con as soon as its principles were discovered. Ben Marks himself "turned out" many of the young men who were later to become notorious on the rag, the wire and the pay-off. He probably contributed more than any other one man to the development of the big store.

The fight-store swindle worked, briefly, like this. The mob consisted of one or more ropers, an insideman, a "doctor," two prize fighters and several minor assistants. The roper traveled about the countryside (usually not far from the store) and steered a mark in whenever he could find one. He posed as the disgruntled secretary to a millionaire sportsman, often a railroad executive, who ostensibly traveled about the country in a private car with a prize fighter, his own personal doctor, a trainer and staff of servants. In order to indulge his sporting instincts, he would match his fighter against any other fighters who could get any backing from their own communities, and of course he bet heavily on the fight. Many fight stores used some local bruisers for their fighters; Ben Marks engaged a famous ex-champion of the prize ring and his brother, who was also a prominent pugilist.

The roper told the victim that he had been selected for a part in this scheme because he could be depended upon. The roper's problem was this: he has been abused and neglected by his employer, who, he says, is really an old skinflint. He has decided to quit his service—but not without making some money for himself. The next fight, for which he is now making arrangements, will be held in Council Bluffs. He has contracted with his employer's fighter to "take a dive"—pretend to be knocked out—in the tenth round. His employer will bet heavily on his own fighter. He, the secretary, cannot personally bet against his employer; hence he needs someone with money who will bet heavily on the other fighter, then divide the proceeds. It is a sure thing.

If the mark was interested, the roper moved him into Council Bluffs to look the situation over. He met the millionaire executive (the insideman) and his fighter. Everyone talked of the coming fight, with the millionaire calling wildly for large bets, and waving money under the mark's nose. As soon as the victim was convinced that he could win heavily, he was sent home, procured his money, contributed something to the purse, and made his bet. Often he was made stakeholder as a mark of the high esteem in which he was held—although, without his knowledge, the satchel containing the money for all the bets was "switched" and he was given a duplicate full of paper, just in case he should yield to temptation.

The fight was held before a very limited audience, for in those days prize fighting was illegal in most states and prize fights were held clandestinely, like cock fights today. However, for the mark's benefit, the fighters put on quite a show. In the sixth round, something happened which no one had counted on. The millionaire's fighter delivered a terrific right over his opponent's heart and he fell to the ground, spurting blood from his mouth. All was confusion. The millionaire's "doctor" came forward with his stethoscope and pronounced the fighter dead. The mark was dazed; the millionaire collected the bet (which was already in his possession, since he had taken the satchel with the stakes in it) and everyone was in a hurry to get out of town before the local authorities got wind of the fight and arrested them for being accessories to manslaughter. Thus the mark blew himself off and the con man split the amount of his bet.

Buck Boatwright, who had this type of store in Joplin, Missouri, Webb City, Missouri, and Galena, Kansas, around 1900, made several innovations in the fight store and raised it to a high peak of perfection. Buck introduced the idea, later used in the pay-off, of furnishing the mark with part of the money for the play; his outsideman carried the millionaire's money in a satchel and, with the insideman (Buck) calling for bets, the outsideman would slip several hundred dollars out of the satchel and surreptitiously give them to the mark so that he could start by placing that much of a bet. This was important, for it "tightened up" the mark and made him ripe to be put on the send for more money. Buck also made some use of shills, who bet on the millionaire's fighter with money which Buck furnished; the mark was thus impressed with the amount of money he would win when the fight was over, and would raise his own bet as high as possible—another principle which was later used in the pay-off. Boatwright placed all this money in a small safe which stood against the wall and the mark was impressed with the sheaves of greenbacks he saw being stored therein—not knowing, of course, that the safe had a door in the back from which the money was removed by an assistant in the next room who handed it to another shill to bet. This device was later to become one of the strongest elements in the modern big store.

Wrestle stores and foot-race stores worked on the same general principle as the fight store, with foot racers or wrestlers taking the place of the prize fighters. The stores were quite crude at first and $5,000 was regarded as a "banner score." However, technique rapidly improved and stores spread over the country, prominent ones, in addition to those operated by Ben Marks and Buck Boatwright, doing quite a business and breaking the ground for the big-time games to come. One of the biggest of these early stores was opened in Hot Springs, Arkansas, in 1902, by Eddie Spears and George Ryan, who did their own fixing. Most of their scores were taken on the fight or foot-race racket. A short time later this store came to grief. At about the same time (1902) Byron Haynes of Colorado Springs opened up a fight and foot-race store which operated for some time. George Ryan also roped for this store, and it fell to his lot to rope the first really lucrative mark ever taken into a fight store. The score was $50,000 and caused a sensation in the underworld. The mark beefed, but the fix was secure and there were no serious repercussions. In Springfield, Illinois, the Keystone Kid operated fight, wrestle, and foot-race stores. In Scranton, Pa., the Narrow Gage Kid and Pretty Billy, both from Chicago, opened a fight store and did their own fixing. It enjoyed its greatest prosperity from 1906 to 1908. Later the Narrow Gage Kid opened his own fight store in Philadelphia with Tim O'Leary doing his fixing for him. In 1911, Gad Bryan and his partner, Jim O'Hara, later owners of the Bowie Race Track, opened up a fight store in the old Junction House in Baltimore. They did their own fixing.

The store for the early con games was a crude arrangement. Usually it consisted only of some place (often a saloon or a room off a saloon) in which to play the mark, and a private ring in which the "fights" took place. The mark was taken on the strength of the "con" which the roper "threw into him" and on the sight of the bag full of money which he had seen the millionaire bet on his fighter. Since he wanted to trim the millionaire rather than the store, as he does in the present-day big-con games, little attempt was made to build up the atmosphere of the store; in this respect the fight store remained similar to the older mitt and monte stores.

The fight store and its prototypes flourished prosperously for about fifteen years, then waned in popularity in favor of the modern big-con games which had meanwhile been developed. But the fight game was really a big-con game in principle. It offered the victim an opportunity to make money by swindling someone else; it displayed large sums of money to arouse his cupidity; it employed shills to stimulate his gambling instincts; it had an excellent device for fleecing him and sending him on his way; and the scores were phenomenally large for that time. Confidence men discovered that, as in modern big-con games, the fix was frequently too delicate to be handled by a saloon keeper and consequently was negotiated directly by the proprietor of the fight store. But the games lacked subtlety. The proposition it offered to the sucker was too bare-faced a swindle. The store was not mobile like the modern big stores; it could not be knocked down and concealed between plays. And when prize fights became legal, the appeal to the average sucker decreased. By 1915 the game had practically disappeared and the big-con games had replaced it. But the principle was sound and even today an occasional touch is taken off with it.

## 2

There were no clean breaks between the short-con games and the fight store, and in turn between the fight game and the modern big-con games, but rather they overlapped one another, with the fight stores constituting an intermediary stage between the short-con and the big-con games. Let us return briefly to the turn of the century for the origins of the present-day confidence games, of which there are three: the wire, the rag and the pay-off.

The wire, the first of the big-con games, was invented just prior to 1900. It was a racing swindle in which the con men convinced the victim that with the connivance of a corrupt Western Union official they could delay the race results long enough for him to place a bet after the race had been run, but before the bookmakers received the results. For this game two fake set-ups were used. The first was a Western Union office, complete with operators, telegraph instruments, clerks and a "manager"; some mobs economized by sneaking in and using real Western Union offices until the company put a stop to it. The second, where the actual play took place, was a horse-poolroom with all the paraphernalia which would naturally be used in such a place—a ticker or telegraph instrument, tables and chairs, a large odds-board on which results were chalked, a cigar counter, a bookmaker, etc., and a staff of shills who won and lost large sums of cash to stimulate the victim's desire for easy money.

The pay-off, another form of racing swindle, followed in 1906. In this swindle the victim is permitted to share in the illicit profits presumably taken by operators who are fleecing gambling clubs by means of fixed races. The victim first bets with money furnished by the con men, is then sent home for a large sum of money, and is fleeced. In the pay-off, the store is either a horse-poolroom as in the wire or, usually, a more luxurious club, elaborately furnished with impressive appointments. Of course, a large number of telephones, wired so that they can be rung at will from a concealed switch, are always a part of the set-up. The ever-present blackboard is there, too, with a board-marker who wears headphones which are supposed to be wired directly to the "track service" which all bookmakers get. These phones are sometimes attached to a loop which slides on a wire overhead, so that the marker can move rapidly about, at the same time continuing to receive the race results. The atmosphere created is one of reckless plunging and betting, and the store makes a most effective stage upon which to enact the play.

The rag developed shortly after the invention of the pay-off, when con men found that the principle of this game could be applied to stocks and convinced the victim that the insideman of the mob was the confidential agent of a powerful Wall Street syndicate which was breaking the small branch exchanges and bucket shops by manipulating the stock prices on the New York Exchange. Their agent buys or sells according to their instructions and of course has a sure thing. As in the pay-off, the initial investments for the victim are made with money furnished by the operators, then he is "put on the send" for a large amount, and fleeced. For the rag the store depicts a broker's office complete with tickers, phone service, brokers, clerks and customers. The same board which did duty for the races is often turned over to reveal a set-up for recording stock prices. The board-marker performs in an identical manner, except that he chalks up changes in stock prices instead of race results. Charley Gondorff, at the height of the rag swindle in New York City, made use of a legitimate broker's office on the second floor of a prominent mid-town hotel after hours for his big store. Most mobs, however, set up their own brokerage establishments.

Although today the best con men prefer to use a store, occasionally, under certain pressing circumstances, they play the mark without one. This is called "playing a man against the wall." The mark, who never sees a store, is kept in a hotel room while the con men bring him his winnings from the investments they claim to have made for him in the gambling club or brokerage. Naturally, this form of the swindle is hardly as effective as exposing the mark to the suggestive influences and the impressive demonstration of the store. But many a mark has been swindled that way. For instance, Frank Norfleet, a Texas rancher, was swindled twice in rapid succession for a total of $45,000 and never saw anything but the exterior of the Fort Worth Cotton Exchange after dark and the lobby of a legitimate broker's office in the Dallas Cotton Exchange Building where the con men claimed they were dealing.

When the big-con games came in, out went the more primitive stores which sufficed for the mitt, monte and fight games, the bare rooms sparsely furnished with a few chairs and a table. The store was now a much more pretentious institution where men high in the social and financial world could be played for scores which ran into the hundreds of thousands of dollars, a prosperous establishment which was well calculated to arouse the larceny in the soul of the mark once he saw it in action. The roper no longer connived with the mark to swindle the insideman, but all three conspired to beat the store. The most effective swindling device which man has ever invented was now in the hands of the confidence men.

But a big store will never beat a mark; it will not take off a score by itself. It is effective only when it is manned by good professionals, and when the props and personnel are used most strategically. Little by little, con men discovered which parts they could fill best; some showed special talents which they developed and perfected to a truly remarkable degree. Division of labor increased and, in direct proportion, specialization became essential. The post of manager developed and some managers, like Willie Loftus (the Sleepy Kid) became real experts in stagecraft and direction. The shills were no longer mere local boys who got a dollar or two for putting up fake bets on a prize fight; they were skilled professionals, good actors and competent con men in their own right, the backbone of any successful store. The size of the touches increased until most good con men have, at one time or another, helped to take off at least one that ran into six figures. Thus the crude and unpretentious store originated by Ben Marks grew to assume a great importance; it became the big store of modern times, owned and financed by the insideman, set up and operated by a manager under the insideman's direction, protected by powerful politicians, and supplied with victims by a corps of expert ropers who scoured the country for wealthy men who liked the "best of it."

While many grifters before the advent of the big-con games had been actors of a sort and certain grifting teams had learned to complement one another's little acts in order to obtain the desired reactions from the victim, there was no organization, little division of labor, and much lost motion. The invention of the big store reduced all big-con games to a broadly conventionalized pattern—leaving ample room for individual variations from the pattern to take care of individual idiosyncrasies among marks and to give grifters an opportunity to develop individual techniques—while at the same time it provided a standardized background against which certain methods, perfected by trial and error, were known to be successful. Specialization made for maximum efficiency; histrionic abilities were cultivated with the support of costume, stage setting, and rehearsal; the efforts of all participants were synchronized with the result that the size of scores increased precipitously and losses were reduced to an absolute minimum. In other words, con men, following trends current in the legitimate world, have employed techniques very similar to those used by big business in order to make mass production effective.

By 1898 the wire had started in New York. Christ Tracy, a fine insideman, opened up the first of the big stores there in that year. His phenomenal success soon became known; the big store was "dynamite." By 1900 Charley Gondorff, John Henry Strosnider, 102nd St. George, Limehouse Chappie and Larry the Lug had all come to the big city and set up stores of their own, each with its own manager, ropers, shills, etc. These men were the best in their profession, destined to remain in business for many years and to take off a high proportion of large scores. A host of fly-by-night places came and went, but few of them ever enjoyed either the prestige or the success that these insidemen brought to their stores. The pay-off and the rag followed rapidly and both are still played there.

Chicago, long a center for short-con activities and ridden with short-con men, gamblers, fight-store men and thieves, swung over to the big con very easily. In 1902 Jim the Rooter opened the first wire store in that city. He was followed by Ora Cornell in the same year. Limehouse Chappie moved his store from New York in 1910 or thereabouts and Barney the Patch, who had John Henry Strosnider doing the playing for him, opened a successful store at the same time. The Yellow Kid Weil also began operations at about this time. These men played the inside for literally hundreds of good ropers who brought well-to-do farmers, merchants and bankers into Chicago. When the pay-off developed, these men all adopted the new game and left the wire for any second-raters who cared for it.

When the pay-off was invented in 1906, the first store for that game appeared in the same year in Seattle, Washington. It was owned and operated by Hazel, Abbot and MacSherry, the last-named later becoming a famous insideman. The second store, manned by the same crew, opened a year later in Oakland, California. This was followed by a store operated by Kent Marshall in San Francisco where Golden Gate Mike handled the fix, which was now becoming a problem. The next store appeared in Spokane, Washington, the next in Salt Lake City. By this time the news of the strength of the pay-off had spread and stores were mushrooming all over the country.

At first, as was natural, New York and Chicago were the centers for the most lucrative big-con activities. They were railroad centers which made the victims readily available, the machinery for the fix was already set up, and the type of high life which con men love was right at hand. However, as the politicians demanded increasingly large payments, as the police grew ever more avaricious in their shakedown tactics, and the fix became not only more expensive but also more complicated and less reliable, many con men of the better class chose to find small cities which could be easily "righted up"; here they located and, avoiding the competition of the bigger stores, operated with much greater profit and security. Furthermore, this movement away from the large cities was hastened by the fact that both New York and Chicago had the name of harboring swindlers and con men of all kinds. It was much better psychology to take the victim to a smaller city for the trimming. Hence many of the best stores scattered out over the country and in towns like Rochester, Minnesota, and Amsterdam, New York, some of the very best professionals were to be found.

At one time or another during the past thirty years, big stores were established in most of the cities of the United States, but these were ephemeral. The fix went bad, con men found better pickings elsewhere, or the surrounding districts ceased to yield a supply of victims. Gradually certain cities became well known because of the success of the stores located there. In these cities con men gathered for both social and business reasons; the fix was solidly established; every facility was available for trimming a mark.

These cities, known as "right towns," are indelibly identified with the big store because at one time or another since 1900 the best big stores have prospered there and the finest ropers brought their victims there to be trimmed. If we arrange the more important ones in the form of a chart we can see, in a general way, both the chronological development and the geographical spread of the big store.

| *City* | *Type of Store* | *Proprietor or Insideman* | *Approximate Date Established* |
|---|---|---|---|
| New York City | wire store | Christ Tracy | 1898 |
| | wire store | Larry the Lug | 1900 |
| | wire store | Charley Gondorff | 1900 |
| | wire store | John Henry Strosnider | 1903 |
| | wire store | 102nd St. George | 1904 |
| | wire store | Limehouse Chappie | 1904 |

(Later these became pay-off and rag stores.)

| *City* | *Type of Store* | *Proprietor or Insideman* | *Approximate Date Established* |
|---|---|---|---|
| Council Bluffs, Iowa | fight and foot-race store | Ben Marks | 1900 |
| Denver, Colorado | short-con stores pay-off and rag store | Lou Blonger: Kid Duff Elmer Mead (The Christ Kid) | 1900–1923 |
| Chicago | wire store | Jimmy the Rooter | 1902 |
| | wire store | Ora Cornell | 1902 |
| | wire store | Limehouse Chappie | 1907 |
| | wire store | Barney the Patch John H. Strosnider | 1911 |
| | rag and pay-off | Yellow Kid Weil | 1910 |
| Joplin, Missouri | fight and foot-race store | Buck Boatwright | 1901 |
| Galena, Kansas | fight and foot-race store | Buck Boatwright | 1901 |
| Webb City, Missouri | fight and foot-race store | Buck Boatwright | 1901 |
| New Orleans, Louisiana | wire, pay-off and rag store | Crawfish Bob | 1902 |
| Colorado Springs, Colorado | fight and foot-race store | Byron Haynes | 1902 |
| Hot Springs, Arkansas | fight store | Eddie Spears | 1902 |
| Springfield, Illinois | fight store | George Ryan The Keystone Kid | 1904 |
| Scranton, Pennsylvania | fight and wrestle store | The Narrow Gage Kid Bill Keeley | 1906 |
| Philadelphia, Pennsylvania | wire stores | Limehouse Chappie 102nd St. George | 1908 |
| Baltimore, Maryland | fight store | Jim O'Hara Gad Bryan | 1908–1913 |

| *City* | *Type of Store* | *Proprietor or Insideman* | *Approximate Date Established* |
|---|---|---|---|
| | | The Narrow Gage Kid | 1914 |
| Miami, Florida | pay-off stores | Frank MacSherry | 1910 |
| | | The Boone Kid | |
| | | Gad Bryan | |
| | | Claude King | |
| | | Doc Sterling | |
| | | Barney the Patch | |
| | | Big Alabama Kid | |
| | | Limehouse Chappie | |
| Minneapolis, Minnesota | wire, pay-off and rag store | The Twin City Kid | 1910 |
| Excelsior Springs, Oklahoma | fight store then pay-off | Conk Jones | 1910 |
| Quebec, Canada | pay-off store | Eddie Mines | 1911 |
| | | Claude King | |
| Montreal, Canada | pay-off store | Eddie Mines | 1911 |
| | | Limehouse Chappie | |
| | | John Henry Strosnider | |
| | | Wildfire John | |
| Savannah, Georgia | wire, pay-off and rag store | Big Alabama Kid | 1911 |
| Omaha, Nebraska | pay-off store | Tom Denison | 1911 |
| | | Omaha Blackie | |
| Kansas City, Kansas | wire, pay-off and rag store | Jack Porter | 1911 |
| | | Danny Shay | |
| Buffalo, New York | wire store | Niagara George | 1912 |
| | | Kid Duff | 1915 |
| | | The Postal Kid | |
| | wire store | Limehouse Chappie | 1919 |
| Atlanta, Georgia | wire, pay-off and rag stores | Big Alabama Kid | 1913 |
| | | Claude King | |
| | | Clyde Smith | |
| Louisville, Kentucky | wire, pay-off and rag store | A police official | 1914–1917 |

| *City* | *Type of Store* | *Proprietor or Insideman* | *Approximate Date Established* |
|---|---|---|---|
| Rochester, Minnesota | wire, pay-off and rag store | The Clinic Kid | 1915 |
| Memphis, Tennessee | pay-off store | Mike Haggarty | 1915 |
| Amsterdam, New York | wire, pay-off and rag store | Charley Gondorff | 1918 |
| Troy, New York | wire, pay-off and rag store | Bruce Upshaw<br>The Postal Kid | 1918 |
| Detroit, Michigan | pay-off and rag store | Detroit Paul | 1919 |
| Mt. Clemens, Michigan | pay-off store | Curley Carter | 1920 |
| Palm Beach, Florida | pay-off and rag store | Barney the Patch | 1920 |
| Atlantic City, New Jersey | wire, pay-off and rag stores | Charley Gondorff<br>Barney the Patch | 1920<br>1922 |
| Reno, Nevada | pay-off and rag store | William Graham | 1927 |
| Toledo, Ohio | pay-off and rag store | Nibs Callahan:<br>Eddie Mines<br>Little Bert<br>J. J. (Mickey) Shea | 1919 |
| Havana, Cuba | pay-off store | Frank MacSherry and many others | |

The advent of the big store brought about two major changes in confidence games. First, the rather shaky fixing machinery of the old days had to be discarded or bolstered up to cushion the heavy repercussions caused by separating important persons from large amounts of money. The friendly saloon-keeper no longer sufficed. The fix had to be pushed into high places. The chief of detectives, the chief of police or the sheriff in each locality were the logical persons to delay or prevent prosecution of the con men. They were bought by the dozens. These men, in turn, had to have the protection of prominent party politicians and the cooperation of police judges, prosecutors, district judges, and even, in some cases, federal judges and state senators. Modern con men must be able to buy officers, judges and juries; they do it so successfully that many a top-notcher has never served a prison sentence.

Second, the size of the touches (the gross amount taken from the victim) has increased beyond the fondest dreams of old-timers. Exact information on the size of touches is exceedingly difficult to obtain, for neither the con man nor the victim likes to discuss them; when they do, their testimony in any given case may differ. The reason for this is that either the insideman has cheated his partners and wishes to conceal the exact size of the score, or that the victim has some reason of his own for raising or lowering the size of the score if the case becomes public. And only a very small proportion of the touches taken off ever come to light. The really big ones come from wealthy and prominent persons who cannot afford to admit that they have been swindled on a con game. Collection of reliable data is rendered more difficult by the fact that con men do not discuss the size of touches readily, even among themselves; it is a matter of etiquette that one is not asked directly about the size of a touch he is known to have taken off. But news leaks out and travels fast; the essence of the gossip which circulates in the underworld is often a fairly accurate index to the facts in any particular case.

Before 1900 the scores were universally small. Touches in monte and mitt stores were considered good if they went as high as $500. The tip might bring as much as $1,500 or $2,000 but was more often played for less. The *spud* and the gold-brick games might bring scores of $1,500. *Wire-tapping* was played for whatever the operators could wangle from the victim and the score usually came in installments. Scores of $5,000 from the fight and foot-race stores were considered highly satisfactory. Grifters worked feverishly for what would look like pin money to modern big-con men.

With the introduction of the big store for the wire, Christ Tracy took off the first known big score—$50,000 taken from a Broadway music-store owner. In 1902, George Ryan matched this score in the foot-race store, which was on its way out while the wire was in its infancy. Once the principle of the wire was established and con men learned that big scores could be taken off, they became common. Most of the good ones ran from $50,000 to $100,000, with one as high as $200,000 appearing occasionally.

The World War brought a crop of millionaires and submillionaires whose purses were swelled out of all proportion to their knowledge of investments. As often as not these men had made their money slightly on the shady side and to them the rag and the pay-off appeared as very logical methods of taking profit. There was a boom in the big-con games which kept con men working day and night to take care of the rush. "The stores were kept busy all the time," says one con man. "You had a hard time getting a mark played for. The joint wanted to know how much your egg would blow. If it was ten grand, the insideman would say, 'Are you daffy, coming in here with a measly ten grand?' "

The scores, known during the 1920's as "war babies," increased rapidly not only in number but in size. Representative of this class were the $350,000 which Glouster Jack took from an Australian in Cuba; the $200,000 which Plunk Drucker took from a Cleveland mark whom he fleeced in Buffalo; the $250,000 which the Indiana Wonder took from a wealthy Pittsburgher; the $375,000 which Big W——— and Charley Gondorff took from a New Britain banker; the $375,000 taken by the Hash-house Kid from a visiting Englishman in Montreal; the $245,000 taken by Louis Mushnick from a British sugar merchant in Cuba. And there were an infinite number of smaller ones—up to $50,000 or $100,000—which were simply lost in the shuffle. Stores in the centers for con games like New York and Miami were, in those boom years, running full blast, with ropers literally waiting their turns to play their marks against the store. Ten thousand dollars became the minimum amount—and still is—for which top-notch professionals would play a victim.

Some con men think that the $375,000 scores taken off by the Hashhouse Kid and Gondorff are the largest; certainly they are the largest which are generally recognized. Rumors of larger ones float about, but they cannot be verified, even though there may well be some basis for them in fact. Typical of these is the gigantic score rumored to have been taken off by the Big Alabama Kid shortly after the close of the War. Estimates of its size run from $1,000,000 to $2,800,000. The roper is supposed to have been a novice who was never paid in full for his share of the score. Whether or not this tale is true, it is certain that many large scores must lie buried in the memories of three men only—the roper, the insideman and the victim. And con men are not always either modest or truthful in estimating the size of the scores they have taken off.

The tendency among con men to exaggerate the size or number of their touches is the source of much good-humored ribbing. A tale is told about Jack Jewett from Texas and the Umbrella Kid from New York, partners for many years. Jack liked to draw the long bow when he told about the touches he and the Kid took off. If they took off $10,000, Jack made it $50,000 when he told the tale. One night, so it is said, the two were invited to a party given by some big-con friends. So the Kid lectured Jack in advance. "Jack," he said, "when you tell about scores tonight, be careful. And if you make them too strong, I'll give you the office by coughing. Then you'll know you're getting them too high and can cut them down."

"O.K.," said Jack. "I'll try to be reasonable." The party was going along fine and talk shifted to big touches that had come off recently. The boys knew Jack's failing and played on it by solemnly telling of tremendous scores. Finally Jack could restrain himself no longer.

"The other day," he said, "I was walking down the street and cut into a mark. He was a soft one, so right there I played the pay-off against the wall for him and beat him out of $80,000." The Kid coughed pointedly. "Excuse me," said Jewett, "it wasn't $80,000. It was $75,000." The Kid coughed again. "Maybe, now that I think of it, it was only $70,000," said Jack. The Kid coughed desperately. Jack turned to him in annoyance and blurted out, "Kid, I'll not take another grand off that touch if you cough till doomsday!"

It is just as difficult to secure reliable information on the number of touches any mob takes off as it is to get the facts on the size of any score. However, it is the consensus of opinion among con men that any roper who gets from two to four touches a year is doing quite well. If he should get as many as eight, he is very lucky. And many ropers are fortunate if they get one, while a few others go through an entire lifetime with only one touch—their first one—to entitle them to a place in the big-con rackets. Often a tendency to fictionalize regarding the number or size of touches is the roper's natural method of trying to bolster up his self-confidence and maintain his status in his profession. On the other hand, a really successful roper has no occasion to lie about his exploits. It is an established fact that one week in February, 1922, Jackie French brought into the Florida store the following marks and beat them:*

* These facts were verified by Postal Inspector Graham, the nemesis of modern con men, who supplied them to District Attorney Philip Van Cise during the Den-

| | |
|---|---|
| P. R. Nicholson from Dillonville, Ohio | $110,000 |
| George Pohling, a Philadelphia brewer | $200,000 |
| John G. Scott, a Britisher | $25,000 |
| Albert Seurin, from Cleveland, Ohio | $13,000 |

(This mark was tied up, but did not complete the play.)

As the war-boom died away, the big scores became less frequent. During the depression years a touch of $25,000 was considered a very respectable one and now we occasionally hear of one for $75,000 or $100,000; another war-boom may supply another crop of "war babies." But one suspects that the day of the big scores taken off in quantity is temporarily over in the United States. With the increasing power and effectiveness of the Federal Government since 1930, the con men have had a hard time of it. Whenever a victim's check passes through the mails the con men are laid open to possible prosecution and almost inevitable conviction, for once the government prepares a case thoroughly enough to bring it to trial, the fix is of little avail and it is almost a foregone conclusion that a federal jury will convict.

In view of these facts, many of the best operators are moving their stores to Cuba, Mexico, South America, Canada and Europe, where wealthy Americans traveling or living abroad supply a perennial crop of victims, not to mention the equally susceptible natives. Well-established stores now operating in Rome, Berlin, Brussels, London, Havana and the Argentine do a large volume of business which is increasingly international in character. However, the domestic stores still operate very profitably and show no tendency to disappear under the sporadic enforcement drives which are directed at them.

---

ver investigation. They are reprinted here by special permission of Colonel Van Cise.

# 3

# The Big-Con Games

## I
## The Wire*

Of the three modern big-con games, the rag, the wire and the pay-off, the wire was invented first. Without it, the rag and the pay-off probably could not have developed. By 1910 it had spread all over the country and scores of $200,000 and higher were being talked of. While it has now waned in popularity in favor of the rag and the pay-off, it is still played with very good success.

The name for the game is an abbreviated form of wire-tapping, from which the idea for the swindle was developed. During the late 1880's and the 1890's there were certain unemployed telegraph operators who traveled over the country looking for some gullible race-fan who could be induced to lay out rather large sums of money

* All names used in the explanation of this game are fictitious.

for the expensive equipment which they represented as being necessary to tap telegraph wires and obtain advance information on the results of a race, hold up these results until the race-fan had time to place a bet with a bookmaker, then advance the post-time and forward the results—with very happy consequences for the fan who had meanwhile bet on the winner. No doubt some of them did do what they claimed to be able to do, in which case they shared the profits with the fortunate fan. But many more acted only in the rather crude capacity of tout. They studied the form-sheets to find likely-looking horses, convinced the fan that they *could* tap the wires, and hoped for the best. If the horse won, of course they shared in the profit; but most of them depended for their profit upon the exorbitant fees which they obtained from the fan in advance in order to buy tools and equipment necessary for wire-tapping. This was known as "expensing" and became a small-time racket. Because it lacked the professional touch, it might well have gone the way of many similar rackets.

However, at this time there were swarms of professional grifters who worked the country over with many types of confidence racket, the immediate ancestors of the present-day big-time games. The idea of a big store, stimulated by old Ben Marks' original experiment and the subsequent success of the fight store, was being applied to many con games with great success. There were mitt stores and monte stores and fight stores and wrestle stores. The big-time grifters of that day blinked in pleased surprise. Why hadn't someone thought of it before? Why not a *wire store*? In other words, why not apply the tried and proved principles of confidence work to the rather clumsy touting efforts of the telegraph operators? If an unemployed telegrapher could get the mark's confidence well enough to extort "expenses" from him, what could any expert insideman do? Once the mark was thoroughly convinced that the race results were being delayed for him, it was immaterial whether they really were or not—*provided he was played against a fake bookmaker instead of a real one.* And so a fake horse-poolroom which took bets was set up, shills were used in place of real betters, fake races were called with convincing fervor, and the results were all that could be desired. Thus the wire store was born. Now it only remained for smart confidence men to study the idea, correct its weakness, refine its strong points, and develop its potentialities.

The modern wire store is operated by one regular insideman who poses as a Western Union official, a variable staff of shills, and a staff of several outsidemen or ropers. These ropers travel the country over looking for victims who have money and can be played for the wire. Some ropers depend largely on luck to enable them to find a mark and do very well by this haphazard method; others are more systematic, resorting to advertisements for "business opportunities" inserted in metropolitan newspapers, and carefully interviewing and sifting out the resulting clientele; the most enterprising have agents who locate prospective marks, investigate their financial standing, and compile a list from which the roper can select the fattest and juiciest. There is one restriction which, though it was formerly ignored especially in New York, is now rigidly observed: the mark must not be a resident of the city where he is to be trimmed.

Wherever the roper finds his mark, he knows that each one is an individual problem and that the play must be varied somewhat for each victim. Consequently, in an account of the wire it has seemed best to simplify it in order to present the general principles of the game without confusing the reader by the infinite possible variations in the play.

In order to visualize the wire in operation, let us assume that a roper whom we shall christen Louis Sanborn has been told that one John Bates, owner of a small department store in Providence, is a prospect for the wire. So Mr. Sanborn visits Mr. Bates, represents himself as the agent for a large corporation which is buying up small stores, and gets his victim's confidence. Mr. Bates is pleased to find a buyer for the business because it has not been too profitable. The two spend several days going over the matter. Sanborn blows hot and cold, then finally decides to buy and makes Bates a very generous tentative offer, subject to the final approval of his superiors. Mr. Bates snaps it up. So Mr. Sanborn takes an option on the business and invites Bates down to New York to consummate the deal.

They arrive in New York around noon and take up quarters at the Fairdale. Mr. Sanborn 'phones his "main office" and reports that their attorneys are occupied with another deal and will not be available until the following day. Then he excuses himself and makes a private call from a 'phone booth to his insideman, whom we shall call Charley Maxwell.

"I have a businessman from Providence," he says. "What time can we play for him?"

Maxwell consults his appointment book. "How about half past two this afternoon?" he asks.

"Fine," says Sanborn. "We'll be there."

When he returns to the room he finds his victim ready for lunch. They go down to the dining room. There, during luncheon, Sanborn plants the first seeds for the play to come. He casually mentions the fact that his cousin is manager of the central office of the Western Union here in New York.

"On my way up I tried to locate a friend in New London," he explains. "Charley wanted to see him about some kind of deal, but he was out of town."

Luncheon progresses. They talk of the pending sale of Mr. Bates' business. When it is time to depart, Sanborn picks up the check and again brings up his cousin. "We aren't in any hurry," he says, "and Charley's office is just around the corner from here. Would you mind walking around that way with me? I think you'll like Charley."

And Mr. Bates does like cousin Charley, for he has a dignified and attractive personality which puts Bates immediately at his ease. He is one of the best insidemen in New York. When they arrive, he is very busy directing the activities of a staff of telegraphers. In the midst of this wholesome hum and clatter the introduction is made.

"Where are you staying, Louis?" asks Charley.

"Over at the Fairdale," says Louis. "Mr. Bates is here on business with me and he is over there too."

"Why, you're just around the corner," observes Charley. "What about our man in New London? Have you talked to him?"

"Not yet," says Louis. "He was out of town."

Cousin Charley rolls up his sleeves another notch and adjusts his green eyeshade. "I want to talk to you about him later, but I can't entertain you here. The inspectors will be around any minute now and it wouldn't look good to have a couple of strangers loafing in the office. I think you understand the situation. Now you two go on down to the hotel and as soon as inspection is over I'll join you there in the lobby. It won't take long. Good-by."

Little does Mr. Bates suspect that the Western Union office he has just been in is entirely fake, that the energetic whir of teletypes was for his benefit only, that as soon as he left, it ceased entirely, the Western Union sign came down, and that cousin Charley put on his coat and dropped his manner of dignified, conscientious executive. The outward appearances have been so convincing, the stage set with such precision, that it does not occur to him to question its authenticity.

Half an hour later, in street clothes, Charley meets Mr. Bates and Mr. Sanborn in the hotel lobby. "It's all over," he remarks, "and they're gone. Now, Louis, how about Brown? You said that you'd find him and bring him along."

Louis explains that he learned that Brown is out of town for two weeks. He ventures to suggest tentatively that perhaps his friend here, Mr. Bates, could be persuaded to fill in on the deal. Cousin Charley looks somewhat shocked at this suggestion and gives Mr. Bates an appraising look.

"How long have you known this gentleman, Louis?" he asks.

"Not very long," answers Louis, "but long enough to know that he is a responsible man, with his own business in Providence. He is O.K. I feel sure that you can depend on him."

Mr. Bates' very natural discomfort in this situation is quickly allayed by cousin Charley, who turns upon him full force the benign rays of his personality and suggests that they talk the matter over confidentially. Mr. Bates begins to feel that he likes Mr. Maxwell even better than he does Mr. Sanborn. Charley Maxwell already "has his con."

They go up to Sanborn's suite and relax. Mr. Maxwell rises to the occasion and "tells the tale" with such dignified sincerity that even the cynical Mr. Sanborn is touched by his fine acting. He explains to Mr. Bates that he has worked for a heartless corporation for years; that he has had advancement, but never what he had been promised and assured; that the company has neglected him when it should have promoted him, and that he has decided to resign.

We must not assume that Mr. Bates is a fool. He has been about a bit himself, he manages his own business and he flatters himself that he knows a good deal about people. If he ever saw character, there it is in Charley Maxwell. He is not so much touched by the facts which

Maxwell has outlined, but by the manner in which they are presented. Instead of a dissatisfied, disgruntled employee, he begins to see before him a man with the makings of a fine executive who has been neglected and wronged.

"And," Mr. Maxwell adds, "I have decided that when I resign, I will not be poor. I know how to swing a deal by which I can make a very good profit without hurting my company in the least. But I must have the assistance of an honest and dependable man, one who is able to put up some funds in return for a share of the profits. Louis' friend, Mr. Brown, was the man I had in mind. Now he cannot be located. I must act quickly, for I may not have the opportunity a second time. Are you interested?"

Mr. Bates is chary. Is Maxwell trying to make a touch? What is this deal? Is it legitimate? How much would he have to invest? And, though he does not say so, the really serious question is: *How much is the profit involved?* He stalls for more information.

Mr. Maxwell drops the question of financing and tells him about the deal. He explains that through his central office pass the race results for all the bookmakers in the city, that the horse-poolrooms are growing fat on the profits from gambling on races, that rich men with inside information can win through the bookmakers, but that the poor fellow with only a form-sheet to guide him always loses more than he makes. He says that he has worked out a system whereby he can beat the bookmakers at their own game by delaying the results long enough to 'phone them to his assistants who are to be stationed next door to the poolroom and who will bet on the races after they are run. Then the results will be released, and of course their bets will pay a very neat profit. And no one will suffer but the rich and dishonest bookmakers.

Once the mark has gone this far, he seldom backs out. If he does, further pressure may be put on him or he may be dropped altogether. But we will assume that Maxwell's smooth voice and sincere manner have had their effect. Bates likes the proposition and sees in it a high profit with no risk. It is a sure thing.

"Now," says Mr. Maxwell, aside to Mr. Bates, "Louis doesn't understand much about this business and I will count on you to take the responsibility of seeing that everything goes all right. You and he go on down to this address on 48th Street and look the place over. Then go into the drugstore next door and wait for a call from me at three sharp. I'll give you the name of the winner and hold up the results just long enough for you to go next door and place your bet. I can't hold them for more than three or four minutes. That way we can see whether or not our system will work, and of course you and Louis can keep anything you win for yourselves. If it works out, we will want to try something bigger."

Mr. Bates and Louis follow the instructions they have received. They visit the poolroom and find there all the paraphernalia that go with a booking establishment. Races are chalked on the blackboard. The ticker is thrumming merrily. Prosperous gentlemen are winning and losing large bets nonchalantly. The caller calls the races with great zest. Bets of $10,000 to $20,000 are laid casually. Very large amounts of cash are changing hands like nickels in a crap game. Everywhere there is cash. The patrons peel off large bets from fat bank rolls or from bulging wallets. The cashier counts out $40,000 winnings without batting an eye. Louis and Mr. Bates are much impressed. A little of the fever of that atmosphere has worked its way into Mr. Bates' blood.

Three o'clock approaches. They return to the drugstore. Maxwell gives them, shall we say, Seabiscuit as winner. They hasten back and plunge into the thick and throbbing atmosphere. Both Mr. Bates and Louis put a ten-dollar bill on Seabiscuit to win. Mr. Bates feels a queer sensation of mingled guilt and triumph. It is a wonderful feeling to bet on a sure thing, even for ten dollars. They have hardly placed their bets when the caller says the magic words, "They're off!" Then he calls the race. Seabiscuit wins, at 4–1. Our pair of innocents collect fifty dollars each. The larceny in Mr. Bates' veins begins to percolate. He can already see a fortune stretching out ahead of him. Why, there is no limit—except the resources of the bookmaker—to what one could make out of this thing. And there are thousands of bookmakers.

They look about them while they await the next race. The same air of dignified, restrained feverishness prevails. No one seems to notice them. Mr. Bates looks the crowd over. It is not large, but it is sporty. Brokers with pasty faces. Sportsmen, tanned and casual. A financier with a Vandyke and highly tailored clothes. The thick blue haze wherein mingle the thin silver streams from a dozen fine cigars. They are betting, joking, absorbed in themselves.

Mr. Bates is a little taken aback at the nonchalant way in which these men handle money. He likes it, and would like to feel that he is a part of it. But he knows that he isn't. He turns to his friend Sanborn. The next race is coming up. They retire to the 'phone for more information. Then they bet fifty dollars each on War Admiral to win at 4–1. He does.

This nets them $250 apiece. "I think I'll shoot the works on the next race," says Mr. Bates. Sanborn counsels caution. After all, this thing is just starting. This is only an experiment to see if their plan will work. Charley knows what he is about, and perhaps they had better do as he says and place only small bets. But Mr. Bates is hooked. He returns to the telephone, awaits a horse, and comes back with the firm intention of placing the $250 on his nose. Louis cautiously refrains from betting this time.

Mr. Bates hurries to the window to place his bet. He

has the $250 in his pocket, ready to be laid. But there are several men just ahead of him. They are laying down very big bets. He cannot help noticing the fat, sleek piles of fives, tens, twenties, fifties and hundreds in the cashier's drawer. He sees the piles of bills on the shelf behind the cashier. He sees the deft hands swiftly paying out and taking in thousands of dollars. He grows impatient. Time is short. The race will be called any moment now. He pushes the line along, but it doesn't seem to move fast enough. He shifts his weight from one foot to the other and peers ahead. Only one man, now. Laying a fifteen thousand dollar bet. Will he never get that money counted down? The man moves casually away, biting the end off a heavy cigar. Mr. Bates removes the wadded bills from his pocket. Challedon. Charley said Challedon to win.

"They're off!" shouts the caller.

Mr. Bates stands there, futilely fingering his money. Betting is closed. Challedon. . . . Where is Challedon? He lags to the rear. He is under wraps. The caller reads off the ticker with such animation that he might as well have been an eyewitness. Will Challedon never make his move? Here it is. They enter the stretch with Challedon moving up. He is booted home a winner. And 6–1. Mr. Bates does a little sketchy mental arithmetic and wonders why he wasn't just one ahead in the line at the window.

He doesn't know it, but he has been given the "shut-out" or the "prat-out," a clever method of stepping up the larceny in the veins of a mark when the manager feels that he is not entering into the play enthusiastically enough. It may be repeated several times so that the mark is fully impressed with what he has missed. The shills who surround the mark at the window usually play for more than the mark is being played for; if the mark is being played for $25,000, the air is full of $50,000 bets; thus the mark always feels like a piker instead of a plunger. Furthermore, ambitious marks must not be allowed to get too much of the store's cash into their pockets.

Mr. Bates returns to Louis. "Tough luck," says Louis.

A suave-looking gentleman approaches them. He is quiet, polite, but authoritative. And just a little condescending. Mr. Bates doesn't know just why, but he feels embarrassed.

"Are you the gentlemen who have been placing these small bets?" he asks, waving a pair of slips.

"We just made a fifty-dollar bet, if you call that small," says Louis.

The manager looks at them with patronizing good nature. "Well, I'll have to ask you not to place any more small bets here," he says. "We have other poolrooms for working men. Small bets make too much bookkeeping for us." He smiles and gently starts them toward the door. Mr. Bates feels patronized. He doesn't like it.

"How much does a man have to bet here?" asks Louis.

"A thousand dollars is usually the lower limit," answers the manager, smiling. "Beyond that, you can go as high as you like. Come back, gentlemen, some other time."

As they pass the doorman, they see Maxwell coming down the street. "Did it work?" asks cousin Charley. "If it did, we can all make a fortune."

"We won a couple of hundred dollars apiece on two bets," volunteers Louis. "But we never got any further. They called us pikers because we didn't bet high enough."

"Never mind that, my boy," answers Charley. "When the time comes we will arrange to bet high enough to suit them. Let's go over to the hotel. I want to discuss this thing further with you in private."

Up in the suite at the Fairdale Mr. Bates hears what he wants to hear.

"This particular poolroom," says cousin Charley, "is the one that I have marked to work on. I know that they have very extensive financial backing. Their volume of business must be tremendous."

Mr. Bates, with a mind full of greenbacks, reflects that it certainly must be.

"They can lose a million and never miss it," continues Charley. "My plan is to take eight or nine hundred thousand in four or five days, then quit. What do you gentlemen say?"

Mr. Bates and Louis agree that it would indeed be a desirable course of action.

"But we have to have cash to finance it," says Charley. "That is why I was so concerned about Brown. He could dig up the cash we need. Let's see, I believe you were thinking that you might raise some for us?"

"How much would you need?" asks Mr. Bates, fearful of appearing too anxious.

"Do you think you would be willing to finance it?" asks Charley. "After all, you know, I haven't much except my salary and Louis here is just getting a start. How much can you raise?"

Mr. Bates studies. He figures on an envelope. His mind is a whirl of mortgages, real estate, government bonds. It may take a couple of weeks to sell his business. Bonds would be the quickest. Government bonds.

"I think I could pick up twenty-five thousand within the next couple of days. Or maybe sooner," he adds, mindful of the potential Mr. Brown. "Is your friend definitely out?"

Mr. Maxwell is very cool and practical. "I hate to let Brown down," he muses. "But I think this arrangement will be fine. How much did you say you could raise? Twenty-five thousand? How is this money? In cash?"

"No, no," says Mr. Bates, "in bonds. Government bonds. I'll have to have my banker sell them and forward me a draft for the proceeds."

"That would be fine," says Charley.

"Now," says Mr. Bates, "how do you intend to split the profits? I would want to pay you whatever is right, but if I put up the money, I ought to get a good share of the profits. Otherwise it wouldn't pay me to get into it."

Mr. Bates suddenly feels important. All he needs is the information. He has the cash. That is the important thing. These men can be paid off at his own price if he finances it now, quickly, before someone else is cut in.

"I have thought that over," says cousin Charley. "Since the plan is mine, I think I ought to have at least fifty per cent. And we should cut Louis in for about twenty per cent for his co-operation. That would leave you thirty per cent which would make you a very good return on your investment."

Mr. Bates doesn't like that arrangement. He wants to cut those men out of all he can. Of course they must have something, but why let Louis in on it at all? And Maxwell. Why, he would go to prison if this thing ever became known. He schemes and argues. As they dicker, Maxwell humors him by working out a compromise whereby he and Bates will split ninety per cent of the profit, and Louis will get the remaining ten. Mr. Bates still feels that they have been too generous with Louis. He moves immediately to 'phone his banker in Providence. But Maxwell interposes.

"This deal must be kept absolutely secret," he argues. "If you 'phone in for money in a hurry, your banker may become suspicious. You know how bankers are. He may feel that you are making a mistake to dump a block of bonds like that on the market right now. It will be a little more expensive, but much safer if you catch a train out of here this afternoon and talk to your banker personally tomorrow. Explain that you are buying some real estate here in the city and want to pay down that much cash."

"But," interposes Bates, turning to Louis, "what about that appointment with your lawyers?"

"Don't worry about that," says Louis. "I'll take care of everything for you. Just send me a telegram as soon as you know when you'll be back and I'll fix things up at the office."

"That's right," says Charley. "And you'd better add a note in that telegram which will let me know how much money you are bringing. But we don't want anyone to suspect you are bringing it. So let a thousand dollars equal, say, one 'bushel.' Then you can say, 'Bringing twenty-five bushels' and I'll know you are prepared to go right ahead with the deal."

This stage of the game is known as "the send." It is a strange fact that, once a good insideman "tightens up" a mark, he can be sent anywhere for his money and will usually return despite all obstacles. For example, during the week of July 3, 1939, the metropolitan papers carried stories on the case of Mr. Leonard B. Reel, a public accountant of Beach Haven, New Jersey, who, with his wife, was put on the send from Mexico City. The couple flew to Philadelphia and brought back $74,000 which they lost on the rag to the Velvet Kid. They reported that they made the trip with some difficulty, having been forced down en route by storms four different times. If the con men think that they can get away with using the mails, they may not use "the send."

Mr. Bates agrees that it will be best to make the trip. There must be no slips. For a moment he fears what might happen if this scheme came to light. Then he remembers that he is only financing it. He feels better. Also, the $250 in his wallet will more than cover his expenses on the trip home. Mr. Bates watches his pennies. But on the other hand, is it safe to leave the deal open here? Suppose Brown—or someone else—turned up with the ready cash?

"You have decided definitely that I am to finance it?" he asks.

"Yes, indeed," says Charley. "Here is my hand on it. We'll shake hands all the way around. That swears us all to keep this deal absolutely secret."

They all shake hands, though having Louis cut in on the deal still sticks in Bates' crop. After all ten per cent isn't much, and Louis still holds the key to the sale of his store. Well, he'll get that ten per cent back and more when Louis' company takes up that option.

Three days later he is back in New York with a draft for $25,000. He is at a high pitch of excitement. This business turns over a profit quicker than anything he has ever seen. And he gets a strange sense of elation—the same feeling, magnified a thousand times, that he felt when he had that first ten dollars on Seabiscuit and watched him romp home. He has a sure thing.

Maxwell takes him to a bank which has been fixed. Mr. John Bates endorses the check, and now has $25,000 in cash. It burns holes in his pockets.

"This afternoon I think we can work," says Charley. "I'll find out what the best odds are, you stay near the 'phone booth, and I'll tell you what to bet just before each race. I'll get any last-minute change in odds as they come through over the wire, and we'll take all that into consideration. We'll work the same as we did the other day. Now hold on tight to that money." Then he goes back to directing the destinies of a minor province in the great empire of the Western Union.

The next few hours are critical ones for the con men. Between now and post-time the mark is most likely to have a "brain-blow" and lose his head. Marks have been known to go to the police with the whole story right at this point, and a "wrong" copper might lay a trap for the con men and get the mark to co-operate. Or the mark might worry about so large a gamble and look up some friend or acquaintance to consult about the matter; of course any of these might tip the whole thing off. Occasionally the victim insists on seeking the advice of his wife, in which case wiser con mobs encourage such a move, for they have learned that such a consultation usually works in their favor. Some marks simply get cold feet at the last moment and go on about their business, or return home.

So a "tailer" is put on Mr. Bates during all the time that he is not with either of the con men. The tailer, a man of ample experience in such matters, can tell immediately by the mark's actions how he is getting along. If he consults the police, the tailer reports back immediately and the con men may simply not see him any more, or they may 'phone him and tell him that the Western Union has become suspicious and that the deal must be postponed. However, if he has consulted a "right" copper or detective, the con men know that they are safe, for they can pay their way as soon as the score comes off. They go right ahead and play for him knowing that the police will not "knock" him or tip him off to what is happening. If it seems necessary, the insideman himself or his fixer will go down and have a chat with the officer in order to be sure there will be no slips. Meanwhile, Mr. Bates, if he has had any traffic with the police, feels better in the knowledge that the officers of the law are not suspicious of the men with whom he is dealing or of the deal (if he lets that out) which he is contemplating.

Meanwhile, Louis stalls the victim along with the pending sale of his store, which, during the play, fades into the background. Some marks become so feverish that, during the period of the tie-up, they apparently forget all about the original reason for their coming to the city where the big store is located, or resent the roper's attempts to continue negotiations for the business while this big deal is in the air.

Post-time finds Mr. Bates and Louis haunting the 'phone booth, awaiting the call which will come sometime during the afternoon. Bates hugs his $25,000. Louis handles his quarry skillfully, knowing just how to arouse his anticipations and how far to go in quieting the doubts which may be troubling his mind.

At last the 'phone jangles. Mr. Bates rushes into the booth. It is Maxwell.

"Hello," he says, "is that you, Louis?"

"No, this is John Bates."

"Well, I've got the winner. Hurry right on over and place the money on Flying Lill. Call Louis to the 'phone, will you?"

Louis talks briefly to Charley. "O.K.," he says. "I understand. Place it all on Flying Lill. Good-by, Charley."

They hurry over to the poolroom and plunge into the atmosphere of synthetic excitement. There on the odds-board is Flying Lill, 5–1. Mr. Bates feels a momentary sinking in the pit of his stomach. His mouth is dry and his hands tremble. Louis takes the bills from his hands and pushes them through the cashier's window. "Flying Lill to win," he says. "Twenty-five thousand."

The cashier gives him his slip and begins to count the money. "They're off!" calls the announcer, and the next two minutes are hectic ones. It is Unerring by a length. Flying Lill second. Lady Maryland third.

Mr. Bates is stunned. *Unerring won.*

"Wait a minute," says Louis, "there must be something wrong. It isn't official yet." He looks with mingled sympathy and anxiety into Mr. Bates' ashen face.

But it is official. The announcement cuts through the smoke and clatter like a great somber gong. It is official.

"We've lost," says Louis, and they go out into the street.

It may occur to Mr. Bates that he has been betrayed. His mind is probably such a chaos that he cannot think at all. He may break into sobs immediately, and wildly tear his hair. But we will assume that he is a gentleman and that he restrains his emotions and reserves his judgments until he learns what has happened. Louis has already solicitously begun the "cooling out" process which will pave the way for Maxwell's smooth patter.

They meet Charley, who can only partly conceal his jubilation, a short distance from the Western Union office. He is talking in terms of winning $125,000. Mr. Bates tells him that Louis bet the horse to win, but that it placed and they lost. Charley turns on Louis in a fury. "Don't you know what the word *place* means?" he roars. Louis tries to justify his mistake on the basis of their misunderstanding of the word *place*. But Maxwell will have none of it. He rakes that young man over the coals until he hangs his head in red-faced shame and humiliation. Mr. Bates is very likely to come to Louis' defense, on the grounds that he, too, misunderstood. Then Mr. Maxwell turns on him and gives him also a piece of his mind. But finally he cools off.

"Well," he says, "we'll never make that mistake again." Then he takes Mr. Bates in hand in such a way that the "cooling-out" process is perfect and Mr. Bates lives only until he can raise enough money to give the plan a second trial. When Charley Maxwell cools a mark out, he stays cooled out. And if he has decided that the mark is good for another play—as about fifty per cent of them are—he will "feel him out" to see whether or not he can raise more cash; some marks have been beaten four or five times on the same racket. If he knows he has been swindled, or if he cannot raise any more money, he is "blown off" and disposed of as quietly as possible. Let us assume that Mr. Bates, being the perfect mark, is good for another play. Mr. Maxwell retains his confidence to such an uncanny extent that he will do almost anything he is told to do. So he is "put on the send" again for $20,000, which he borrows, using real estate as collateral.

The second play takes up just where the first left off.

The only delay is caused by obtaining Mr. Bates' money. Louis knows how to handle the deal regarding Mr. Bates' business and assures him that everything is going along fine, but that his corporation is going to investigate the department store further before they sign the final papers. Usually, if the mark is good for a second play, he is by this time so wrapped up in the wire that he has practically dropped the legitimate deal. Some con mobs will send a tailer along home with the mark to see if he consults the police before returning. The tailer may pose as an agent for the corporation which is interested in the mark's business.

The big store, the boost, and all the necessary stage-settings are again called into play. When the time comes to make the big bet, the sting is put in a little differently. Over the 'phone Mr. Maxwell gives the mark Johnny J. at 6–1 to win. Mr. Bates and Louis bet the $20,000, making sure that there is no misunderstanding this time regarding that tricky word *place*. The betting is heavy all around them, though Mr. Bates does not realize that those bank rolls have seen much service as props. The $50,000 in cold cash laid down by the better just ahead of him is real money; it makes an impression.

"They're off!" says the caller. The room quiets. The smoke drifts in swirls. The gamblers listen with polite eagerness. It is Johnny J. by a neck.

Mr. Bates feels a great exhilaration; his fingers and toes tingle; a warm wave of relief sweeps over him. His horse has won $140,000. Now to take his share and build it up into a fortune.

"Let's cash it right away," urges Louis, "before something happens to it."

Mr. Bates waves the ticket before the impassive cashier, who is imperturbably stacking big bills; Mr. Bates has never seen so much loose cash. It is everywhere. The cashier looks at him with polite indifference.

"Cash this, cash this, please," says Mr. Bates, pushing the ticket under the grating.

"Just a minute, sir," says the cashier. "I'm sorry, but those results are not yet official. Wait just a minute."

"Flash!" says the caller. "Flash! A mistake in colors. It was Silverette by a neck, Johnny J. second, Technician is third. This is official."

Mr. Bates vaguely hears a man beside him say to his friend, "I'm very glad that horse disqualified. I had $7,000 on Silverette."

"I'm not," says his friend. "That damned Johnny J. cost me just twenty thousand. . . ."

Mr. Bates is dazed. He remonstrates with the manager. He cries and curses his luck. He suspects that he has been swindled but doesn't know how. The manager is polite, firm and impersonal. The heavy play goes right on for the next race. Louis, crying and complaining as if it were his $20,000 which went glimmering, leads him out into the street. The outside air only intensifies the terrible feeling of loss and despair in Mr. Bates' heart. To him money is a sacred thing. This is terrible.

Outside on the street they meet Charley. He looks tired and worried. He is nervous and distraught. He listens absently to the tale of woe. "Yes, that is terrible," he agrees. "But right now I am in terrible trouble myself. The Western Union detectives have been investigating the delay in race results and I'll be lucky if I only lose my job. If they pin anything on me, I'll go to prison. Maybe all three of us."

Mr. Bates hasn't thought of this angle since Charley first explained the deal to him. Fear now adds its agony to despair. They talk over the possibilities of arrest. Maxwell advises that Bates and Louis leave town as quickly and quietly as possible. They return to the hotel. Louis obligingly gets the time for the next train to Providence. It leaves at 10:00 P.M. Mr. Bates, worried, nervous, broken, agrees to take it. Charley promises that, if this thing blows over, he himself will raise enough money to play the game again and will give Mr. Bates all his money back, and some profit to boot. Then he leaves, so that he may not be picked up. Louis draws Mr. Bates aside.

"How much money do you have?" he asks.

Mr. Bates looks in his wallet. "Less than fifty dollars," he answers. "And I have to pay my hotel bill."

"Well," offers Louis, "I have nearly a hundred and fifty. You have had a bad break and I hate to see you stranded. You have been a fine sport to take it the way you do. Here, let me lend you seventy-five to get home on. You can pay it back any time. And remember," he adds, "our auditors will be at your place next week. Then I'll have everything in good shape at this end and we'll close the deal."

Mr. Bates takes the money which is pressed on him. He is surprised. Louis is a pretty nice fellow after all. He is ashamed of the way he has felt about him recently. Still in a daze, he shakes the proffered hand and Louis departs. "I'll be back about nine-thirty," he says, "to see that you get to the train safely. Wait for me in the lobby."

From now on, it is up to a local tailer to keep close tab on Mr. Bates to see what he may do, reporting any tendency he may show to consult the police. Mr. Maxwell may have him paged to the telephone and continue the cooling process by 'phone. The tailer watches closely; if, after this conversation Mr. Bates consults the house detective or a detective he has stationed in the lobby, the tailer reports immediately to Maxwell, who puts the machinery of the fix into operation. Or, Louis may deliberately delay his arrival at the hotel to see his victim off. As the time for departure approaches and Louis fails to appear, Mr. Bates may get nervous and make a 'phone call to the police, or consult a detective already stationed in the hotel. The tailer can predict the mark's reactions with a good deal of accuracy, for he has had ample opportunity to study at first hand the psychology of the trimmed mark.

Just before ten, at the tailer's signal, Louis appears with a good excuse for lateness, bundles Mr. Bates carefully into a cab, hurries him to the station, buys his ticket for Providence, and puts him on the train. He waits solicitously until the train pulls out.

As soon as the mark is safely on his way, Mr. Maxwell meets his roper, the manager and the boost at the hangout. He is a meticulous bookkeeper. He gives each one a plain envelope containing his share of the score, and drops a word about an appointment for eleven-thirty on Wednesday. And so the big store goes on.

There is one fundamental weakness in the wire; the victim must furnish his own money.

## 2
## The Pay-Off*

Like the wire, the pay-off sprang from a humble beginning. It came as a bright idea to two hungry race-track touts in the city of Seattle. Their names were Hazel and Abbot. They seem to have been ingenious touts, for they are credited by their contemporaries with being the first to advertise in the newspapers for clients. Even so, money was tight in 1906.

A contemporary who knew them well and himself had a finger in the early development of the pay-off says that Abbot gave him the following version of the inception of the greatest of all confidence games.

The touts had been working the race-track at Seattle and were very discouraged because they could hardly make a living. "This touting is a dud," said Hazel. "We've

* The name of the victim in this chapter is fictitious.

got to get something new or we'll starve to death. The fans are getting hep to this old racket. I've been thinking that if we gave a mark a horse and then paid him off after the horse won, it would convince him that we were in the know."

"That's fine," said Abbot, "but how are you going to get him a winner?"

"That's easy," said Hazel. "I'll pick up a mark at the track and then you come around. I'll point you out to him. Then I'll put you away as that big plunger who won all that money at Frisco last winter. Then you cut in and tell your story. I'll ask you to win us our hotel bill. I'll give you a fin and get the mark to give you a fin. Then you can tighten us up not to talk about the race as it is fixed. You take the money and go away and tell us to watch No. 10. That's all. The horse will be nameless, but no matter. The horse will win. I'll come back and give you the tickets, but you hold both of them, as they will be phony. . . ."

Thus, in a crude form, was conceived the very simple principle which could be applied to either races or stocks, and which has accounted for no one knows how many millions in illegal plunder taken by con men in the past thirty-odd years. But what Hazel and Abbot had invented was not the pay-off as we know it today; it was really a crude form of what is now known as the "short pay at the track" and is still played by touts who have the temerity to face the possibility of a prison sentence; very few have. Furthermore the touches almost always "come hot"—that is, the mark is likely to suspect that he has been swindled—and there are no facilities at the track to cool him out.

During the 1906 racing season Hazel and Abbot played their little game at the track, but they were not satisfied with it. They took off very small touches because they could take only the ready money the mark had on him at the track. The touches came too hot, and, seeing the protection enjoyed by other species of the grift which were played against one form or another of the store, they took their idea to two smart grifters who were engaged in other forms of swindling.

These were the Boone Kid Whitney, later famous as a big-con man, and a friend named Frank MacSherry, later a fine insideman. They were very much impressed by the fact that Hazel and Abbot almost always got a touch, even though it was small. So they put their heads together and planned a layout for a pay-off store, the first in the country; it was rigged like a horse-poolroom, and had a boost composed of professional shills while professional ropers from other rackets brought the marks in. I have been unable to discover who roped the first victim, but I do know that MacSherry played the inside for him and the Boone Kid acted as manager and owner of the poolroom, a small establishment located between Seattle and the race-track. The first score was not large, but the ravenous way in which the mark took the bait showed the con men that they had something too good to throw away.

They played their game around Seattle, for a while, then decided to move their store down to Oakland, near where Hazel and Abbot got their start as touts. But the end was inevitable. The game had great possibilities but was too crude; the fix went wrong and they paid the price of a jolt in prison for their originality; Hazel and Abbot, being touts, could not stand the gaff and never played their little game again.

But the word had gone about in the underworld and smart con men were studying this new game. The third store was opened in San Francisco by a man who also held—and still does—the convenient post of local fixer, and a powerful one he was, too. Kent Marshall, a fine con man by both instincts and training, played the inside, and this time there were no slips. These men knew what they were doing when they tinkered with a con game. The pay-off was well established by 1907, but was almost unknown off the West Coast. The rest of the story of the pay-off is closely intertwined with the history of the big store, without which it could not have developed; suffice it to say here that, as soon as the news of this new swindle transpired, stores appeared like magic in almost all of the larger cities of the country. By 1915 it had outstripped its rival, the wire, to become the most lucrative of all rackets and remains so today.

Con games never remain stationary; the principle may be old, but the external forms are always changing, for con men know that they must adapt their schemes to the times. This is especially true of the big con. A good grifter is never satisfied with the form his swindle takes; he studies it constantly to improve it; as he learns more about people, he finds a way to use what he has learned. So the big-con men over the country began to improve the pay-off in every way possible. Many of them brought to it the benefit of their experience on the wire. They tried out new ideas, discarding those which failed and developing those that worked. Consequently, the pay-off as we know it today is not only a far cry from the crude little game which Hazel and Abbot started back at the Seattle race-track, but also a great improvement over its sister-game, the wire. Let us watch it work.

Mr. James Ryan is riding the ocean liners between New York and points south, sometimes going as far west as New Orleans and Galveston. He has connections with a pay-off store in West Palm Beach where a Maine Scotchman, John Singleton, plays the inside. The store is one of the best; Mr. Ryan is a discriminating roper and brings in only the fattest of marks; Mr. Singleton is an insideman of the first quality who, despite the sarcasm and bad temper which make him difficult personally, never lets his personality interfere with his profession and has a reputation for giving any mark a good play.

About four in the afternoon Mr. Ryan boards the steamer. He goes to his stateroom, bathes, shaves and puts on a dinner jacket. Then he goes into the bar, where he sips a drink in a leisurely fashion. There sitting at the bar is a heavy-set, well-muscled man with money written all over him. Mr. Ryan looks him over carefully. He has a feeling that this is his man. It has been months since he has had a touch. He hopes that this man is traveling alone. He watches from the corner of his eye so that he may finish his drink just as the stranger finishes his. Then he "cuts into him" and starts a casual conversation. He orders himself another drink and offers one to the stranger, who accepts. They chat briefly and Mr. Ryan learns that the stranger is from Boston.

The roper never says that he is from New York or Chicago because many marks tend to suspect big-city folks. Usually he picks a small, solid town in the same state from which the mark hails. Ropers travel so extensively that they know almost every town of any size well enough to claim residence there.

And so Mr. Ryan tells the stranger that he is from North Adams, Massachusetts. He mentions a banker in that town. The stranger knows him. They introduce themselves. The stranger is Mr. William Fink. He is a real-estate broker. He looks Mr. Ryan over and feels that he is rather a fine fellow. They hobnob in a friendly fashion. Mr. Ryan finds out discreetly if Mr. Fink is traveling alone. He is. They make a date for dinner.

Mr. Fink is going to Miami. Mr. Ryan is going there too. It is his first visit there. Could Mr. Fink give him any information about accommodations there? Mr. Fink has reservations at the Courtland Hotel and recommends it highly. Mr. Ryan intimates that he will stay there too, since he is a stranger.

During the voyage the two see a good deal of each other. Mr. Fink finds Mr. Ryan an extremely attractive fellow, well informed on many subjects, and with a keen and ready wit. He is a most agreeable traveling companion. They talk freely and confidentially, each one lying to the other, as men do on the strength of a shipboard acquaintance. Mr. Ryan finds out about Mr. Fink's hobbies. He listens with extraordinary sympathy to Mr. Fink's exploits on the golf course. Yes, he knows many of the courses on which Mr. Fink has played. They tire of sports.

Mr. Fink has a twinkle in his eye for every pair of pretty legs on the first-class deck. Mr. Ryan waits for Mr. Fink to broach the subject of women; once he does, Mr. Ryan has several well-told exploits to contribute to the conversation. He knows a very convenient and handsome woman in Boston; he gives Mr. Fink her address and suggests that he call her up on his return. They have drinks. Mr. Ryan usually picks up the checks and does the tipping. He is free, but not too free, with his money. The topic of investment is broached. Mr. Ryan says, "I was lucky in the depression. I got a tip to sell instead of buy just before the crash, and now I'm fixed." Mr. Fink reciprocates with the troubles of a real-estate broker. He considers himself a shrewd businessman and says as much. Under the polite attentiveness of his friend, he may even lie a little. He gives generously of his mercenary wisdom.

Ryan then decides that this mark is good for at least $25,000, maybe more. He'll see what John thinks about it. He sends a radiogram: ARRIVING MARCH 10 MIAMI WITH UNCLE GEORGE. COMING SOUTH FOR HIS HEALTH. JAMES.

They dock in Miami and ride together to the hotel. Mr. Ryan observes what sort of accommodations the mark has reserved, then inquires for something a little more expensive. After tipping the service men liberally, he takes temporary leave of his friend.

From his suite Mr. Ryan 'phones Mr. Singleton. "Uncle and I just arrived," he explains. "Where can I see you?"

John says, "I'll be very glad to see you. Meet me at the cigar store about eight o'clock. Good-by."

That night at eight they meet and talk the situation over. John looks in his little book to see how many marks are ahead and when Mr. Fink can be conveniently played. They set a tentative date and time. "What do you think we should play him for?" asks John.

"I'd say the ponies," says Ryan. "He is a real-estate man and seems to know a lot about investments. He ought to be good for twenty-five grand and maybe more. And he likes the best of it."

"O.K.," says John. "We'll give him the hides. What kind of an egg is he?"

"Well, he's no lop-eared mark," says Jimmy. "He knows what it is all about. And he may be hard to handle. He is a hefty baby with plenty of moxie. I'd guess he'll be hard to cool out."

"If he gets fractious, he'll get the cackle-bladder. That cools out those tough babies. Do you want to find the poke for him?"

"We might as well. He's right there in the hotel with me and it would be a better tie-up than the point-out. And no more trouble."

"O.K. When do you want to find it?"

"I think tomorrow noon. I'll 'phone you as soon as I can date him up for lunch."

And so Mr. Ryan returns to the hotel, 'phones Mr. Fink, makes a luncheon date for one the next day, and relays the information to John.

Ryan and Fink lunch the next day in the exclusive coolness of the hotel dining room. Mr. Ryan is full of questions about Miami. They enjoy a most palatable luncheon. As they are about to go, Mr. Ryan looks embarrassed, glances sidewise under the table, and says, "I'm sorry. Is that your foot I'm on?"

"No," answers Mr. Fink. "It's not." He looks under the

table, bends over, and comes up with a fat wallet in his hand.

"What's this?" he asks, astonished. "Somebody has lost a pocketbook. Is it yours?"

Mr. Ryan pats his breastpocket. "It's not mine," he says.

"Let's see who it belongs to."

Mr. Fink opens it up, laying the contents on the table. There is a stack of fifty-dollar bills, twelve in all. Here is a membership card in what we shall call the Turf Club, made out, shall we say, in the name of Henry E. Lamster. And here is a telegram-code with two telegrams, also addressed to H. E. Lamster. Here, in a small compartment, are a pair of race-tickets, and in another, a newspaper clipping. They look at it. It is captioned with a picture of a man shielding his face with his hat, and labeled Henry E. Lamster. They read the clipping. It is from a West Coast paper and describes the phenomenal race-track winnings of one H. E. Lamster. They conclude that Mr. Lamster must own the billfold.

"Shall we inquire at the desk to see if we can find this fellow?" asks Mr. Ryan.

"By all means," says Mr. Fink. "This wallet is valuable."

They inquire of the desk-clerk for Mr. Lamster.

"Yes, he is in Suite 4-E," says the clerk.

"Would you please ring him to see if he is in?"

The clerk rings. "Yes, he is in."

"Thanks, that is all," says Mr. Fink. "Can we have a boy to show us up?"

The clerk signals a boy, and they are off. They halt before 4-E and dismiss the boy with a tip. Mr. Fink raps on the door. It opens just a crack.

"What do you want?" snaps a man within.

"Are you Mr. Henry Lamster?" asks Mr. Ryan.

A curt voice tinged with annoyance answers. "Yes, I am. Speak up. What do you want?"

"We found . . ." begins Mr. Fink.

But Mr. Lamster cuts him off. "Are you newspapermen? If you are, I don't want to see you. You hound me to death. Get out of here!"

"But," interposes Mr. Ryan, "we aren't newspapermen. Have you lost anything? I think we have found something which belongs to you."

"I haven't lost anything," snaps Mr. Lamster.

"Do you have your billfold?"

Mr. Lamster taps his pockets and his brusque manner melts. "My God! It's gone." He looks anxiously at his visitors.

"I think we have found it," says Mr. Fink.

"Well, well, gentlemen. You have saved my life. Do come in," says Mr. Lamster, opening the door wide. There stands Mr. John Singleton, but there is no sign of recognition between him and his roper. His suite of rooms is luxurious. He turns and paces the floor nervously, rumpling his hair. He is a tall, florid, well-proportioned man, somewhat inclined toward stoutness. On the bed are a pair of telegrams.

"I suppose you can identify this," says Mr. Ryan, extending the billfold.

"I think so," says Mr. Lamster, his eyes lighting up. "There should be in it a code-cipher, a membership card in the Turf Club, five or six hundred dollars in cash, and . . . let me see . . . a newspaper clipping. Oh yes, and a couple of telegrams."

"Right, it's yours," says Mr. Ryan and passes it over.

"I can't tell you gentlemen how much I am indebted to you," says Mr. Lamster. "Here, take this cash and have yourselves a good time. These papers were what I was afraid to lose. Here, you will please me very much if you take this money." He riffles the edges of the fifty-dollar bills invitingly.

Both men decline.

"Well, then, you both must be my guests for an evening while you are here. Drinks. Dinner. A show. And maybe some girl friends, eh?" He glances knowingly at Mr. Fink. "Meanwhile let me place a bet for you which will cover your hotel bills while you are here."

"A bet?" asks the roper. "I don't understand what you mean."

"You see," explains Mr. Lamster, "the reason I was so rude to you is that I thought you were newspapermen. You see how they hound me." He takes out the clipping and passes it over to Mr. Fink. "They make life miserable for me whenever they learn who I am. You see, I win a good deal of money at the races and that brings notoriety, which is unwelcome to say the least."

"You mean you have some hot tips?" asks Mr. Ryan.

"Well, in a way, yes. You see it is like this. I work for a large syndicate which ah—shall we say—purchases races wholesale at tracks all over the country. I am just an agent. I place bets for the syndicate to the great—ah—disadvantage—of bookmakers and gambling clubs. Naturally, any publicity is very detrimental to my business. I receive all my instructions in code, and without my cipher I would be unable to carry out my orders." He waves the cipher under their noses. There is a knock at the door.

"Telegram," says a bellhop, and Mr. Lamster signs.

"You mean to say," asks Mr. Ryan, "that you bet on races that are fixed in advance?"

"Well, yes, if you want to put it that way. That is why it would be so simple for me to place a small bet for you which, at favorable odds, should make you pin money at least. Let me place, say, fifty dollars apiece for you gentlemen and if things work out as I expect, you will make a neat killing. Let me see, I think I have something here."

As he decodes the telegram, Mr. Ryan turns to Mr. Fink (if Mr. Fink has not already turned to Mr. Ryan) and asks, "What do you think of it? I think I'll let him win my hotel bill."

"We might as well," says Mr. Fink. "It doesn't cost him anything."

"Here, gentlemen, is a very good thing," says Mr. Lamster. "You must excuse me for half an hour. Here are drinks and cigars. Help yourselves. Just make yourselves comfortable and I'll be right back."

"Put something on it for us," calls Ryan, half in jest.

Mr. Ryan and Mr. Fink sample the liquor and cigars. There is Seltzer water and ice. They sit back and speculate upon this peculiar person they have met. "He may be just a nut," observes Mr. Fink, "but at least it isn't costing us anything. And this is good whisky." Mr. Ryan comments upon the sad state in which the racing world finds itself, when the race-fans haven't a ghost of a chance and a big syndicate takes all the sport out of the thing.

Before long Mr. Lamster lets himself in. He takes from his pocket two sheaves of bills. "Here is a couple of hundred apiece," he says. "Have another drink."

The two men count their money and Mr. Fink begins to covet mightily the power that this man has. Another telegram arrives. Mr. Lamster decodes it rapidly. "Here's another one," he says. Then, turning to Ryan, "Here, give me that $200 I just made you."

Mr. Ryan hands it over.

"Now yours," he says to Mr. Fink, who obediently surrenders his $200.

And before either can protest, he has picked the bills from their fingers and hurried out.

He is not gone long. When he returns he hands each man $600 in crisp greenbacks. Mr. Fink is very much impressed. Why in no time, he could build up that $600 into a fortune. . . .

The con men may play for their victim that afternoon.

They may let him sleep on it if they feel that he is not yet securely hooked. Let us assume that, as a tribute to Mr. Fink's conservative and substantial virtues, they allow him to contemplate overnight the phenomenon of $600, now reposing in his wallet, made in the twinkle of an eye—and without any risk or investment whatever on his part.

His doom is set for the following day at four.

That night Mr. Ryan and he dine together and go to a night club afterward. Mr. Ryan doesn't want anything spectacular to happen to that $600 which Mr. Fink has in his pocket. Mr. Ryan seems to have formed a very good opinion of Mr. Lamster. Mr. Fink likes him too; in fact, he would like to know him better; he does not suspect Mr. Ryan of fostering this feeling gently, but nevertheless effectively. This is the first step in "switching" Mr. Fink's confidence from the outsideman to the insideman, a difficult and delicate step which must be successfully negotiated if the pay-off is to reach its maximum in effectiveness.

The next day the roper visits Mr. Fink in his room. He proposes exactly what Mr. Fink has in his own mind—that they look up Mr. Lamster and see if he will give them some more horses to bet on. They find him in his suite, busily decoding telegrams.

"I'm very glad you called," he says. "I need someone I can trust, and I know from the way you gentlemen returned my wallet yesterday that both of you are O.K. Now I am going to give you a chance to make a little money. They are beginning to suspect me down at the Turf Club. I'll have to stay out of there for a week or so. But this guest card will admit you without question. And here is a horse in the fifth race. Bet him to win. And I'll give you a blank check. I don't know who I'd rather accommodate this way."

"But how do we do it?" asks Mr. Ryan.

"Well, you still have the $600 you won yesterday?" asks Mr. Lamster.

"Sure," says Ryan, producing the currency.

"All right. You have yours, Mr. Fink?"

"Yes, indeed!"

"All right. Here. You give your $600 to Mr. Ryan. That makes $1,200 for the two of you. Now do exactly as I tell you. Mr. Ryan, when the time comes to bet, you make out and sign this check for $50,000. Place it together with your $1,200 on Dancing Cloud in the fifth race. The odds will be about 4–1. That ought to net you—let's see—about $256,000."

"But, see here," protests Mr. Ryan, "I haven't got $50,000 in cash to take up that check. That is a big check to put my name to."

"Never mind that," says Mr. Lamster. "Never mind that at all. Your entrance card here will assure your credit. Then just as soon as you win, you can take up your check without the slightest trouble. You see, I can't send my check or I'd advance you the money. I might as well go myself."

"O.K.," says Mr. Ryan. "But what if we don't win?"

"You can't very well lose," interposes Mr. Fink. "It's a sure thing."

"Mr. Fink," says Lamster, laughing, "you certainly catch on in a hurry."

And so out they go armed with their cards, the check, and information which is to make them a small fortune. Their magic cards get them past the doorman without question. They find the club a swank, private affair, with a carefully selected boost giving it a heavy play. There is deep carpet on the floor. There is a small bar on one side. Bright, streamlined furniture makes the gamblers comfortable. Indirect lighting throws soft glow everywhere. And the big bets are going down thick and fast. They take their time to look the place over. There is still plenty of time before the fifth race. And there is something intoxicating about watching gentlemen lay down $100,000 bets without batting an eye.

They watch the board-marker up in front. His earphones are on a sliding wire which runs up over his head. As he moves rapidly backward and forward, up and down, the sliding wire follows him. He chalks up the races rapidly. There is a low, murmurous hum of voices, a clink of ice in glasses over at the bar. The second flash has just come in. The odds on Dancing Cloud settle down to 4–1.

At their leisure they go to the cashier's window and place a bet of $51,200 at 4–1 on Dancing Cloud to win.* The cashier asks for their credentials, examines them, and accepts the check without question. He gives Mr. Ryan a ticket which calls for $256,000 if Dancing Cloud wins. There is still ten minutes before post-time. Mr. Fink has plenty of time to watch the heavy play going on all around him. It must take nerve to play with money like that. What kind of lives do these men live? he wonders. Their personal fortunes must be unlimited.

The marker hastily puts in the last flash on odds. The fifth race is up. There is Dancing Cloud, still 4–1. "They're off!" says the caller. Dancing Cloud remains under wraps for the first quarter, the second quarter. Then he moves up to third place and holds it easily. In the stretch he makes his move, fights desperately for the lead, takes it, and pounds home under the wire a winner.

Fink and Ryan exchange jubilant glances. It looked bad there for the first half, but it worked! It worked! "Those jocks must know their stuff," observes Ryan, "to pull a race like that. Nobody would ever suspect it."

* Sometimes at this point, if the con men are not sure that their mark is firmly hooked, they allow him to place another small bet or two as "convincers" before the big play is made.

Mr. Fink is drawn to the cashier's window as by a magnet. All around betters are tearing up their tickets—tickets for tremendous bets—as if they were laundry bills. There is much good-natured grumbling at the outcome of this race. Nobody had doped it out that way. Mr. Ryan is right at Fink's elbow with his ticket. Two hundred and fifty-six thousand dollars. That is a lot of money. Ryan moves to cash it.

"Sorry, sir," says the cashier. "Those results are not yet official. The judges' decision will be in in just a moment."

They wait at the window, standing aside so that the betting on the sixth race may proceed. Mr. Ryan calls attention in an undertone to the large bets which are being laid. Mr. Fink has never seen so much money, even in a bank. The shelf behind the cashier is literally piled high with stacked currency. The cash drawer is overflowing. It is actually on the floor.

"The results of the fifth race are official," announces the caller.

Mr. Ryan lays down his ticket. The cashier glances at it and calls, "Bring me $256,000." His assistant lays the stacked bills at his elbow. He begins to count them out, pushing them under the grating to Mr. Ryan.

At this moment the manager steps forward and asks, "How did you gentlemen get in here? This is a private club."

They show their cards. "Hmmm," he says, "you have a pretty big bet here." Then, turning to the cashier, "Did you take this gentleman's check?"

"Yes, sir," says the cashier, and produces it, with a duplicate ticket from his file.

The manager studies the check a moment and looks again at the cards. "Well, you have won this bet," he says quietly. "This money is rightfully yours. We'll put this check through the bank and if they O.K. it, you'll be paid off. We'll impound your money right here, and you stay in the city until the bank reports back. And by all means keep that ticket. It is your receipt."

"But," objects Mr. Fink, "twelve hundred of that bet was in cash. It seems to me that you should honor that bet immediately. Pay us the six thousand and hold the check."

"Not at all," says the manager firmly. "If you wanted that kind of settlement, you should have placed two separate bets. As it is, this is all one bet and will have to be paid all at once. Good day, gentlemen."

Back go our friends to Mr. Lamster in the hotel. He is not particularly perturbed and quiets Mr. Ryan's misgivings about the $50,000 check he has just signed.

"Just be patient and don't get excited," says Lamster, "and everything will be all right. Don't worry about it."

"Can't you give us some more tips, and maybe we could build up what cash we have into enough to redeem the check," suggests Mr. Fink.

"I wish I could," says Mr. Lamster. "But I haven't any more coming through today. That check will have to be taken care of immediately. Why don't you go back and talk to the manager privately and see what kind of settlement he will give you? Ask him to give you a little time on the check and we'll think of some way to cover it."

Ryan and Fink find the club still open and going strong. They ask for a private conference with the manager. He keeps them waiting for some time. Then he ushers them into his private office.

"We are the men who won that $256,000 this afternoon," begins Mr. Ryan.

"What $256,000?" asks the manager, looking at them blankly. "What are your names? The play here is so heavy that I can't possibly keep track of all of it."

"This is James Ryan and I am William Fink," says Mr. Fink, producing one of his business cards. "The bet was made in Mr. Ryan's name."

The manager picks up one of his numerous telephones and buzzes. "Bring in the file on Ryan, James," he says.

The other 'phones on his desk ring busily. Another clerk answers them, taking down large bets. He turns to the manager. "Excuse me," he says, "but Mr. Whitney wants to put $250,000 on Sorteado to win at 3–1."

"That's fine," says the manager. "Take it and ask for more of it. They all have to go round and round before they win. And don't bother me with those details."

The assistant cashier comes in with a file. It contains the betting slip, the check, and a note to the effect that the slip is not to be cashed until the check is cleared.

"Oh, yes," says the manager, "I remember you men now. I was lucky to catch the cashier just paying you off. That was very lax. This club protects its members carefully against impostors and fourflushers. I believe you came in here on rather questionable credentials."

"We have a guest card, but we won't argue about that," says Mr. Ryan. "But please don't send that check back immediately. I can deposit the cash in a local bank very soon, and you can clear it through. But right now I am somewhat embarrassed for funds in my home bank."

"Then you shouldn't have written the check," says the manager. "But I'll give you a chance to redeem this check if it is done quickly. I still have it here. It should go through the bank immediately, but I'll hold it for a short time. You deposit the $50,000 cash in our bank. That will show that you could have paid the bet in case you had lost. That is very important."

"You'll hold my check for, say, a week?" asks Mr. Ryan.

"Yes, although it is not quite regular," answers the manager.

Ryan and Fink go back to the hotel to report their success to Mr. Lamster. Ryan feels quite proud of the concession he has gained, and shows it. Mr. Fink likes him less and less. He would like to see him cut out of the deal entirely. They hold a council to see how the money can be raised quickly. This stage of the game, designed to show the con men exactly how much money their victim can raise, is known as the "breakdown."

"I might have known that you men would get into a jam," says Mr. Lamster, "but now that you are in it, I'll do all I can to get you out. I don't want to see you lose that money. But, on the other hand, I can't afford to interfere with my own business. Mr. Ryan, how much cash can you raise right away?"

Mr. Ryan studies very hard. "I haven't much cash in the bank," he says. "Most of my money is tied up in investments. But I have $17,000 in government bonds. I could cash those on short notice."

"How much can you raise, Mr. Fink? Can you make out the other $33,000?"

Mr. Fink studies. He gets out his notebook and perspires over it. Finally he says, "I just can't make it. $25,000 is all I can possibly raise right now. My investments are pretty well tied up and I can't disturb them. But I could cash some paper and raise the $25,000."

"Well," says the accommodating Mr. Lamster, "I have a bank account here. My boss must never find it out or I'd get fired, but I can let you have the other $8,000 until this thing is cleared up. It won't take long."

"That would be damned nice of you," says Mr. Fink.

"All right, now," continues Lamster, "I think we have everything in hand. It is after banking hours now, but the first thing in the morning we will all go to my bank and get things moving. I am well connected there and I am sure that they will co-operate in every way. Where does your money have to come from, Mr. Ryan?"

"My securities are in the People's Bank at North Adams, Massachusetts. I'll telephone the bank in the morning to turn them into cash and send them right down. How long will it take you to get yours, Mr. Fink?"

"I'll have to 'phone Boston," says Mr. Fink. "Mine will be here all right."

Here we are assuming that the con men take a chance with the Federal Government and use the mails to transport the money. Often the mark is "put on the send" as described in the account of the wire.

Mr. Fink is somewhat disturbed over the division of the proceeds. Ryan evidently expects to repay Lamster's $8,000 and take half of the $256,000. That isn't right. If he wants half the proceeds, he should put up half of the capital. Otherwise, they should split it proportionally and give Lamster a share too. That would be only right. He mentions it to Ryan. Ryan hedges, but leaves the impression that he doesn't expect to include Mr. Lamster at all. The irritation that Fink has been feeling for Ryan during the past day flares into definite dislike; the influence of Mr. Lamster looms larger and larger in his mind. This fellow Lamster is one of the finest fellows he has ever met. Nothing small about him. And Mr. Fink cannot abide small people.

At this point the mark is usually "tied up." That is, he is placed in the custody of the roper and never allowed to be alone until the bitter end. It is done something like this.

Mr. Ryan excuses himself, or Mr. Lamster makes a private appointment with Fink. When they are alone, Mr. Lamster speaks thus: "Mr. Fink, I wanted to talk to you privately because I have observed that you have a good deal of character and that you are always to be depended upon. This is just a start. I feel sure that I can make a substantial fortune at this business. You and I understand each other pretty well. There is no reason why you can't go along with me in it. But it is absolutely necessary that we have complete secrecy. Are you willing to assure me that you will protect my confidence in every way?" (At this point the insideman sometimes goes so far as to swear the mark in on a convenient Gideon Bible; but in view of Mr. Fink's obvious integrity, we will not subject him to that ordeal.)

Mr. Fink is only too willing to comply with this request.

"Now about this man Ryan . . ." continues Mr. Lamster.

"I don't like him," says Mr. Fink with some heat. "He is a little too greedy. He wants half the profits without putting up half the capital. He impresses me as being a rather small man."

"I am sorry to say that you express my sentiments exactly," says Lamster. "But that is really neither here nor there. The serious point is this: can he be trusted?"

"I don't think so," says Fink.

"Well, perhaps you are right. And I think you understand how important it is, not only for me but also for you and Ryan, that this thing be guarded very carefully. I have talked with Ryan about it and he doesn't seem to appreciate that point as he should.

"Now what I want to ask is this: For our protection, will you keep a very close watch on Ryan? I mean stay with him at all times. Don't let him out of your sight a moment, for he may see or talk to someone who will tip the whole thing off. Don't let him shake you under any circumstances. And don't let him suspect that you are watching him. Now I will be very busy for the next few days, but I will 'phone you at least once a day and you report to me if everything is going nicely. If Ryan gets out of hand, just let me know and I'll be right up and give him a talking to. By the way, could you get him to share your room?"

Here it is sometimes customary to shift the mark to another hotel. The insideman suggests a quiet and obscure hotel where they will be safe from the newspaper reporters who are in and out of the lobby of the big hotel. The mark induces the roper to move with him and they stay together until the mark is trimmed.

"Perhaps I could," says Fink, "but I'm not anxious for that much of his company."

"Well, it is for the best interests of all of us," says Lamster. "And I know that you can arrange it without making him suspicious. Now, I'll see you at the bank at nine in the morning."

Although Mr. Fink has no inkling of it, the "switch" is now complete. His confidence has been transferred from Mr. Ryan to Mr. Lamster and the tie-up is complete. From now on he won't let Ryan out of his sight. This may be a little hard on the nerves of Mr. Ryan for stormy times are ahead, but it leaves Mr. Lamster free to handle other marks whom other ropers are bringing into the store for a play. And, lest we feel too sorry for Mr. Ryan, his nerves are strong. He has been through this many times before.

That night Fink persuades Ryan to check out of his suite and share a room. Ryan isn't particularly interested, but Fink points out that they may be there some time and it will be much more economical. Ryan finally agrees. They move in together and the eagle eye of Mr. Fink misses no move which might be interpreted adversely. Most of all, he tries to keep Ryan from coming in contact with outsiders. Mr. Ryan, who knows just how far to excite his suspicions so that he will not become bored with his vigil, seems to be always just on the verge of telling the whole plan to some stranger.

Next morning at nine they meet at the bank. Mr. Lamster seems to be well known there. He waits upon the president, introduces his companions, and explains that both these men want to have some assets transferred from up north as quickly as possible. The president is most obliging, for he receives a commission on whatever Mr. Fink will yield.

He has both Ryan and Fink make out checks for the amount they want transferred. Ryan signs his for $17,000 and Fink for $25,000. Mr. Lamster leaves his own personal check for $8,000. The banker assures them that he will open their accounts as soon as the money arrives.

The monotonous period of the "tie-up" now continues. Mr. Ryan, who shows increasing tendencies toward irresponsibility, is subject to the most rigorous examination. All his motives are suspect. Every move he makes is watched by Mr. Fink, who reports once a day to Mr. Lamster. Fink comes to feel that he and he alone stands between Mr. Lamster and disastrous publicity. Ryan talks mostly about the $256,000 they are going to split. He wants to go out and paint the town red. Fink trembles when he thinks of what a few well-placed drinks might do. They eat in their room. They sleep in their room. They read magazines. It is much safer if Fink does not see the newspapers.

Fink experiences half-day periods of elation during which he anticipates strongly the money they are to make; these are followed by periods of worry and depression. He alternates between feelings of warm, cozy security and the cold, clammy fear that all will be lost. This thing isn't real. Yet it is, painfully real. He conjures up all sorts of things which might go wrong with their scheme. He grows concerned because his money does not come right away. He froths and fumes at Mr. Ryan, whose job it is to answer tactfully all his questions and allay all his fears—without seeming to do so.

When he gets too nervous, or when Mr. Ryan's nerves fray, Mr. Lamster visits the room briefly to assure him that everything is working out all right. Fink reports on Ryan, who gets a good, sound talking-to. Mr. Lamster explains the workings of his syndicate and how the horse-gamblers are being beaten. But Mr. Lamster is having troubles of his own now in Miami. He has to lie low because the reporters are hounding him. If they locate him and write him up, his game in Miami is done. Otherwise everything is fine and he will soon make a huge killing. And Mr. Fink mustn't worry because the banker will notify Mr. Lamster just as soon as the money comes through. Fink looks forward to these visits from Lamster; they always make him feel better. This situation may continue for anywhere from several days to several weeks. Let us mercifully end this tie-up after a week.

The bank sends word that Mr. Ryan's money has come. Then Mr. Fink's. Mr. Lamster suggests that they go down to the bank to see if everything is O.K. They do. Everything is in good order. The account is opened in Mr. Ryan's name, since both the betting slip and the check are already in his name. Fink now sticks closer than ever to Ryan, for nothing must happen to that money.

Then all three men go to the Turf Club. Mr. Lamster waits outside. Fink and Ryan go in. The play still goes merrily on. Mr. Fink recognizes some of the customers. Some of the faces are new. But all are playing with money at a scandalous rate. They ask for the manager. They wait. And they wait. The telephone buzzes incessantly. The sheet-writer takes bets over the 'phone for tremendous sums. Prominent names in the sporting world go with them. Business proceeds with smooth precision and breath-taking speed. Everyone studiously ignores them. More delays.

Then the manager sees them. He does not remember them. He has to identify their bet. He apologizes, but he just can't keep so much in his mind. He calls for the familiar file.

"That clears it up," he says. "Now, I suppose you gentlemen want to take up your check?"

"That's right," says Mr. Ryan. "I now have the cash in the bank to cover it. Do you want to call at the bank to verify it?"

"My dear man, I'd think you would see that I can't get away from here during business hours. Of course, I can't go with you to the bank. You bring the money here, our cashier will check it and then you will be paid off."

"But $50,000 is a lot of cash to carry around on the street."

"Well, that is your look-out. I think it will be safe to bring it over here. Just show it at the cashier's window and our man will check it. Good day, gentlemen, I am very busy."

The buzzing 'phone on his desk emphasizes this remark forcibly.

Fink and Ryan go outside and report to Mr. Lamster, who has waited in a conveniently sheltered doorway. He agrees that this is the proper procedure. They all go to the bank and draw $50,000. The banker offers them a little satchel to carry it in. Mr. Fink takes charge of it just to be sure that nothing happens. Although Mr. Fink does not suspect it, an armed tailer follows them from the door of the bank to the entrance of the big store.

When they arrive at the Turf Club Mr. Ryan takes over the money, for he must show the cash. Mr. Fink is in a cold sweat. Just as they are about to enter, Mr. Lamster produces a telegram from his pocket. "It is Jitterbug in the fourth race at 3–1," he says, and quickly puts the telegram in his pocket.

Mr. Fink sees a fortune within his grasp. They have the money. They will soon be paid more. With his share on Jitterbug . . .

"Last flash," says the caller and chalks busily.

This time Mr. Lamster goes in with them. They go to the cashier. Mr. Ryan lays out the $50,000, explaining what they want. The cashier rings for the manager. It is O.K. The cashier begins to count out the $256,000. Mr. Ryan presents his slip. The cashier pushes stacks of bills at Mr. Ryan, who can hardly keep track of the rapidly growing piles. Mr. Fink's scalp is tight and his palms itch.

"Why don't you place it all on Jitterbug?" asks Mr.

Lamster over Mr. Fink's shoulder. "The fourth race is up."

"That's a good idea," says Mr. Ryan, and shoves all the money back to the cashier. "Put it all on Jitterbug to win," says he and turns away, shaky and nervous. Fink is stunned by the speed with which it happened. But it is the right thing to do. Lamster was right. A delicious prickly sensation spreads over him. The beads of perspiration stand out on his brow; his collar chokes him; a bottomless pit yawns in his stomach. He knows how it feels to play with big money.

The cashier writes out a slip calling for $1,020,000 if Jitterbug wins.

"They're off!" says the caller.

Mr. Ryan turns immediately to Mr. Lamster, showing him the ticket. "My God! man," exclaims Lamster, "you bet this horse to win. I said *place.* That horse will run second."

Mr. Fink thinks he is going to faint.

Mr. Lamster grabs the ticket, buttonholes the manager who is just passing and pleads with him to change the ticket to place instead of win. The manager is firm. Lamster begs frantically. But it is no use. Jitterbug places.

Mr. Lamster seizes Ryan by the throat. "You dumb s—— of a b——!" he says. He shakes Ryan like a rat.* The manager tries to step between them. He apologizes for causing the trouble, but protests that he couldn't change the bet after the horses were running.

Mr. Fink's senses are beginning to return. He sees Mr. Ryan struggling and protesting in Lamster's iron grip. They reel back and forth against a sea of cigar smoke and startled faces. A murky red fog settles over everything.

* Sometimes the insideman strikes the roper and knocks him down. One roper adds, on reading this manuscript, "Yes, and if he happened to be sore at me for winning a few dollars from him in the last poker game, he'd hit me a lot harder than was necessary."

"He ruined me too," shouts Fink. "Let me at him! He ruined me. Oh, he ruined me." He lashes out wildly at Mr. Ryan. The manager and the cashier step in and try to stop his wild lunges. "You *will* lose my money!" he shrieks, and breaks away from the men who are restraining him, picks up a metal chair and charges at the struggling men, swinging it over his head. Lamster is still shaking and cursing Ryan, who now begs for his life. Fink has a glimpse of Lamster's white face, distorted with rage, his eyes bulging. He catches the glint of a pistol in Lamster's hand. Lamster breaks from Ryan and backs up a step. The heavy report stops Fink in his tracks, the chair poised awkwardly over his head. Ryan is on the floor, gasping. Fink lowers the chair and gazes at Ryan, who twists and groans. Mr. Fink, appalled and fascinated, steps closer. A stream of blood spurts from Ryan's mouth, spattering Fink's face and shirt. He feels it, warm and slippery, on him. The spectators close in. Lamster is in action. Fink feels himself hurled through the onlookers. They are in the street. Lamster rushes him into a cab. They hurry to the hotel.

There, they take stock of the situation. "I'm afraid I killed him," says Lamster.

"If you hadn't, I would have," says Fink, shaky and fearful. He pours out two drinks.

Mr. Lamster regains his composure somewhat. "I never should have done a thing like that," he moans. "I should never carry a gun. When I lose my temper, I go crazy. But now it's done. And the terrible thing is that you're implicated as an accomplice. I hope the poor devil doesn't die."

Mr. Fink is incapable of speech. He is sickened by what he has been through. He thinks wildly of his family, his wife, his friends, his business; a trial, prison, maybe—

"We can't sit here like a couple of fools," says Mr. Lamster. "Here, let me help you get that blood cleaned off you. Now you do as I say and we'll beat this. Get out of here quickly and go to the La Tosca Hotel in New Orleans. I'll give them the run-around and meet you there in a couple of days. Now follow my instructions and I'll get you out of this."

He helps Fink pack. Fink scurries wildly around the room with his hands full of neckties. Lamster finally gets all his things into his suitcases, hurries him down the stairs and out the side entrance into a cab.

"Don't worry about checking out," he says. "I'll pay the hotel bill and you can square it with me later. See you in a couple of days. Good-by, and good luck."

This method of "blowing the mark off" is called the *cackle-bladder* from the small bladder filled with chicken blood which the roper conceals in his mouth. It is not used except when the mark goes wild and is hard to handle, or where the mark feels sure he has been swindled.

And Mr. Fink is furtively off to New Orleans. But he never meets Mr. Lamster at the La Tosca Hotel. After he has been there several days, he receives a letter from Lamster. Ryan has died. He describes his difficulties with the authorities, warning Fink that he will be picked up in New Orleans, and advising him to move to a hotel in St. Louis, where they will meet. A second letter reaches him in St. Louis sending him to Detroit. From Detroit he is moved to Cleveland. He is furtive and frightened. He has sent home for more money. It is used up. He wires for more. He is moved to Philadelphia. There he receives a pathetic letter from Lamster telling how he has been harried by the police, and saying that he has managed to get enough money together to flee to Europe until the thing blows over. After that, he will get in touch with Fink again and they will recoup their fortune. Good-by and good luck.

Mr. Fink is now close to home. He returns to Boston because he doesn't know what else to do. He has been swindled, but he hardly realizes it. In his heart he nurses a lifelong hatred against James Ryan. His one aim is to conceal his loss from his family and his business associates. For a long time he is apprehensive about being picked up by the police. But they never molest him. By and by he doesn't worry much about it any more, though sometimes he awakes at night to see Ryan's face, contorted and hideous, writhing in the dark. And sometimes he wonders—whatever became of Lamster? He was one hell of a swell fellow.

## 3
## The Rag*

In the rag we see the principles of the pay-off applied to a deal in stocks or securities. Its present form, which is a direct adaptation of the pay-off, has been used for about twenty-five years.

However, let us revert for a moment to the time before the origin of the rag to see what technique was formerly used by confidence men who dealt in stocks. By 1880 stock swindles were common. By 1900 the con men had perfected a technique, entirely different from the stock swindle now used, which had only one serious weakness—the touches were not very large compared to those taken off by the modern rag. As was the case in most of the earlier and more primitive forms of confidence swindle, the use of the store was not known. The older form of the stock swindle worked this way:

The roper, whom we shall call Will Finley, had connections with a brokerage office in New York from which he obtained lists of the persons who bought stocks by mail. From these lists he culled likely-looking prospects whom he interviewed. When he found one living, say, in Mar-

* All the names used in the descriptions of stock swindles in this chapter are fictitious.

ion, Indiana, who he felt sure would take the bait, he told him this story:

"Mr. Eggbert, I have information that there is a man in Indianapolis who has three thousand shares of stock in the Bird Cage Gold Mine. The stock hasn't been quoted for a long time. Everyone thinks it is worthless. But I have a friend who works on Wall Street and he tells me that the old mine has come to life. It promises very good returns for anyone who holds the stock. Smart brokers are now quietly buying it up in blocks for next to nothing.

"Now this fellow who has the stock is about to die of consumption. He has no idea that the stock is going up, and I understand he is pretty hard up. I think he would sell it for anything he could get out of it. His name is White. He is staying at the Henry Clay Hotel there. I haven't seen him, but the desk clerk says he is very sick and may not live. If his stock could be bought at the right price it would make the buyer a good profit. I haven't the money to swing the deal, but if you could finance it, we could split fifty-fifty on the profit and both make a nice little thing out of it."

Mr. Eggbert has owned some stocks now and then and likes to speculate in them. This sounds like just what he is looking for. But it will have to be investigated. He wants to look into it. Mr. Finley suggests a personal investigation. They set forth to find Mr. White.

They visit Mr. White in his hotel room. White has been selected for his tall and slender physique—a build not hard to find among con men. His face is skillfully made up. His hands are waxy and almost transparent against the white sheets. He coughs red ink into a towel. He reclines against the pillows. His cheeks are flushed. His eyes are starry bright. He doesn't look as if he would live a week. The shades are drawn and in the semi-darkness a satchel reposes beside his bed. In it are three thousand shares of perfectly worthless Bird Cage mining stock, beautifully engraved and embossed. This stock is practically all of his worldly goods.

In this pitiable state he meets Mr. Eggbert and Mr. Finley, who have concocted a story to allay any suspicions which Mr. White may have regarding their motives for buying the stock. "We are acting for the executors of the estate of the late John Bowling," says Mr. Finley. "We have heard that you have a small block of Bird Cage mining stock."

Mr. White admits that he has three thousand shares, inherited from his father.

"Well," says Mr. Finley, "this estate must be settled up. But it cannot be cleared up until we secure a controlling interest in the old Bird Cage Mine. The stock is almost worthless, but we must buy up fifty-one per cent of it before January first. We can't offer you much for the stock, but we have come to see you with a view to talking the matter over."

It is with difficulty that Mr. White arouses himself enough to talk about the matter. His cough racks him. Yes, he is interested. He knows the stock isn't worth very much on the market. But it is all the property he has and he wants to get all he can out of it. He needs cash badly.

"What will you offer me for it?" he asks.

"We are hardly prepared to make you an offer on it," says the cautious Mr. Finley. "It isn't even listed on the market, and probably is worth very little. We would have to investigate it before we can make you an offer. But we are prepared to offer to take an open option on the entire block, and make you an offer a little later."

"Well," says the cadaverous Mr. White, "I need cash very badly. What would you consider a fair price for the option?"

"We can offer you $25," says Mr. Finley, and Mr. Eggbert nods assent.

"That isn't very much," complains Mr. White. "But if that is all you will give, I'll have to take it."

"Very well," says Finley. "Here is the option form. You sign it and we will pay you the $25."

The deal is completed and the two men leave Mr. White racking his piteous life away. They congratulate each other on the wisdom of their move. Now to find out something about what the stock can be sold for to the right people. Mr. Finley has the names of three brokerage houses, one in New York, one in New Orleans, and one in Chicago, all furnished by his friend on Wall Street. They go to a telegraph office. Wires are sent to all three asking for quotations.

These wires are picked up at their respective destinations by accomplices who have been notified just when to expect them and they are waiting at the telegraph offices to pick up the messages sent under their respective names. Immediately they wire back offers to buy blocks of any size of the stock. New York offers $3.50. New Orleans $3.75. Chicago $4. That looks good.

Fortified with these telegrams, Mr. Finley and Mr. Eggbert decide that they will try to buy the stock for $1, and at most $1.25 or $1.50. They decide that cash on the line will make a strong impression on Mr. White. So Mr. Eggbert either goes home for the money while Mr. Finley attends to pressing business in the city, or, more desirable still, Mr. Eggbert signs a check and has the bank in Indianapolis open up an account for him immediately. Just as soon as the cash is on hand they hover like vultures over the dying victim.

The hotel room is still hushed and dark. Mr. White looks even more waxen and deathlike than before. They offer him a dollar a share. He declines, contending that his father paid $50 a share for it and that it must be worth much more than a dollar. They haggle. Mr. White holds out stubbornly. They finally compromise at $1.50 per share and Mr. Eggbert pays him the $4,475 in cash.

They leave the hotel feeling that they have made a fortunate deal. It is very comforting for Mr. Eggbert to think of that telegram from Chicago offering $4 a share. A neat profit of $7,500, to be split in half—$3,750 apiece.

Mr. Finley pleads very pressing business in Indianapolis which will hold him there for some time. He proposes that Mr. Eggbert go to the brokerage house in Chicago to cash in the stock, and Mr. Finley, in return for this accommodation, will pay Mr. Eggbert's expenses when they divide the money. Mr. Eggbert lusts for the $3,750 profit and agrees. Mr. Finley sees him to the train for Chicago, admonishing him to guard the package of stock with his life. Mr. Eggbert, armed with the telegram and the address of a brokerage house which does not exist, departs with joy in his heart. He will be back tomorrow, he promises.

Back at the hotel Mr. Finley knocks with a pre-arranged signal upon Mr. White's door. Mr. White, who has played 'possum lest Mr. Eggbert return for something, now admits his partner. He resembles a frowsy corpse in his short nightshirt, his gangly joints protruding grotesquely. But he is very agile for a sick man.

"The egg has blown," says Mr. Finley cheerily. "Now he can play hide and seek around the Village for a while. I've got the touch right here. Get a move on and get that grease-paint off. You look like a damned scarecrow. You give me the fan-tods. We've just got time to check out and get down to the shed before the 4:40 pulls out."

And Mr. White makes prodigious noises in the bathroom.

This game was, within limits, very successful. It was played both in America and abroad by American confidence men as the best and most effective stock swindle which, up to 1910, the con men had been able to devise. The only capital needed to operate it was a bundle of worthless stock. But it lacked the advantages of play against a store, with a permanent fixer to take care of trouble. The convincer, in the form of the telegrams, was rather weak, and there were no facilities for cooling the mark out; it depended too heavily upon a single factor—the roper's getting the mark's confidence and holding it. However, the game prospered—and still does, as a matter of fact—even though it is largely supplanted by the rag.

The modern rag constitutes an application to stocks of the fundamental principles of the pay-off; in fact, most big-con ropers will bring in marks for either the pay-off or the rag;* usually it is not until the roper has brought the mark into town and has had a talk with the insideman that it is decided which game to play him for. As a general rule—though there are many exceptions—the mark is played for the game he is least likely to know something about. Thus a broker would probably be played for the pay-off since he might know too much about stocks to be fleeced by the rag; on the other hand, an experienced race-gambler and sportsman might be easier to play on the stocks, for he might suspect the race-game. But any big-con man will tell you that brokers and bankers have taken the hook for the rag, and hardened race-track plungers have been trimmed by the pay-off.

Let us call the intended victim of the rag Mr. Asa Savage. He has met a very affable gentleman, whom we shall

* Most mobs change the settings in their big store to fit the game which is being played at the moment; that is, if the pay-off is used, the gambling club props are used; if the rag is being played, the brokerage office is set up in place of the gambling club.

In cities where the mobs are well established and have excellent political connections (as, for instance, in Denver during the 1920's) separate stores for each type of game are maintained. These stores are more or less permanent and are very convenient because once a mark is roped, he can be played immediately on either game without the necessity for changing props between plays.

call Charles Meade, on the Pullman coming into Denver. Mr. Meade has decided that Mr. Savage is well fatted for the kill and he has him firmly in tow, although Mr. Savage feels no suspicion. They have moved into Denver and are established there.

Mr. Meade immediately gets in touch with his inside-man, who shall be named Daniel Duff during the play.

"Well, Kid," says he, "the savage is here. He is a wholesale fruit merchant from Dallas. He is here for the convention. I think he'll go for fifty or sixty grand. I have him parked over here in the Granada Hotel."

"What does it look like?" asks Duff, who is well equipped to give their man a fine play in almost any kind of store on almost any kind of game.

"I think he craves the rag," says Meade. "He has already copped some dough in stocks and I guess he is about due to blow some."

"Can we play the point-out for him?" asks Duff.

"I think that will suit him fine," answers Meade. "He likes to hike in the fresh air. He's hipped on it. And he gets up early in the morning. I'll take him to breakfast about seven. You park in front of the hotel dining room and I'll pick out a table by the window. When I give you the office, have the driver pull away from the curb. That will give him the first flash. Then I'll walk him around until about nine. You plant yourself in the car over on University Boulevard. Then we'll give him the play right away."

"O.K.," says Duff. "I'll see you there."

The next morning Mr. Savage and Mr. Meade breakfast together. They have ham and griddle-cakes, for strenuous times are ahead. There is no use to play for a mark when he is faint with hunger. As they are enjoying their meal, Mr. Meade suddenly rises in his seat and peers through the window which gives directly on the street. Mr. Savage has a glimpse of a large, chauffeured limousine pulling away from the curb.

"Did you see that man in that big car?" asks Meade. "He looks to me like a friend of my uncle's down in Fort Worth. Let me see, what was his name? Duff, that's it. Duff. He was in on some deals with my uncle. He's some kind of a big-shot in Wall Street."

"He certainly drives a swell car," says Mr. Savage. "But I didn't get a very good look at him."

"If he is staying here in Denver, I'd like to look him up," says Meade. "But I suppose it would be impossible to find him."

Conversation turns to the stock market, and Mr. Savage holds forth at some length on his investments. They finish breakfast and Mr. Meade picks up the checks.

Mr. Savage likes Mr. Meade. He is a native Texan. It is pleasant to hear that drawl up here in Colorado. And Mr. Meade is such a quiet, mild-mannered man with pale blue eyes and a kindly face. He is past middle age, with a sizable nest egg laid away. And he knows some of the people in Brownsville where Mr. Savage lived as a boy. He shares Mr. Savage's penchant for walking and seems to appreciate Mr. Savage's effort to acquaint him with Denver. They get along very well.

After breakfast they start out for a brief walk before Mr. Savage goes out to attend the convention he has come up for. The air is crisp and invigorating. The trees are blossoming out with the first warm days of spring. Mr. Meade produces two of the long, strong stogies which Mr. Savage has smoked for years. They walk briskly and Mr. Savage volubly discusses the problems of the wholesale fruit business.

Suddenly Mr. Meade seizes his companion's arm and calls attention to a large car parked by the curb. Savage recognizes the big Packard. A distinguished-looking gentleman with a deeply lined face is sitting in the back seat busily engaged in studying a sheaf of telegrams through a pince-nez.

This method of tying up the mark is known as the point-out. It does not have the advantage which finding the leather has of immediately obligating the insideman to make investments for his two benefactors, but in the hands of first-rate confidence men it produces very good results.

"Do you see that man over there?" asks Meade. "Why, that is Mr. Duff. He is the man we saw at breakfast. I was sure I wasn't mistaken. He made over a million on the stock market down in Fort Worth. The papers were full of his pictures. I'll bet he is doing the same thing up here."

Mr. Savage finds himself headed, willy nilly, for the unsuspecting Mr. Duff.

"I wonder if he remembers me," muses Mr. Meade. "Maybe we could get him to give us some tips."

Mr. Duff glares in annoyance over his glasses at the two strangers who are peering into the car. Mr. Meade extends his hand.

"What are you doing up here?" he asks.

"I don't believe I know you, sir," says Mr. Duff icily. "Are you a reporter?"

"Why, don't you remember me?" says Mr. Meade. "I'm Charley Meade from Brownsville, Texas. Judge Smith from Fort Worth is my uncle. I was visiting him last winter. Don't you remember, he introduced us up in his chambers? You and the Judge had just cleaned up a lot of money on the stock market. Don't you recall?"

Mr. Duff remembers. "Yes, yes," he says. "And the old Judge certainly did think a lot of you. Told me you were the only one of his kin that really gave a damn about him." Mr. Duff laughs genially and Mr. Meade joins in. "The old Judge is quite a character. And a very shrewd man, let me tell you that. He and I have been in on many a deal together. If it hadn't been for the newspapers, we would have cleaned up another million in Fort Worth. But the reporters got wise and they ruined me. For heaven's sake, don't let it be known that I'm here, or they will hound me to death. Look here what they did to me down in Sacramento."

He produces the conventional newspaper clipping, much like the one used in the pay-off except that it recounts Mr. Duff's phenomenal exploits in stocks in that community.

Mr. Meade agrees to silence. He introduces Mr. Savage with the enthusiasm which native Texans show for one another.

"I can vouch for Mr. Savage," says Meade. "He is one square shooter. He knows a lot of the home folks down in Brownsville. You don't have to worry about his letting anything out.

"Mr. Duff," says the roper, "I have always wanted to invest on one of your tips ever since the Judge dealt with you, but I never had a chance to ask you. Would you consider giving me a tip or two, just to make expenses?"

Mr. Duff hesitates. Then he warms up and says it will be a pleasure to serve any friends of old Judge Smith. Mr. Meade fishes out his wallet and extracts fifty dollars. "Why don't you give him fifty, too?" asks Meade, turning to the mark.

Mr. Savage may consider himself a plunger and hand over fifty. If he demurs, Mr. Meade waves his hand generously and says, "That's all right. You don't know this man, Mr. Savage. Just invest that fifty for both of us, and we'll divide any profit."

Mr. Savage feels properly put in his place, and wonders why he didn't agree to invest fifty also. If there were to be any profits, he would have made twice as much. Mr. Duff takes the fifty, puts it in his wallet, chats a moment, looks at his watch, and says he must be at the exchange when it opens.

"Now be sure," he cautions them, "never to breathe a word of this—least of all to a reporter. Good-by."

"But where will we see you?" asks Meade. "We are over at the Granada. Where are you staying?"

"Oh, that's right," says Duff. "I'll want to see you soon. You are over at the Granada. Well, you go on over there and I'll call on you there some time this morning. Good-by." Mr. Duff speaks to the driver and the big car purrs away.

"Who is that fellow?" asks Savage, once Duff has gone.

"Why," says Meade, "he is an expert stock manipulator. The Judge told me all about how he works. He is an agent for a combine of big Wall Street brokers who are trying to break up the branch stock exchanges and bucket shops. They have millions behind them. They control the rise and fall of prices of large blocks of stock, and then tip him off whether to buy or sell. He makes plenty of money at it. He can hardly lose."

"Oh," says Mr. Savage, and contemplates this vast idea.

Usually the insideman tells the tale, as he did in the wire and the pay-off, but here, for the sake of variety, the roper tells it. There are several advantages in having the insideman tell it. First, the insideman is almost always a better operator than the roper; he has had unlimited experience in handling marks and has an uncanny sense of how to deal with people. Second, it is a very propitious moment to bring the mark under the influence of the insideman, who will control the play from this point on. Third, the mark already knows the roper and it is comforting to him to have someone he knows to talk the matter over with; when the mark sees the roper convinced by the insideman's story, the power of suggestion is brought to bear on him.

The two men return to their hotel. Mr. Savage skimps his first morning sessions at the convention so that he may be back when Duff returns. He has just returned to the room when Mr. Duff 'phones from the lobby. They tell him to come on up. He enters. He has taken on added stature in Mr. Savage's eyes. He is a genuine capitalist. And he looks the part.

"Well, gentlemen," says Mr. Duff, "I invested that fifty dollars for you along with a deal of my own. The returns were just $150—not much, but enough to pay your hotel bill. Here it is."

He takes out an envelope where the earnings of Mr. Meade and Mr. Savage are kept, separate from his other numerous transactions.

"Thank you a lot," says Meade. "Here, Mr. Savage, is your half."

Mr. Savage may need no second offer. But the chances are that he feels compelled by etiquette to refuse. Mr. Meade insists. Mr. Duff interposes.

"Here, here, gentlemen. Why argue about it? Mr. Savage, I'll take your half. And Mr. Meade, I'll take yours. And I'll invest both of them when I get back to the exchange. Then there will be no argument. You can each have what your share nets you."

He pockets the money, putting it carefully back into the envelope. They chat a bit, and Mr. Savage is very much impressed with Mr. Duff. When he goes out, Mr. Savage wishes that he had the nerve to add a hundred more to the seventy-five which will be invested for him.

Just after lunch Mr. Duff stops by again. He hands each man $225, and waves away their thanks graciously. "It is certainly a pleasure," he says, "to do a favor for friends of the old Judge. His friends are always my friends."

In playing Mr. Savage, we have, in order to prevent the game from becoming unduly complicated, assumed that Mr. Duff is the permanent insideman, that the mark has been roped by a single roper, and that it has been possible to move him directly to the city where the big store is located. Ordinarily the best ropers work in pairs and give the mark several convincing plays before he is moved to the big store, as described in *The Mob.* Here a single roper and the permanent insideman are giving him the convincers.

This sort of play goes on for some little time—perhaps for the rest of the day, perhaps well into the next day. As soon as Duff and Meade decide that Mr. Savage is thoroughly hooked, the big play begins. By this time we shall say that Mr. Savage has made $1,500 from the humble $25 put up for him by Mr. Meade, and that he now has the money in his pocket. Both he and Mr. Meade want Duff to keep on investing their money for them.

But Mr. Duff is a very busy man. He must make a flying trip down to Albuquerque and back. He doesn't see why they can't make their own investments. He will introduce them at the exchange and furnish them with the necessary information which he receives regularly by wire from New York. He seems to have taken a great fancy to Mr. Savage. And Mr. Savage feels that Mr. Duff is very agreeable and democratic to be such a power in the financial world.

"But, gentlemen," says Mr. Duff, "what are you going to make your money with? Not that little $1,500 apiece I made for you, surely. Does either of you have a bank account here?"

Neither one has.

"Well," says Duff, "here is a blank check. Now follow my instructions. Make this check for, say, $100,000." Mr. Savage is frightened at the thought of signing such a check. Mr. Meade hesitates because he says he never could make good a check of that size.

"You will never have to," says Duff. "Just follow my instructions and that $100,000 will double itself. Then you can take up the check and have a hundred thousand clear profit. Oh, yes. Here, Mr. Savage, give Mr. Meade that $1,500. Now, Meade, add your $1,500. Now you have $103,000 to invest. Gentlemen, you can't make money without money to play with. Now, Meade, that check. Have you got it signed?"

He inspects the check and seems satisfied that everything is in good order.

That afternoon they are taken to the brokerage office and introduced to the manager as friends of Mr. Duff. "Give them anything they want," says Duff. "They are friends of mine and I might add that they have very good connections down Texas way. Their credit is gilt-edged. I can vouch for that."

Then he takes Meade and Savage cautiously aside. "Watch American Petroleum closely," he says. "You will observe that even now it is very active. Buy $103,000 worth as soon as it goes under 3. It will fluctuate somewhat to throw any speculators off. Then the big orders will come through. When it reaches 5¾ sell and sell quickly, for it won't hold there long." Then he departs for Albuquerque.

The brokerage is doing a thriving business. Conservative, substantial-looking businessmen, brokers with cigarettes always alight, financiers, all buy and sell stocks and securities in very large blocks. Some of them deal in cash. Most of them have accounts. There is plenty of money in evidence, and it changes hands rapidly. The cashier always has a ready stack of "coarse ones" where they are visible to the customers. And the clerk at the cashier's elbow is taking orders at the 'phone almost faster than he can write them out. "Yes, sir, Mr. Johnson," he is saying, "yes, 50,000 shares of Consolidated Copper at $12.25. . . . Yes, Mr. Forester. How many American Can? 15,000? Yes . . ."

This is, of course, the big store for the rag. It is a first-rate replica of a broker's office, with the staff of brokers, board-markers, clerks, etc., and with tickers and stock-board rapidly reflecting the ups and downs of leading issues. Mr. Savage does not suspect that the entire set-up is fake, or that all the customers are shills, carefully made up and instructed in their parts. They talk incessantly of stocks. They live stock, stock, stock. They plunge just as heavily as the boost for the pay-off did on the horses.

They watch American Petroleum. It is quoted at $3\frac{3}{4}$. Very shortly it moves. $3\frac{5}{8}$ is chalked on the board. Then $3\frac{1}{4}$. Then $3\frac{1}{8}$. Then 3. Meade and Savage grow tense. Then $2\frac{7}{8}$. They invest their $103,000 in American Petroleum. Almost immediately, it goes down on the board to $2\frac{5}{8}$. Half an hour later it is down to $2\frac{1}{2}$. Mr. Savage feels a little apprehensive about his $1,500. But this is exactly what Mr. Duff had said it would do. Then it drops to $2\frac{3}{8}$. There it stays. Then it moves again. Up to $2\frac{7}{8}$. Mr. Meade and Mr. Savage sit back comfortably in their chairs and watch the board through the haze of cigar smoke. The chatter of stocks, the hum of the ticker makes them feel a sense of elation. Business is good. Mr. Savage is calling attention to their issue. It moves again. The boy puts up 3. Then $3\frac{1}{8}$. Then $3\frac{5}{8}$. The afternoon passes. It is near time for the markets to close. Their stock moves again. And rapidly, again. They can see that big blocks of it are being bought up in New York. It is up to $5\frac{1}{8}$. Then $5\frac{3}{4}$. There it holds. Mr. Duff had said sell at $5\frac{3}{4}$.

They approach the cashier's window with their receipt. The cashier is busy cashing receipts for men ahead of them. They wait. Mr. Meade holds the ticket. The cashier looks at it, and begins to pay them their $206,000. But the manager interposes.

"I have just had word from the bank that there are no funds to back this check," says he. "Which one of you men is Mr. Meade?"

"I am," says Meade. "Mr. Duff said that arrangements had been made here for us to have credit if we needed it."

"I know he did, but a hundred-thousand-dollar check is a pretty large one to put through without any account in the bank. I had no idea you wanted time on a check that large."

Then he turns to the cashier and puts him on the carpet for having accepted such a large check. The cashier says he thought Mr. Duff had vouched for these men. The manager says that he did, but no amount was specified and that it was wrong to let them deposit a check for that amount. The cashier still has the money (or the check, as the case may be) in his hands to pay them off. Mr. Meade and Mr. Savage contend that they made the investment in good faith, and that they should have their profit. The manager agrees.

"I will hold this check for a short time," says he. "And meanwhile your profits will be impounded in our vault. When you deposit $100,000 in the bank to take up the check, you will be paid. But we can't hold it long. It is a bit irregular to hold it at all. I don't mind telling you that it is only because Mr. Duff is vouching for you that we can do it."

Mr. Savage raises the question of the $3,000 in cash. Couldn't they be paid off on that part of the investment?

The manager looks at the receipt which Mr. Meade holds. "It is true," he says, "that you invested $3,000 cash. But this is entered as a single purchase and must be settled for as such. It is now almost closing time, gentlemen. You must excuse me. Don't let that matter of the check wait too long."

"I think we can arrange to take care of it one way or another," says Meade. "Just hold it here and give us a little time."

They return to the hotel to await the return of Mr. Duff. Then they will give Mr. Savage the breakdown to find out how much he can really invest.

From this moment on the mark is tied up with the

roper, as in the pay-off. Next day Mr. Duff returns and is acquainted with the situation. He tries to help them discover a way to raise the necessary $100,000. They try frantically to scrape it all together. Mr. Savage can get $55,000. Mr. Meade sells some bonds for $20,000. He also borrows $12,000 more by wire from a brother in San Francisco. They now have $87,000. Where in the world will they turn up the other $13,000? Mr. Duff comes to their rescue. He will arrange to loan them that much in order to save their investment. He has treated them both like brothers through all this. Mr. Savage resolves to reward him with a handsome gift when this is all settled up.

Now the parallels to the pay-off continue. Mr. Savage is kept tied up until his money comes. The days of agony, sweat and worry follow. Time drags with leaden slowness. The money comes. Mr. Meade gets his also. Mr. Savage is taken to the bank and an account is opened for him. Mr. Duff not only makes everything smooth sailing through the bank but makes his word good and contributes $13,000 as he has promised.

They are requested, as in the pay-off, to bring the money to the brokerage to show that they could have paid had their stock gone down instead of up. They remove it from the bank. Meade is given the package. He shows it at the cashier's window to be checked, as in the pay-off. Mr. Savage sees the fortune he has dreamed about for the past ten days suddenly within his grasp. The cashier is pushing out the packs of bills, sealed with little tan labels, to Meade, whose arms are full of them.

Suddenly Duff steps forward with a telegram. He speaks swiftly of its contents to Mr. Meade. It is an order to sell up to 20,000 shares of Gypsum Consolidated at 20½.

"You handle 11,000 of it and put up this money as security. I'll take the rest. Between us we'll clean up."

Mr. Duff steps back to talk to Mr. Savage. He explains

how this stock is to be sold short on a tip, then bought in at a much lower price, and delivered at 20½. Mr. Savage sees a vast fortune developing. He speculates and figures. Mr. Meade turns about with the cashier's receipt. Mr. Duff looks at it aghast.

"My God! man," he roars. "You bought 11,000 shares. I meant for you to sell that block. Sell it short! Don't you see this telegram? *Sell!* Now you've ruined us all. . . ."*

The world reels for Mr. Savage. His house of cards has slithered down and buried him in the ruins. He vaguely hears Duff berating Meade in the strongest of language. Meade is begging and pleading. He says that Duff did not tell him to sell. He said that they could *handle* 11,000 shares. He thought they were going to buy it. He turns to the manager, who has come over when the trouble starts.

All three start to talk at once. The customers form a knot about the three men. Finally Mr. Duff succeeds in making the manager understand what has happened. Meade, white-faced and tearful, begs the manager to countermand the order.

"I can't possibly do that," says the manager. "That order has already been 'phoned in to New York. Look at that board. Gypsum Consolidated has already begun to drop. The only thing you can do is to raise more margin, and raise it quickly if you want to save your investment. Look, there is Consolidated at 18⅜. What is that new quotation? 17¾. That stock is falling rapidly. Gentlemen, I'll have to sell you out!"†

Mr. Savage feels the numbness which comes with disaster. Somehow he and the insideman find themselves out on the street. Meade is beside them sniveling and

* The stock in this confidence game is all bought on margin, so that it would be impossible to hold the stock until it goes up again without raising more margin to save the investment.

† For a slightly different method of playing the mark on the rag, see *Fighting The Underworld,* Van Cise, Philip S. Houghton, Mifflin Company, 1936.

crying. Savage feels murder in his heart. He would like to tear that cringing, stupid Meade into shreds. Duff tries to drive Meade away; he follows them up the street. Duff becomes very abusive and Savage joins in. They head for the hotel.

At the desk Mr. Duff is given a telegram. They go up to the room. Duff pours Savage a good drink. "This has been a terrible blow," he says. "A drink will straighten you up. Then we'll think about how you can get that money back."

The door opens and Meade comes swiftly in. He is pleading, begging, apologizing, weeping, howling. He has lost heavily. He is ruined. He wants just one more chance to recoup. Won't Duff have pity on him and take him back for another deal tomorrow so that he won't be penniless? Won't Savage or Duff loan him a hundred dollars to live on until he can get on his feet? He is completely broke, and his poor brother will go bankrupt because his $12,000 is gone.

In this account it will be observed that Mr. Savage is being given only one play—the play for the "little block," as the first big plunge is called. There are several methods of lining him up for the "big block," or second play, provided the con men decide he is good for another play. For instance, when Duff and Savage return to the hotel after the swindle and Meade follows them crying, and begging to be forgiven for his mistake, Meade confesses that he lied during the "breakdown" when they were trying to raise the money. He says that he had more than $32,000, but that he was afraid to invest all of it. Now, however, he is convinced, and if Mr. Duff will let him in on another deal, he has $23,000 more which he is willing to put up in order that they can all make back what they have lost. Mr. Savage is called upon for his share on the second deal. Mr. Duff forgives Meade and agrees to help them recoup and so the second play is on.

However, in our version, Mr. Duff is firm. He denounces Meade mercilessly. He pushes him out of the door and bolts it from the inside. Then he turns to Savage.

"Look what they gave me downstairs," says he, pulling out the telegram.

It reads: WHAT TROUBLE DENVER? PROCEED LOS ANGELES FOR FURTHER INSTRUCTIONS.

"What does that mean?" asks Savage.

"It means that the big boys in New York know what has happened when that order to sell wasn't carried out. Now all their manipulation is for nothing. And I think the brokers here are suspicious. I've got to go to Los Angeles and wait till they get another set-up ready for me to work on. You certainly have had a tough break. I think I can help you get some of that money back. You go right on to the Avocado Hotel in Los Angeles. I'll follow you just as soon as I settle up some business here. You be very careful that Meade doesn't follow you, for he may suspect that we will work together again. I'll take you down to the eleven o'clock train and see that he doesn't follow either of us. Now let's get your things packed and get started."

The same precautions regarding the police as those described under The Wire are taken here.

Mr. Savage is still in a daze. The faint glimmering of hope which he sees bolsters him up. He drags himself out of his chair and listlessly prepares to leave. He doesn't quite know why he feels that he should follow Duff's instructions, but he cannot think for himself. He is glad Duff is there to think for him. He packs and Duff sees him off, cheering him with many promises.

But Duff never shows up at Los Angeles. He writes Savage to proceed to San Francisco, as he has had trouble with the authorities at Los Angeles. Savage waits in San Francisco until further word comes. He is instructed to move to San Antonio. There he receives a telegram from

Galveston: SYNDICATE BROKEN UP. EVERYTHING WENT BAD. SAILING SOUTH AMERICA TODAY.

Savage is broke. He is tired and discouraged. The weary road he has traveled, the strain and tension under which he has lived for the past three weeks, have left him almost a nervous wreck. He goes home to Dallas and takes up again the broken threads of his wholesale fruit business. But deep down in his heart he hopes that some day again he will find Duff, and together they will be able to make a fortune.

Another form of blow-off for handling recalcitrant marks is the "button." If the mark gets out of hand, two burly detectives appear with a warrant for the insideman, who is charged with fraudulent stock manipulation (in the pay-off, with swindling the bookmakers). The manager accuses the mark and the roper of being accomplices to the swindle. The insideman admits his guilt but protests that they have nothing to do with it and talks the detectives into allowing his friends to go free. Then the insideman is led away while the roper cools the mark out and gets him to another city. However, neither the button nor the cackle-bladder is used extensively unless the mark really causes trouble, although Curley Carter, in his store in Mt. Clemens, Michigan, used the cackle-bladder almost exclusively. "It's a lot easier to just plug the roper and watch the mark light a rag," he laughed.

## 4

In treating these big-con games, the wire, the rag and the pay-off, composite illustrations have been used. That is, an ideal mark has been placed in an ideal situation so that the reader may see the games progress with few variations from the norm. This is done because no two marks are ever played in just the same manner. Both the roper and the insideman vary their techniques infinitely to suit the situation. And the situation is determined by first, the mark—his intelligence, his interests, his business, and the amount of native larceny in his blood. Second, by the physical conditions under which he must be roped and played, where he must be taken, how long he must be held there, how closely his normal and natural movements will coincide with the movements which the con men desire him to make, conflicts, if any, between the demands of his ordinary business and the demands on his time made by the con game, the distance he must be sent for his money, the ease with which he can liquidate his property, and possible interference by outsiders such as members of his family, bankers, attorneys, etc. Third, the relations with the law maintained by the con men in the city where the store is located. The final decision as to how the mark is to be played rests with the insideman; even with the detailed information (based on careful study of the mark over a period of several days) brought in by the roper, the insideman is frequently forced to vary his play considerably as he goes along, depending upon his wide experience and his acutely developed "grift sense" to guide him.

Whenever a mark objects at any stage of the game, his arguments are met immediately by one or the other of the con men; for instance, if, after the convincers, the mark wants to back out, the roper professes to be so thoroughly convinced that he offers to sign an agreement by which he will buy out the mark's interest in the deal for a liberal consideration; usually, after one of these "chills" the mark comes back into the deal with greater confidence than he has ever had before. Any one play may involve a great number of deviations of this sort, impossible to include in a written version of the game because it is impossible to determine where any given mark may balk, and it is even more difficult to foresee how the con men might meet his objections. Hence, it seems much better here to present an hypothetical case that the reader may not be lost in a maze of details.

Big-time confidence games are in reality only carefully rehearsed plays in which every member of the cast *except the mark* knows his part perfectly. The insideman is the star of the cast; while the minor participants are competent actors and can learn their lines perfectly, they must look to the insideman for their cues; he must be not only a fine actor, but a playwright extempore as well. And he must be able to retain the confidence of an intelligent man even after that man has been swindled at his hands.

The reader may be able to get a better view of the situation if he will imagine for a moment what would happen if, say, fifteen of his friends decided to play a prank on him. They get together without his knowledge and write the script for a play which will last for an entire week. There are parts for all of them. The victim of the prank is isolated from everyone except the friends who have parts. His every probable reaction has been calculated in advance and the script prepared to meet these reactions. Furthermore, this drama is motivated by some fundamental weakness of the victim—liquor, money, women, or even some harmless personal crotchet. The victim is forced to go along with the play, speaking approximately the lines which are demanded of him; they spring unconsciously to his lips. He has no choice but to go along, because most of the probable objections that he can raise have been charted and logical reactions to them have been provided in the script. Very shortly the victim's feet are quite off the ground. He is living in a play-world which he cannot distinguish from the real world. His natural but latent motives are called forth in perfectly contrived situations; actions which, under other circumstances, he would never perform seem natural and logical. He is living in a fantastic, grotesque world which resembles the real one so closely that he cannot distinguish the difference. He is the victim of a confidence game.

Every reader probably feels sure that *he* is proof against con games; that his native horse-sense would prevent him from being made a victim, that these tricks which seem so patent in print would never ensnare him. Perhaps so. But let him remember that competent con men find a good deal of diversion in "playing the con" for one another, and that many a professional has suddenly realized that he is the butt of a practical joke in which all the forces of the big con have been brought to bear upon him.

Now, confidence men do not go about burdened down with bales of script written out in advance to take care of every situation which may develop. They do not write out anything. But they know from experience the situations which are likely to come up, and know their lines letter-perfect for those situations. Then there are a number of stock variations which can be used if the office is given by the insideman. All the players know these variations by rote, and can swing into their routine at the given signal.

These variations aside, all big-con games fall into the same general pattern, the fundamentals of which were outlined in the early pages of this book. The rather remarkable but well-established fact is that men who have been beaten once will come back again—and again, and again. Truly, "you can't knock a good mark."

# 4

# The Mark

## I

People who read of con touches in the newspaper are often wont to remark: "That bird must be stupid to fall for a game like that. Why, anybody should know better than to do what he did. . . ." In other words, there is a widespread feeling among legitimate folk that anyone who is the victim of a confidence game is a numskull.

But it should not be assumed that the victims of confidence games are all blockheads. Very much to the contrary, the higher a mark's intelligence, the quicker he sees through the deal directly to his own advantage. To expect a mark to enter into a con game, take the bait, and then, by sheer reason, analyze the situation and see it as a swindle, is simply asking too much. The mark is thrown into an unreal world which very closely resembles real life; like the spectator regarding the life groups in a museum of natural history, he cannot tell where the real scene merges into the background. Hence, it should be no reflection upon a man's intelligence to be swindled. In fact, highly intelligent marks, even though they may tax the ingenuity of the con men, respond best to the proper type of play. They see through the deal which is presented, analyze it, and strike the lure like a flash; most con men feel that it is sport of a high order to play them successfully to the gaff. It is not intelligence but integrity which determines whether or not a man is a good mark.

Stupid or "lop-eared" marks are often played; they are too dull to see their own advantage, and must be worked up to the point again and again before a ray of light filters through their thick heads. Sometimes they are difficult or impossible to beat. Always they merit the scorn and contempt of the con men. Elderly men are easy to play because age has slowed down their reactions.

Most marks come from the upper strata of society, which, in America, means that they have made, married, or inherited money. Because of this, they acquire status which in time they come to attribute to some inherent superiority, especially as regards matters of sound judgment in finance and investment. Friends and associates, themselves social climbers and sycophants, help to maintain this illusion of superiority. Eventually, the mark comes to regard himself as a person of vision and even of genius. Thus a Babbitt who has cleared half a million in a real-estate development easily forgets the part which luck and chicanery have played in his financial rise; he accepts his mantle of respectability without question; he naïvely attributes his success to sound business judgment. And any confidence man will testify that a real-estate man is the fattest and juiciest of suckers.

Businessmen, active or retired, make fine marks for big-con games. In fact, probably the majority of marks fleeced by the big-time confidence men are businessmen. Their instincts are sound for the confidence game, they respond well to the magnetic personalities of roper and insideman, and they have or can raise the necessary capital with which to plunge heavily. "In prohibition days," notes one con man whose identity cannot be revealed, "a businessman turned bootlegger was a prize package. You couldn't miss. Do you remember that big bootlegger from Cincinnati? R—— was his name. He got tangled up with a government dick while he was in stir at Atlanta. He blew $200,000 against the pay-off. After beating him out of that money, we turned him over to a faro-bank mob from Chicago and they gave him the best of it for about fifty G. They gave him the last turn. There were hundreds taken the same way. It was a perfect in to the mark."

Bankers, executors in charge of estates, trustees and guardians in charge of trust funds sometimes succumb with surprising alacrity. To the con men, anyone who has access to funds with which he might speculate is a potential mark. Even church funds frequently find their way into grifters' pockets. Several years ago Big W—— roped a pious and respectable church trustee from New Britain, Connecticut. Gondorff was said to have played him against the big store and he was reputed to have yielded over $300,000. Ironically enough, the con men were acquitted—or rather Gondorff was acquitted and his roper took it on the lam and was never tried—but the church trustee got a good stiff jolt in prison for misappropriating funds. "He was a very religious man," said Gondorff, dryly, "but I guess the temptation for the dough was too much for his scruples."

Religious scruples often seem to fail a mark at the crucial moment. One confidence man who has contributed liberally to this study attributes his facile knowledge of the Bible to the long nights spent in solemn prayer with devout marks who sought moral support from a Divine Providence which, so it might appear to the pious mind, may sometimes select confidence men as instruments of vengeance against one who covets his neighbor's goods.

Professional men who have prospered in their work or who have married money also contribute their share of marks. Doctors, lawyers and dentists sometimes yield good results, though most operators do not like to play for lawyers. Even an occasional college professor is played for, with scores which are said to be quite discouraging. Con men feel that professional men as a class are notoriously gullible; they readily fancy themselves as adept at financial manipulation as they are in their own fields of specialization. One dentist from New York state, fortunately having married very well, has been played against the big store more than half a dozen times. He has become somewhat of an institution among grifters. One meets another on the road and asks, "Do you have anything good in tow?" "No," says his colleague. "Well," suggests the other, "why not go up and rope that dentist? He'll always go for twenty grand."

One would naturally expect bankers to be well aware of the nature of confidence games, and consequently to be too wary to be taken in by them. Most of them are, but some make perfect marks. With a Yellow Kid Weil or a Charley Gondorff on the inside, any one of them will meet his match in wit, financial sagacity and shrewdness. Bankers, if they can be played at all, can be counted on to plunge heavily, for they can dip into bank funds with a view to reimbursing the bank once they have taken their profit. Several instances of that ironical spectacle, one mark roping another, are reported by a mob operating in Florida. When a mark who is brought in expresses a desire to talk the matter over with his banker, he is (under certain circumstances) encouraged to do so. Sometimes, the banker comes back with him, both of them well heeled for the play. Thus two marks flourish where only one grew before.

Wealthy or retired farmers are putty in the hands of competent operators. Many ropers specialize in retired farmers, ranchers or fruit-growers, and one distinguished confidence man, Farmer Brown, devoted most of his checkered career to nefarious bucolic swindling; his rural make-up, his pastoral manners, his back-country speech, and his unbelievable clothing, reinforced by an open and naïve personality, proved to be deadly to literally hundreds and hundreds of farmers throughout the West and Midwest. In the years following the World War they poured millions into the hands of willing confidence men.

An occasional police officer is taken—though that practice is generally frowned upon by professionals. However, within very recent years a Los Angeles captain of detectives was roped in Europe by Stewart Donnelly, brought to the United States for his money, then moved to Montreal where Kent Marshall played the inside for him. He yielded $38,800 according to Marshall, but that figure does not check with the amount made public in the newspapers. "He wasn't dumb," said Marshall, "he just thought he knew all the angles to the big con. He had headed the con-detail for years. It was two weeks after he got back home before he suddenly tumbled that he had been played for the pay-off."

Other tales regarding the fleecing of police officers float about, but cops seem to react much the same as any other mark. One comes to me from Havana which is interesting because of the method used to rope and tie a Texas sheriff who was vacationing there. He frequented the hotel lobbies, where he did a good deal of boasting about how many thieves and criminals he had shot in the course of his term as peace officer. The grifters in Havana decided to trim him properly. So an expert pickpocket was commissioned to pick his pockets clean. The grifters tore up his boat tickets for home and gave his wallet to the pickpocket. Meanwhile he discovered his loss and "beefed gun" at a great rate. He yelped about the hotel, telling everyone his tale of woe. Then a smooth roper approached him, listened to his troubles, and loaned him money to go home on. Just before he sailed, he was given the point-out, the insideman told him the tale, and he was given the convincer. He returned to Havana within a few weeks with $80,000 in a money belt. Also, rumor has it that the great fixer, Lou Blonger, was once given a fine trimming on the big con, but I have been unable to unearth any very definite information about it.

Not all marks are men. Since the World War, big-con men have played for women with increasing success. Middle-aged women—married or single—are especially susceptible, for sooner or later the element of sex enters the game. Some ropers are particularly adept at picking up women because they know how to use their personalities, their clothes, their manners, all to the best advantage. Most of them deliberately compromise their victim by inducing her to sign the hotel register for both of them, then sharing a room or suite with her. Thus the con men usually preclude any retaliatory action on her part, for often she is a woman whose position would be damaged by the evidence on the hotel register, regardless of whether or not she had actually been intimate with the roper. One successful roper tells me that he often finds, when he is playing for a man accompanied by his wife, that a little amorous by-play with the wife facilitates the play. "I always treat charwomen like duchesses," he laughs, "and the duchesses like charwomen."

But no profession, occupation, race or sex has a corner on the never-failing supply of marks. "Anyone with money," reflected old Buck Boatwright, dean of modern confidence men, "is worth playing for. Just bring him in, and I'll take something from him."

## 2

The mark is wary game. Like most game, he migrates, and his migration is his undoing. The wily roper, armed only with a smooth tongue, a deep disillusion regarding the motives of mankind, and some notes on human psychology which are not to be found in the textbooks, knows how to stalk his quarry.

Although marks may be plentiful, they do not walk heedlessly into the traps of the confidence men. They must be stalked for days and even weeks before the kill. This strenuous field-work is done by the roper, who travels far and wide, in this country and abroad, in his diligent search for promising material.

Ropers employ various methods for flushing their game. But most of them depend solely upon chance and casual contacts to provide them with marks. A con man never meets a stranger. Within a quarter of an hour he can be on good terms with anyone; in from twenty-four to forty-eight hours he has reached the stage of intimate friendship. And so most ropers swing back and forth across the country or ride the passenger liners, knowing full well that sooner or later they will meet their man. And they do. Most marks are gathered into the net on one or another of our transportation systems as a result of what appears to be a most casual contact.

A few years ago, before the American public turned wholesale to travel by automobile, the Pullman car was the roper's best hunting ground. "If you were on a train bound for Florida," said Old Man Russell, a fine wireman of the old school, "you might notice a clean-cut man traveling alone. You would tab him and when he went into the smoker or lounge car you would tail him there. That would be your first contact."

This one contact is all a first-class roper needs, provided the mark has the necessary cash and the proper temperament. And it doesn't take a skillful roper long to find that out. For a good roper is first of all a good listener. In a short time he knows where the mark is going, what business he is in, what his financial standing is, and has collected an amazingly intimate fund of information regarding the mark's hobbies, his family, his friends, his extra-marital exploits. Many ropers agree that often marks can be played for the same day they are picked up, but most con men feel safer to allow the mark plenty of time to become thoroughly hooked.

The ease with which people make traveling acquaintances may account for the great number of marks which are roped on trains or ships. When a mark is off his home ground, he is no longer so sure of himself; he likes to impress important-looking strangers; he has the leisure to become expansive, and he likes to feel that he is recognized as a good fellow. The natural barriers to friendships with strangers come down. He idles away time chatting and smoking in a way he would not do at home. And the roper knows how to play upon the festive note which is always latent in a traveler away from home.

Occasionally it happens that a fortunate roper has more than one mark in tow on the same train or boat. If he cannot handle both of them, he may turn one of them over to another roper with whom he gets in touch along the way. If the second roper scores with his victim, the first of course collects the standard fee—ten per cent—for "putting the mark up."

"You can't always tell which mark is better," wailed one roper, who once turned a most unprepossessing mark over to his friend, Joe Furey. "The mark I kept was a fat-looking baby, but he blew up and didn't yield a cent. The one I put up for Joe was the kind you don't bump into. He went for a hundred grand and didn't think anything about it. And all I got was a measly ten per."

Vacation cruises are often fine hunting grounds for ropers. The High Ass Kid was once riding a boat to Cuba when a friendly, talkative gentleman came up to him in the bar and started a conversation. He practically roped himself. "That egg just blowed a hundred and fifty grand for tying into the wrong man," laughed the Kid. Almost every roper has had a similar experience at some time in his life.

Summer resorts catering to a high type of vacationers, golf links, health spas and country clubs also furnish their quota of lucrative marks. The Hashhouse Kid, a roper from Minneapolis, was playing golf on a private course adjoining a country club outside Ottawa. He played a few rounds with a visiting Englishman, then steered him to Montreal where he played him against the store and took $375,000 from him on the pay-off. Many of the best con men include slacks and golf clubs as a regular part of their traveling wardrobe.

One roper reports that he operates with some success wherever vacation cruises come ashore. "In Havana," he says, "I meet each cruise ship that comes in. When the tourists are herded off for a shore excursion, I fall right in and mingle with them. I talk about the trip and they naturally think I'm one of the party. Then I tie into a mark and stay with him until I sound him out. If he looks good, we play the point-out for him and tie him up on the pay-off. The last time I worked there, I cut out a fine old Scotchman and sent him right home to Dingwall, Scotland, for $100,000."

The roper who depends upon casual contacts will find marks anywhere that well-to-do folk congregate. Sometimes they fall right into his lap. Says Bill Howard, a con man from Detroit, "I was standing one night in the bar room of the Tod House in New York. Just as I was leaving, a stranger asked me for a match. That match cost him $100,000." Needless to say, Bill made friends with him, let Gondorff tell him the tale, and the next day he went home for his money, which he lost like a gentleman. "When Charley put him on the train, he was satisfied that a great mistake had been made," said Bill.

While luck plays a large part in bringing the mark and the con men together, not all ropers are willing to wait for the law of averages to operate. Many of them have agents who "put up" marks for them for ten per cent of the score. Any professional criminal may put up a mark if he locates one; some have permanent connections with confidence men and collect a steady income from this source. For instance, Overcoat Kelly acted for many years as general agent for ropers working out of Minneapolis. Many good con men got their start by first putting up the marks for established con men to trim. Most fruitful of these agents are the professional gamblers who ride the trains and steamships and, as a convenient source of additional revenue, put up marks for the big store. From the many itinerant gamblers who act in this capacity, we might cite the two most skillful and prosperous old-timers—Eddie Mines of Hamilton, Ontario, and Wildfire John of Chicago. Mines is strictly a gambler—and a fine one—but Wildfire occasionally ropes and steers a mark on his own.

Some grifters will put up other underworld folk as readily as they will legitimate marks, and on occasion this cannibalistic tendency backfires with amusing and embarrassing results. Once A—— C—— sent for a con mob to come to Little Rock to trim a sucker gambling house which was taking some of her husband's business. They were instructed to register at the hotel and wait for A——'s husband, who would give them the necessary information. When they arrived at the hotel, the roper wandered out into the dining room and found gambling going on behind a screen. He played for a short time, then left, saying that he would bring in a friend later in the evening. Up in the room the roper said, "Boys, I have spotted the joint. It is so soft you can put your finger in it." After dinner they gave it a play and cleaned up more than $5,000. The next morning they called A—— and she aroused her husband. "We certainly found that sucker joint easy enough," said one of the con men. "We took them for five grand last night."

"Where did you find it?" asked C——.

"Right down in the hotel dining room," said the con man.

"Jesus Christ!" howled C——, "that's my joint."

While most men who put up marks are grifters or other underworld folk, it is an interesting and significant fact that often con men have good marks put up for them by legitimate citizens who have no underworld connections except an acquaintance with the con men whom they assist. Many of these respectable agents take no commission, but put up the mark only to help the con man, or, more frequently, to secure revenge upon someone. It is a strange fact that some marks will put up another mark for a con game on which they have just been beaten; they may even beg for permission to watch the process; they seem to feel that they would get a sort of satisfaction from knowing that someone else has taken the bait and found a hook in it; probably nothing would bolster up their deflated egos more than watching the play, but no nonprofessionals ever get into the big store.

One of the proprietors of the old Bon Ton Livery Stable in Des Moines seemed to get pleasure out of putting up marks for the men who swindled him. After being fleeced himself on *the tip,* he looked up the con men and asked them to fleece some of his acquaintances, refusing any commission. A prosperous cattle-buyer who once ran for mayor of Sioux City, Iowa, hung around with con men and located fat marks as a favor to them.

However, the ten-per-cent arrangement extends beyond a simple agreement among ropers. Many persons from the respectable and legitimate world accept their commission with never a qualm. F—— H——, one-time proprietor of two hotels in Chicago, purloined promising-looking guests from his own registers and put them up for con men at a commission. One Dr. A—— of Des Moines located fat marks among his patients and put them up for ropers. A traveling representative for a well-known Cincinnati safe manufacturer, one W——E——B——, ferreted out wealthy marks (to which his business gave him ready access) throughout Iowa and Nebraska; because of the sure-fire quality of his marks, he received the rather high commission of 33⅓ per cent. But sometimes he seems to have lacked the courage of his convictions. One roper says of him: "B—— always introduced me to the mark and then lit a rag out of town. He seemed to have an unholy fear that something would go wrong." A former railroad executive who was later interested in a prominent midwestern baseball club also acted as agent for con men for many years. W—— S——, originally from Paris, Kentucky, bought a hotel in Kansas City; a pair of con men took him there for a nice round sum which ruined him and his business. Later on in a St. Louis hotel he accosted the man who had roped him. S—— was a husky, flaxen-haired Kentuckian who had the reputation of being dangerous; the roper was much relieved to discover that S—— only wanted to recoup his losses by putting up several wealthy marks in St. Louis. The con men obliged him, and S—— went happily on his way with his commission tucked in his pocket.

But enough of these hypocritical folk who pimp away the purses of their friends. They are mentioned only as illustrations of the fact that larceny makes strange bedfellows.

Other lambs are brought to the slaughter through newspaper advertisements. The roper puts an ad like this in a metropolitan newspaper:

> BUSINESS OPPORTUNITY: For an honest, reliable businessman with $20,000 to invest for a large return. References exchanged.

From the surprisingly large number of persons who claim to have the character and the money to qualify for this investment, the roper selects those who seem to merit an interview, then from these selects one or more to be played.

Sometimes a mark is found by answering bona fide advertisements seeking purchasers for farms, real estate or established businesses. The roper pretends an interest in purchasing the property, offers the victim a high price, then under the pretense of consummating the deal, steers the owner to the city where the big store is located and "switches" him over to the pay-off, the wire or the rag. Prosperous farmers and small-town merchants who have laid by comfortable nest eggs are often visited at home after they have been investigated and found suitable.

Strange as it may seem, there are authenticated instances of a man's looking up a con man in the hope that he can profit from a con game. "I remember one winter in Miami," said the Postal Kid, "when there was a mark hanging around trying to meet someone who played the pay-off. He had read about it in the papers and had brought along a bank roll to see if he could make some money at it. But none of the grifters would pay any attention to him. They thought he was batty, until one day the Leatherhead Kid found out that he really had the money.

So the Kid played the point-out for him right there. They moved him to the store and he went for twenty-five grand. When it was all over, the mark said, 'I'll go home and raise some more money, and we'll clean up next time.' This savage just thought things broke that way. You couldn't knock him."

The Square Faced Kid tells a tale in similar vein. "One day I went into Dan the Dude's place," he said, "and Dan gave me what he thought was a good subject for the wire. He was an old gentleman about seventy years old. So I went over to Plainfield to see him. He was a spunky old boy and looked like a good mark. So I moved him to the City and we told him the tale of the wire. Then he blew up. 'Young man,' he said, 'I've been swindled by that game. Not only that, but I've been swindled by every other crooked game in the country—the gold brick, the green-goods game, three-card monte, the shell game, the eight-dice game, and a braced faro game. And do you know, they all took me good. Now I've been reading in the papers that there is a new game out. It must be all right, for it's the only game where they pay you off. It's called the pay-off and I'd be interested to take a whack at it if you can dig one up.' He thought the game was on the up and up because they paid you off. He was the only perfect sap that ever was born."

And Joe Furey—whose statements must be discounted because of his reputation for tall talk—adds, "At that time [1925–1929] marks were so thick in Florida that you had to kick them out of your way."

## 3

The sagacity of Buck Boatwright's philosophy that any man with money is worth playing for would not be questioned by any experienced con man. The first thing a mark needs is money.

But he must also have what grifters term "larceny in his veins"—in other words, he must want something for nothing, or be willing to participate in an unscrupulous deal. If a man with money has this trait, he is all that any con man could wish. He is a mark. "Larceny," or thieves' blood, runs not only in the veins of professional thieves; it would appear that humanity at large has just a dash of it—and sometimes more. And the con man has learned that he can exploit this human trait to his own ends; if he builds it up carefully and expertly, it flares from simple latent dishonesty to an all-consuming lust which drives the victim to secure funds for speculation by any means at his command.

If the mark were completely aware of this character weakness, he would not be so easy to trim. But, like almost everyone else, the mark thinks of himself as an "honest man." He may be hardly aware, or even totally unaware, of this trait which leads to his financial ruin. "My boy," said old John Henry Strosnider sagely, "look carefully at an honest man when he tells the tale himself about his honesty. He makes the best kind of mark. . . ."

In most big-con games the initial approach is made to the mark on the basis of his fundamental honesty. When ropers interview prospective marks who have answered "come-on" advertisements it is customary to insist upon character references which will establish the mark's honesty beyond all doubt. Plunk Drucker tells this anecdote which is so typical that one version or another of it is repeated each time a mark is roped. "I had advertised in a Chicago paper for an honest and reliable man with $50,000 to invest for a quick, sure profit," he said. "A redheaded Jew answered the ad. I interviewed him in his office and raised the question of his character. He said, 'Mr. Bannester, to show you how honest I am, I found a pocketbook with $220 in it on the street the other day. I spent three dollars advertising to try to find the owner.'

I shook hands with him and congratulated him on his integrity. I said that showed that he was just the party for a large and confidential transaction." The mark's honesty is always a standing joke among grifters.

Without raising the fundamental problem of the pot and the kettle, it can be reliably said that this attitude among con men is universal and that this almost childish insistence upon dealing with an honest man gets very gratifying results. Thus the mark's ego is flattered at the start, while at the same time he feels a sense of security in the deal because he is convinced that the men he deals with trust and admire him for his honesty. And once a man admits complete and unshakable faith in his own integrity, he is in an excellent frame of mind to be approached by con men. The larceny begins to percolate ever so gently, and by the time it reaches the boiling point, he is helpless to cope with it—even assuming that he sincerely wishes to do so. Often his rationalization mechanisms are so perfectly developed that he never admits, even to himself, that he is fundamentally dishonest.

Many con men feel that marks have one characteristic in common—they are all liars. Whether this is true or not, I have no way of knowing first-hand, but we may assume that, if anyone is capable of giving expert testimony on this point, con men are, since lying is their profession. It is the consensus of opinion among many operators that marks usually lie about how much money they have, what kind of investments they make, how aristocratic their family connections are, and how good they are to their wives and families. Many marks love to dwell on the magnitude of their sexual adventures. These topics might be said to be universal, or almost so, as prevaricatory grist to the mill of most marks. The breadth of variation from these norms is limited only by the ingenuity of the mark and the daring with which he chooses to navigate the uncharted seas of the imagination. Individual forays into fabrication may be amusing or spectacular, but they hardly contribute to the general picture. This tendency of marks to fourflush is, in the end, helpful to the con men. If marks were not so anxious to impress strangers, they would keep their bank accounts intact much longer.

The mark may usually be counted upon to lie (if only by omission) about the way in which he was swindled. This type of dissimulation, of course, takes place when the mark is telling his troubles to newspapermen, the police, or his family. It may be explained in two ways, either of which may be justifiable. First, he may feel that he must protect himself against publicly displaying his own chicanery; that is, he must carefully conceal that fact for business, social or purely egotistic reasons. No con man would hold a mark in contempt for this sort of protective lying. Second, a mark often does not understand exactly how he was swindled, and feels called upon to explain in some logical fashion, both to himself and to others, how he happened to lose so much money. So he fabricates the parts which are not clear to him and builds up a story which he himself comes to believe. This is regarded by con men as natural and looked upon indulgently. But sometimes a mark shows singular daring and originality. He denies he has been swindled, or never mentions the fact; then he swears out a warrant for the con men charging armed robbery, and tells a story which convinces the prosecutor and the grand jury. This is known as a "bum rap" and is contrary to all established canons of lying; it is looked upon by con men in much the same light as a fly-fisherman regards dynamiting fish.

Con men do not assume that fundamental dishonesty is universal in human nature. Any one of a number of simple tests will reveal to the grifter how well his prospect likes "the best of it" and enable him to judge the strength of this motive with uncanny accuracy.

Sometimes he finds otherwise promising prospects whose concepts of honesty and dishonesty are very clearly defined; these men refuse to respond to the lure because their own consciences speak in a still small voice—and they harken. Most con men have met this kind of man, and few of them show any tendency to ridicule him—their only feeling is one of being baffled because the man cannot be beaten. The Big Alabama Kid, proprietor of some of the most successful stores in Alabama and Florida during the most prosperous days of the big-con games, has this to say about honest marks: "Yes, I have seen men who were too honest to have anything to do with the pay-off, and most of them were the nicest men I've ever met. And they weren't knockers, either. You could say to them, 'Just don't say anything about this,' and their word was good. Just really folks."

This sentiment is echoed, often in almost identical phrases, by experienced con men. Truly, "you can't beat an honest man."

But we must remember that, first of all, marks are human beings. As such, their reactions to being swindled are unpredictable, though they do fall into something of a pattern and con men depend upon their "grift-sense" to tell them roughly what those reactions will be. For instance, a mark who is hard to hook frequently exhibits a bulldog tenacity and, once he has taken the hook, can be played for all he has; on the other hand, a mark who is very easily led into a con game may "blow up" before the play has gone far. An "easy mark" sometimes lets his emotions get the better of him and, forgetting himself, sympathizes with the poor roper who has to face the insideman's wrath when the mark is fleeced. Marks who immediately start to cry and complain are easy to handle. Some get violent immediately; some do foolish or ridiculous things. "I remember a redheaded fellow we beat in a Chicago hotel," recalls John Henry Strosnider. "He went haywire in the lobby after we cleaned him on the wire. I remember he had a little red stash, and he pulled it all out a few hairs at a time when he blew his chunk." Some marks are tough and can cause plenty of trouble if they get out of hand. Some are well-bred and take their medicine like men. Laughing marks are usually considered the most dangerous; and there is an iron-clad maxim current among big-con men: "Never beat a mark when he is drunk."

Some marks are mean, grasping and cunning. Just as soon as the insideman tells them the tale, they begin to scheme and connive for a way by which the roper can be done out of his share in the profits, or squeezed out of the deal entirely. Of course, there are really no profits—except what the mark ultimately furnishes—but con men feel that the mark's attitude toward these hypothetical and never-to-be realized profits is justification for a good and proper skinning. In their eyes he is just as much a "tear-off rat" as if he were holding out on actual cash. "Grifters get a kick out of trimming a fink like that," said one con man. "But," he added, "on the other hand, some marks are fine fellows and it is a shame to trim them."

"That's exactly right," said John Henry Strosnider, who, in his thirty-odd years of playing the inside on all rackets, had ample opportunity to study marks first-hand. "Why, some marks are the finest men you would want to meet, and I have heard grifters say, 'It was hard to beat a good man like him, as he was no beefer, and when he blew his cush, he just laughed it off and said it might have been worse. And all the time he knew he had been trimmed. . . .'"

Many con men have fleeced marks who remained good fellows throughout the entire procedure, men whose good nature and restraint seemed inexhaustible.

Once in Shreveport, Louisiana, a con mob made up of Johnny Tolbert, Jerry Mugivan, and others trimmed a

Dutchman named Palmy Rinky on a con game. Palmy had a large saloon just across the street from the police station, and was well connected locally. Sometime later the con men were back in Shreveport beating a gambling house from the outside. They had just collected $3,000 of checks when the management was tipped off. "Stop the play," said the dealer. "These men are cheaters." The house refused to cash the checks. The con men found themselves outside. Two detectives immediately picked them up. They knew that the gambling house operated under very powerful local protection, and it looked bad. Then, too, they remembered the Palmy Rinky business. As the con men were being arraigned, who should come into the police court but Palmy. Their hearts sank. But Palmy had a big smile on his face. He was immediately pleased that the con men had taken the gamblers. "I lost my money and didn't squawk," he said, "why can't they do the same?" Then he used his influence to have the con men freed and, with the aid of the local fixers, he persuaded the gambling house to cash in the $3,000 in checks. Forever afterward those con men had a warm spot in their hearts for Palmy.

Suspicious marks are not unusual; in fact all marks are suspicious at first, but once they fall under the spell of the con men, and once they become fascinated by the play in the big store, most of their suspicions are laid. "Marks don't often get suspicious, or if they do, they get suspicious of details that really don't matter," said Claude King. "When they have a good insideman telling them the merits of the send, and how their paper will be handled by the insideman, who always knows what's best to do, they follow his advice. An insideman is like your mother. Mother knows best. . . ."

Maybe all insidemen do not have the natural touch which Claude King cultivated. At any rate, the mark's suspicions are not always so easily allayed. The roper really bears the brunt of the mark's suspicions while he is tied up; it is during this period that the "sucker feel-out" reaches its peak. The poor roper must be prepared to be awakened from a sound sleep at any moment during the night by some startling question, and promptly invent an answer to it.

In this connection there is a tale told of a crotchety old mark whom Red Lager once had tied up in a hotel in Havana. Frank MacSherry, who was playing the inside, gave the mark the customary instructions to watch the roper so that he could not get out and talk about the deal. Red tried putting on a little play with the mark, pleading all sorts of excuses to get out, but the mark stood pat. As soon as the mark's money came, Red made the "mistake" which cost the old man $75,000. After the roper had gone, the mark looked ruefully at MacSherry and wailed, "Now I wish I'd let him go out. Maybe a car would have hit him and then we would have saved our money. Even if he did talk, you and I could have gone somewhere else and put over the deal. But things happen that way when you've got an airtight thing. I know, because it happened to me right here in Havana! It made a difference to me of about $200,000 just because I wouldn't let that flighty guy out of the room for a week."

But not all marks are so easily quieted. Some grow restive and take precipitous leave without further ado. "Any mark might get a brain-blow," said Jackie French, "and take a powder any time. You just can't do anything about it. He just blows—a message from Heaven."

Mean and vicious marks are sometimes encountered. There are instances of marks who went so far as to plot with one con man against the life of another for profit. Eddie Mines, perhaps one of the best ropers for the tip who ever lived, once found himself in such a situation. Eddie, a kindly, dignified man, interviewed a real-estate man in St. Louis and told him the tale. He was traveling, he said, with the scapegrace son of a very dear friend. The young man had just inherited half a million dollars in securities from his father and was rapidly dissipating the estate. In fact, he was carrying at the time more than $200,000 in a money belt. He was a fool for gambling and the roper feared that his charge (played by Johnny on the Spot) would run through his fortune before he could persuade him to invest it soundly. Eddie sought the real-estate broker's aid in getting some of this money into property. The real-estate man was impressed; he became more than co-operative.

"I have a big farm away up in the country," he told Eddie. "Let's bump him off, and split the two hundred thousand. We can bury him on this farm and no one will ever know what happened to him."

Eddie talked this proposal over with Johnny and their moral indignation was aroused to such an extent that they trimmed their mark unmercifully.

It is only natural to expect that some marks become incensed when they learn that they have been swindled and try to kill or injure the con men, although it is very seldom that any mark actually hurts a con man. Nevertheless, because this is always a possibility, a con man always guards himself as best he can. His greatest danger threatens from other underworld characters. For instance, it is rumored that a well known East Coast gambler tried to have Stewart Donnelly put on the spot for swindling him of $38,000. He hired Legs Diamond to have the killing done, but Diamond was a friend of Donnelly and prevented the execution. On the whole, however, con men show little fear of physical violence from the marks they trim.

Some con men have observed that marks respond to con games differently according to nationality, with well-to-do American businessmen being the easiest. "Give me an American businessman every time," declared one of the most successful of the present generation of ropers, "preferably an elderly executive. He has been telling other people what to do for so long that he knows he can't be wrong." Perhaps it naturally follows that, if a mark has made money in a speculative business, his acquisitive instincts will lead him naturally into a confidence game; in the light of his past experience and his own philosophy of profit, it is a natural and normal way of increasing his wealth; to him, money is of value primarily for the purpose of making more.

"All Latin races like the best of it," says Limehouse Chappie, distinguished British con man working both sides of the Atlantic and the steamship lines between all with equal ease, "but when they lose their dust, they lose it the hard way and are hard to cool out. They get highly excited when they blow, and it takes a good man to see that they are cooled out properly."

The large number of Britishers and Canadians who are swindled on big-con games in America would seem to indicate that the Latins are not alone in liking the "best of it." "People of Anglo-Saxon and Scandinavian extraction have always been easy for me," said Plunk Drucker, one of the Postal Kid's best ropers. "Germans and Swedes are easy. Irish are hard to beat, and, boy, how they can beef! For my part, give me an Englishman, and you can have all the rest. Our dear country cousin just blows his money like the gentleman he is supposed to be. An Englishman is so different from other marks that there is no comparison. He just takes hold with that bulldog tenacity and holds on—until he is trimmed good and proper."

Jews are difficult, but there is a con man's proverb which says, "It takes ten Jews to trim one Greek." And all con men agree that it is next to impossible to trim a Chinese. "I don't know any grifter who would be dumb enough to try to trim a Chink," said Little Chappie Lohr. "I've often seen them watching flat-joints down in Chinatown [San Francisco] that were playing for tourist suckers. They would look on for about five minutes, then walk on with a kindly grin. They're a fly lot, those Chinks. They can smell a crooked joint." Nevertheless, Chinese do occasionally fall victim to confidence men.

**4**

"Once a mark, always a mark," and "You can't knock a good mark" are not meaningless sayings; they have been born of long experience, and express a good deal more of the grifter's philosophy about marks than appears on the surface.

It is easy for the layman to understand why some marks "blow up" when they realize that they have been trimmed. If these marks are not properly cooled out, they may get the mob into serious trouble, or, more rarely, kill or injure the roper. The average reader can readily sympathize with the mark whom Christ Tracy once trimmed for a large chunk in New York. "I've been calling you Mr. Bennett for the past week," said the mark, "but now I'm going to call you the biggest s—— of a b—— in New York." Some years later Christ encountered the mark on the street in Boston. "What are you calling me now, my friend?" he kidded. "I haven't changed my mind since I saw you last in New York," snapped the mark and walked away.

But it is difficult for the legitimate citizen (and sometimes for the mark himself) to understand why a man, once trimmed on a con game, will go back for another dose of the same medicine. Yet it happens all the time. Grifters have an endless fund of stories which illustrate this fact.

"I roped a mark for the last turn at faro-bank in Chicago," said a fine short-con man named Scotty. "Old Hugh Brady played for him. The mark went for about ten grand—all he had at the time. About two years later Old Hughey was strolling down Clark Street and he met Mr. Mark, who was tickled to see him again. He said, 'I've been looking for you for a long time. I've raised some more money and I'd like to play that faro game again.' Brady told the mark that he had moved to another hotel. He rented another room and framed the gaff and took the mark all over again."

The Big Alabama Kid tells of a mark they had beaten in Miami for $50,000. "We figured he was good for a second play," said the Kid, "so we sent him from Miami to Vancouver, B. C., for $30,000 more. He was gone for nearly three months. The store had given him up for lost, strayed or stolen. But one day who should come in smiling but Mr. Bates with a lot of apologies for keeping me waiting so long. He said that his banker had tried to tell him that this deal was a swindle, and wouldn't let him have his money. So he waited until things had cooled off at home and the banker had forgotten all about it. Then he went to the bank, drew out his money, and caught the first train for the South."

The Big Alabama's mark is typical of the man who leaves the big store beaten, only to return as soon as possible with a fresh bank roll, determined to correct the mistake which was made the first time and recoup his losses. It is also quite indicative of the strength of the "con" which has been put into the mark. Some marks would return even years later if they could raise the money and locate the insideman. This is well illustrated by a mark whom the High Ass Kid roped in Texas. He was put on the send and came through with about $45,000. The Kid figured that he would not be good for another play and "blew him off." Some time later, another roper picked up the mark on a train. He steered him to the hotel, when the mark recognized the approach and confided to the roper that he had been through this once before, and that he was looking for the insideman. The roper convinced the mark that he worked for the High Ass Kid with another branch of the same syndicate. The mark said that he already had the money in his home bank, so that he could go ahead with the deal as soon as he found the High Ass Kid. Then the roper, finding his work all done for him, steered his man to another store and took him for $20,000 more. The mark said he would have been back much sooner, but for the fact that it had taken him some time to borrow the $20,000 here and there from friends.

A mark, once hooked, is often most difficult to "unhook." If the operators once get his confidence completely, he is so sure of the deal in which he is involved that he will not listen to reasonable advice even if it is given to him. Many a banker has dissuaded one of his clients from withdrawing his money only with difficulty; some marks proceed with the deal in the face of sound advice to do otherwise. Con men report many instances of this phenomenon. And District Attorney Van Cise* of Denver, in prosecuting the Denver confidence ring, cites the case of one C. H. Hubbell of McPherson, Kansas, who was tied up with the Christ Kid when the officers arrested the Kid. He was being played for $50,000 and was most indignant at the interruption. Even when he learned that he was being played on the rag, he refused to believe it and insisted on posting bond for both the Christ Kid and his insideman.

Once the "con" takes effect on the mark, its strength is surprising. The mark may believe in the validity of the con deal even after the con men have told him it is a swindle; part of this is doubtless wishful thinking, and part the comforting fact to which he always returns when

* Cf. *Fighting the Underworld*, p. 207.

he doubts the scheme—hasn't he already made money by this method? And so he often does ludicrous things because he is unwilling or unable to shake off the "con" which has been put into him. Claude King tells an experience to illustrate this point.

"I had a store in Florida," said he, "and played for a savage who lost ten grand. That was all the jack he could get his mitts on at that time, so I sent him on his way and eased him up. I thought I'd knock him good, so I wrote him that he'd been trimmed and that it was no use looking for us as we were going to Europe. About a year later I bumped into him on the street. He shook my hand and said, 'Mr. MacAllister, you can't get away with it. You can't let me down now. You know, I didn't make that mistake. It was that crazy fellow who introduced me to you. Now I have dug up ten thousand more. You can't keep me out of the deal this time. Just you and I alone will get the money from that poolroom, and we won't let anyone else in on it.'

"I said, 'You've got something there, my boy. We'll do it.' I took him again and he said, 'Well, I guess that is just the breaks of gambling. I'll see if I can't make some more money.' Off he went and I felt sorry for him because he was such an understanding winchell."

Of course, not all marks come back. Many of them, realizing or suspecting that they have been swindled, immediately cause trouble and all the ingenuity and persuasiveness of the insideman is required to prevent serious repercussions; sometimes all that fails and the con men are indicted. But not very often, considering the large number of marks who are beaten.

It is a rather common experience among con men to encounter a mark who knows about con games, or who has known someone who has been fleeced, and to find that the mark is good for a play himself. An old-timer tells a story which shows this type of mark in action. "Jerry

Daley and I had an 8 die store [a short-con game much used by old-timers] in Charleston, South Carolina. We had a famous jockey in our boost. One day he said to Daley, 'Jerry, if I had the money I once had, I'd break that game of yours. I've watched you beat a lot of marks and I notice that you freeze out the players who can't put up the money. Your game is on the level, but you know you have to have money to beat it.' "

Two other old-timers cap this anecdote with a similar one. They tell how they had rented space from a saloon-keeper in Mattoon, Illinois, for an 8 die cloth. All week the saloon-keeper watched the con men trim the suckers who came into the saloon. When Saturday night's business was over, the con men "mitted him in" and took him for $800—his week's receipts.

There are simply no statistics available on the number of marks who are swindled on the big-con games. However, it is estimated by experienced con men that only from five to ten per cent of those swindled ever go to the police. District Attorney Van Cise has very kindly permitted me to use the names of the marks who were known to have been swindled by the Blonger mob of Denver from 1919–1922.*

| *Name* | *Town* | *Amount* | *Date* |
|---|---|---|---|
| W. H. Scherrer | Houston, Texas | $25,000 | 1920 |
| Victor E. Larson | Ontario, California | $15,000 | 1921 |
| Barney Knapke | Ohio | $12,000 | 1920 (Fla.) |
| James F. McGrath | Sayre, Oklahoma | $5,000 | 1921 |
| W. A. Carnes (farmer) | Iowa | $15,000 | 1921 |
| J. L. Tilton<br>Aaron Cobbs | Ottowa, Iowa | $10,800 | 1920 |
| William E. Griffith | Walnut, Iowa | $20,000 | 1920 |

* Collected from Van Cise, *Fighting the Underworld* and reprinted by permission of the author.

| *Name* | *Town* | *Amount* | *Date* |
|---|---|---|---|
| Herbert J. Gray | Exeter, Devon, England | $25,000 | 1921 |
| W. H. Wurzbach | Pueblo, Colorado | $6,800 | 1921 |
| George Kanavuts | Sapulpa, Oklahoma | $25,000 | 1921 |
| Morris Freeman (taken in Little Rock) | Denver, Colorado | $6,000 | 1921 |
| C. H. Hubbell (tied up but lost) | McPherson, Kansas | $50,000 | 1922 |
| Frank Donovan | New Orleans, Louisiana | $65,000 | 1921 |
| John Peck | Kentucky | $19,000 | |
| John Emrich | Fort Smith, Arkansas | | 1921 |
| C. E. Henson | Haskell, Oklahoma | $14,000 | 1920 |
| P. G. Schaible (bank president who did not know he had been swindled until asked to testify) | Chelsea, Michigan | $25,000 | 1922 |
| Frank Norfleet (rancher) | Texas | $45,000 | 1919 (Dallas and Fort Worth) |
| Mr. Unzner | | $19,300 | 1921 |
| Gug Bergstrom (farmer) | Hudson, South Dakota | $10,000 | 1919 |
| E. Nitsche (florist) | Dallas, Texas | $25,000 | 1919 |

Before attempting to draw any conclusions from these figures, perhaps it should be suggested that the Denver situation appears somewhat unusual. Because of the airtight protection enjoyed under Lou Blonger, the con men felt free to "rip and tear"—that is, to grift without restraint as long as they avoided Denver residents. This may account for the fact that small scores occur with greater frequency than they might in the big stores in, say, Miami. I have information regarding several large scores, one of $200,000 taken from a nationally prominent figure, which were made by the Denver mob during the time, but which cannot be printed here because the victims do not wish any publicity. Perhaps it is only chance that more big touches do not appear in this list; perhaps the fact that the large touches usually come from prominent people who cannot afford to admit participation in a con game helps to account for the absence of testimony regarding more large touches. It is also possible that the marks have not always stated their losses exactly. Furthermore, we do not know that this list is representative of the number of touches which were known to the police, for no one knows exactly how many marks complained to the Denver police, were cooled out, and sent on their various ways by the officers who were in league with the swindlers; these names were compiled—and not without difficulty—by District Attorney Van Cise and used as a basis for his prosecution; so powerful was the fix that, at times, this list threatened to dwindle away to almost nothing.

I make these suggestions only by way of cautioning the reader that these figures are probably not representative and that they would not apply to all mobs alike. They are simply the only ones available which apply to the operations of one mob over a significant period of time. And, in the absence of something better, they will have to serve as a basis for calculating the number of marks played and the volume of business handled by a big-con mob working steadily (during the summer season) under full police protection.

If we summarize these figures (including two touches, one for $13,000 and one for $50,000, which were not completed but nevertheless were reported to the authorities) we see that they reach a total of $437,900 taken from nineteen men. If we can assume that this, at a conservative estimate, represents ten per cent of the total, we can estimate that, roughly, the sum of $4,379,000 passed into the hands of the Denver mob during this time, taken from a probable total of 190 victims. District Attorney Van Cise arrived at an independent estimate that the Denver mob took from $1,000,000 to $3,000,000 each season from 1919 to 1922.

The volume of play given different stores at different times varies greatly. When the fix is sure, times are good, and a smoothly working mob has a store, the number of marks increases until the play assumes the appearance of a rush. When the fix fails or when the "heat is on," the number of marks decreases noticeably. It has been my experience that the police departments in those cities where stores are or were located are usually unwilling to permit examination of records with a view to collection of statistics—and even if they were co-operative, there would be no record of those marks who were successfully fixed. Hence, it is practically impossible to give anything like accurate estimates of the number of marks who have been swindled on the big con. Truly, their name is legion.

# 5

# The Mob

## I

A con mob is a functioning unit of the big store. It consists of a minimum of two—the roper and the insideman. When the mark is played against the store (as he usually is in the big-con games) the mob also includes the personnel of the big store—the manager or bookmaker who has charge of the impressive-looking shills, and the minor employees such as board-markers, clerks and the "tailers" who keep tab on the mark while he is not with one of the con men.

The personnel of the store is hardly considered a part of the mob proper for, with the frequent exception of the manager, it consists of floating grifters or con men who have not made a touch recently and are in need of money. Some of the best stores, however, retain their personnel almost intact over a period of months or even years. Other necessary connections for the mob as, for instance, persons who "put up" marks on a percentage basis or fixers (where the insideman does not do his own fixing), are only auxiliaries and not an integral part of the mob, even though their services may be necessary to the smooth functioning of the organization.

Once the store is established, the size of the mob increases even though its essential elements remain exactly the same. If the insideman, who is usually the proprietor of the store, wishes to show a good profit, he must have more than one roper to bring in victims. So he arranges to have several ropers on the road while he stays near the store to handle the marks as they come in. If business is good, he keeps an appointment book after the fashion of a doctor or dentist and plays the marks according to a rigid schedule. As the insideman multiplies the number of ropers working for him, the fundamental relationship between himself and each roper remains the same, with the result that the store becomes increasingly prosperous. If he has a high professional reputation and ropers know that he will give their marks a good play with a minimum of risk and a maximum of protection, he may have as many as forty or fifty ropers working out of his store during a busy season.

As the play given a store increases, the burden of the roper's work increases for he must, since the insideman cannot travel far from the store, assume more and more of the responsibility of gaining the mark's confidence. Consequently, in order to give the mark the convincer in the form of cash winnings which is usually necessary before he can be moved to the store for the big play, ropers frequently work in pairs, each temporarily playing the inside for his partner when a mark is roped. As soon as one of them picks up a mark, he arranges for his partner to meet him at a given point (probably the mark's destination) where the pair find the poke or play the point-out for the victim. The mark finds out all about the deal by which he can make a fortune, after which he is given enough of a play "against the wall" (that is, without the use of a store) to hook him on the scheme and insure his continued interest. Then the first or temporary insideman moves the mark to the city where the big store is located, on the grounds that he has been ordered to report immediately to the headquarters of the racing syndicate or the stock syndicate, as the case may be. He tells the mark that he will take him along and that he can make a much larger investment there. At headquarters the mark meets the high executive in charge of the syndicate (the permanent insideman who operates the store). His confidence is then "switched" to this insideman and he is given the big play.

Although this arrangement complicates the task of bringing in the marks somewhat, at the same time it facilitates the play from the ropers' viewpoint because the mark can be told the tale and given the convincer very early in the game. It also makes for much greater mobility, for the ropers can, after hooking the mark, move him clear across the country, if necessary, to his doom. In fact, the mark can be moved anywhere, once he has had a sufficiently realistic convincer; a captain of detectives from Los Angeles, recently roped in Europe, was moved to Los Angeles for his money, then returned to Montreal for the play against the store there. But a roper who works with a partner pays well for the assistance he receives. If he ropes the mark unaided, he usually receives forty-five per cent of the touch; if he has a partner, each gets twenty-two and a half per cent. It is not often that a roper has such good luck as did the Hashhouse Kid when he roped an Englishman in Canada for $375,000 just the day after his partner, John Singleton, quit him. Thus he collected $168,750 where, had he found the mark a day earlier, he would have received only $84,375.

The permanent insideman keeps the remaining fifty-five per cent of the score, from which he pays the manager ten per cent of the gross score, settles with the banker for from five to ten per cent, gives the shills and other accessories one per cent each (or in some stores, a "consideration" of from $100 to $500 each, depending on the size of the score), and usually splits the remainder with the fixer—unless he is thrifty and does the fixing himself. Whatever set-up is used, the big store is the center for all big-time confidence games; it is "framed" in different ways for the wire, the rag and the pay-off, and different mobs have different working arrangements (though practice is remarkably standardized), but these are differences of detail. The fundamental relationship of the roper to the insideman, of the mob to the store, remains the same.

The roper and the insideman are the principals of any mob. Upon them depends the success of the big store, for, however elaborate a set-up is provided, and however secure the fix, all is useless without the services of a man who can bring in marks, and one who can give them a convincing play. Each must perform a specialized piece of work and needs certain personal qualifications and experience which fit him for the task. Some men, and rare they are, can handle either end with great success, as, for instance, the Yellow Kid, Frank MacSherry or the Jew Kid. Others, like Limehouse Chappie and Charley Gondorff, have consistently specialized in inside work, at which their talent falls little short of genius, but could not steer a hungry man into a restaurant. Grifters like Stewart Donnelly and the Umbrella Kid specialize as ropers. It is rather unusual for a man to be able to handle either end; most first-rate con men specialize in one type of work and perfect their technique in that field until it is a high art.

## 2

The outsideman travels on railways and steamship lines, usually on those lines leading into the city where the big store is located, and preferably those lines which extend far beyond the borders of the state within which the big store is situated; thus he avoids the "home guards" and "short riders" who might be able to cause trouble through political connections in their home state. He "roots out" the mark, makes the initial contact, decides whether or not he is worth playing for, makes a tentative estimate of the game he will respond to best, puts him in touch with the insideman, is tied up with him during the play, and generally assists with the play in the big store. While he is on the road roping, he either lives on cash he has saved from his last score, or borrows from the insideman if he is well known at the store and has an established reputation as a roper; if he is spending some time in the city where the big store is located, he may fill in on the boost for several touches and thus increase his income materially.

Upon the roper falls the responsibility of ferreting out marks to be trimmed; as soon as he ceases activity, the big store must close. However excellent the talents of the insideman may be, they are wasted unless he has good ropers out "riding in" the fools. Without a slow but steady stream of marks coming in, the big store cannot show enough profit to operate in the face of the high overhead, the expense of keeping ropers on the road, and the maintenance of fixed municipal and county officials. Hence ropers are just as essential to the prosperity of a big store as salesmen are to the success of a legitimate business.

"A good outsideman is one who always has a chump to play for," comments one insideman. "You can always spot a good roper by the fact that he is out railroading continually for marks." This extensive travel wears the roper down, separates him from his wife and friends, and keeps him on his toes to pay expenses—for no one knows how long it will be between touches. "There's nothing easy about roping if you want to keep out of stir," said the Postal Kid. "The fear of getting lagged keeps you always under a strain. My friend, it's no bed of roses. Playing for marks is hard mental work. You just try going out and getting a good mark on your own, riding the trains day and night and dodging the dicks. And the cap every day is something terrific. If you play the bank, boy, you have to get yourself a fool quite often."

Not only does the outsideman have to locate and ride in the marks, but he works under conditions which are much less safe and comfortable than those enjoyed by the insideman, who stays near the store, within "right" territory where he can feel reasonably secure from arrest. Hence, most ropers hope some day to open a store of their own and play the inside—but while they are roping, they look with some envy upon the man who plays the marks in the store. "It is pretty soft for him," said one con man. "He can just loaf around, knowing that he has a dozen good ropers out digging up marks. All he has to do is sit around on his can. Nice work if you can get it. . . ." The outsideman, almost constantly working outside the territory which is covered by the protection money paid out by the mob, is continually exposed to the danger of being recognized by a detective and arrested or shaken down, or of being identified by a former mark who may have him arrested in a strange or hostile locality.

I once asked two ropers who were in a merry mood what they considered the qualifications for a first-rate roper to be. Although their answers are not entirely serious, they contain a measure of truth beneath a broad burlesque of the platitudinous style of Dale Carnegie. Said one, "Will-power is the most important asset a con man can have. Have you ever watched a grifter who stayed in one position all his life and never advanced? It is pitiful to see how much mental energy he uses up getting nowhere. If he is a smack-player, he won't try to get up any higher in the racket. Most failures wear themselves out with futile grifting and worry about keeping out of the can. They work themselves into a fever because they haven't the will-power to stop and organize themselves for efficiency and try to get a big mark for the big store.

"Then there is the grifter who works the trains, the ocean liners and the resorts, trying to land a mark for the big store. That's today—but tomorrow he meets a pretty girl and decides that he could not possibly leave home to travel. So he changes his direction toward the shed in his home town, Chicago, and falls back on the smack. Yes, he has a goal all right, but he hasn't the will-power to keep on the track. Yes, I think will-power is essential to success on the grift. The grifter who can develop his will is increasing his roping force, adding to his horse-power, and building up character which will eventually carry him to the big store with a fine mark. Trained and disciplined, the will can be a most valuable and useful tool. Of course, there are grifters who will object to any talk of training the will. They will talk wisely of the need for self-expression and the inhibiting effects of any kind of discipline. But you will find that grifters who do this do so because of their inordinate desire for self-indulgence. Their psychology," he concluded with a twinkle in his eye, "is not the quill."

The other said, "I couldn't say what you *must* have to be a good roper, but I can tell you some of the traits you better *not* have. Never permit yourself to be bored. If you gander around you will always find some mark you can trim. But some heel-grifters think it is smartly sophisticated to appear languid or condescendingly wise. That is really stupid. Tie into any mark. He may have it in the jug.

"Never ask a mark embarrassing questions. You know

how *you* feel when someone lets the cat out of the bag. Take it easy with any fool, and always lead your ace.

"Never boast about your rags, but brag about your long cush. That will lead him along to brag about his long jack, and then you're getting somewhere, brother. If he is a hard-shelled Babbitt, why you're one too.

"Never advance political views unless the fink asks you to do so. It is good to 'yes' him. And always be on the feel-out regarding his sporting tendencies in an easy way so as not to raise his suspicions. Marks are sometimes prejudiced against sporting.

"Never give detailed accounts of a trip, accident or personal ailment unless your mark evinces an avid interest in all the details. Just a hint about sex, and if he's interested, you've got something to work on. Tell him about the married woman you know and leave the impression that you would like for him to meet her. They love it.

"Never interrupt a fink while he is talking. Be a good listener and he will immediately conclude that you are a young man of some note. Just listen carefully to the lies he tells you. Marks are chock full of lies.

"Never be untidy or drink with a savage. There is nothing worse than drinking when you are trying to tie up a mark. You've got to have your nut about you all the time. You need what little sense you've got to trim him—and if you had any sense at all, you wouldn't be a grifter."

In all seriousness, however, the most important qualification for a roper—so important, in fact, that he would starve without it—is what is known in the underworld as "grift sense." No one, it seems—not even the grifters themselves—can say just what grift sense is. It appears to be a faculty which the grifter is acutely aware of when he needs it; a something that "clicks" within him, telling him when he meets a mark that he can beat, enabling him to sense at once whether or not the man is good for a play and to chart the mark's probable reactions to the game; it guides him materially in eliciting the proper response from his victim, and "tells" him how to handle the particular man in question. There is nothing occult or supernatural about it; yet it is there and every con man follows its promptings unconsciously, just as a tightrope walker reacts instantaneously and without question to his highly developed sense of balance. Probably it is no more than a highly sensitized and elaborately co-ordinated set of reactions to people and to situations, but a satisfactory explanation of it remains to be found and stated by the criminal psychologist. Whatever grift sense is, one thing is certain: it is a very real and useful faculty; without it no con man, regardless of what other brilliant attributes he might possess, could ever rope or play a mark.

Grift sense appears to be inherent; con men testify that experience may be helpful in attaining a high state of perfection, but all agree that the grift sense must be there first. Sometimes it manifests itself at an early age. Some grifters, like the Yellow Kid, who as a lad bought cheap watches from pawnbrokers or thieves and peddled them around Chicago saloons for as much as fifty dollars, possess it as mere boys. The Yellow Kid really sold his story, not the watch. The Jew Kid was roping marks for the Furey Boys when he was only fifteen; the Yenshee Kid likewise at fifteen was roping marks on the street for old Larry King. Joe Frog, as a farm boy in Iowa, was fascinated by the flat-joints with a circus and when he was picked up as a "stick" for one of them, his grift sense cropped out and he knew that he had found his life's work; he followed circuses acting as a stick until he finally persuaded a grifter to take him on as a regular. Many of the first-raters started when they were very young.

Others do not discover that they have grift sense until later in life. Some competent con men are turned out on the big con after they have been beaten at a confidence game, when they suddenly realize that they have ability in that line also; then, without benefit of early training or valuable experience on the short con, they go to work with a professional mob. Had Buck Boatwright never been trimmed on a con game, he would in all probability have continued as a successful railroad engineer and one of the best insidemen who ever trimmed a sucker would have been lost to the big-con rackets. Training and experience are of course important, but without grift sense they count for little, as can be seen from the ——— family. Two of the brothers, C—— and F——, are rated at the top of their profession, while Brother G——, who worked under the very best of tutelage, never succeeded. "G—— was always a blank as a grifter," said a former roper for C——. "His brothers were tops, but he just didn't have grifting sense."

In addition to grift sense, a con man must have a good deal of genuine acting ability. He must be able to make anyone like him, confide in him, trust him. He must sense immediately what aspect of his personality will be most appealing to his victim, then assume that pose and hold it consistently. If the mark is a wealthy farmer, he must assume those characteristics which he knows will arouse the farmer's confidence and friendship. He must be able to talk over the farmer's problems with sympathy and understanding. Frank Norfleet, a rancher, himself a victim of the big con, illustrates this point admirably. In his account of the swindle, he describes his loneliness, his desire to find some friendly face in a strange city. In his case, his wish was soon gratified, for Tex Cooper soon noticed his condition and promptly took him in tow. Norfleet found that Tex knew stock so well that he readily accepted him as a mule buyer.

Yet the roper must never leave the impression with a rural character that he is a sharper or that he is too clever or slick to be trusted. With business or professional men he reveals other facets of his multiple personality and, in a remarkably short time, has established himself on a very friendly footing with them.

He must also be able to look a mark over and make rapid, accurate estimates of the mark's financial status, his susceptibility to the principle of confidence games, and the best methods of playing him. "After the roper has been with the mark for a while," says the Postal Kid, "he knows all about him and has decided what would be a good play for him. He feels him out about everything in a roundabout way, but the mark doesn't know that he is telling the roper the tale that will lead to his downfall." Says Claude King, a fine international con man, "A good roper is one who knows what to do with a mark after he has roped him. He must have grift sense and know how to handle marks at the critical stages of the swindle. He must be able to revive them when they are chilling and tell them a convincing story which they believe for the pure quill. The roper is always a fine judge of human nature. He knows how to play on the mark's weak points."

Once the outsideman has roped a mark, his work is just beginning. Then he must move the mark to the hotel (where the insideman also locates) and find the leather or play the point-out for him. This puts the mark in contact with the insideman and "ties him up." These steps are, in themselves, little dramas which must be enacted with great naturalness; one false move and the mark suspects that his new-found friend is not all that he seems. If he acts his part well, the mark suspects nothing, for the sequence of events is built up with most convincing logic and plausibility. After the mark has taken the bait, and while he is making the easy money which prepares him for the final plunge, the roper has complete charge of him; that is, he has him tied up, although the mark firmly believes that he is keeping the roper under control at the confidential suggestion of the insideman. "Put a thief to watch a thief," laughed one con man. "I'll bet some old-timer thought of that."

During the long and often hectic period when the mark is tied up, the outsideman is responsible for him; the final success of the venture is held in his hands. The Postal Kid describes the tie-up thus:

"When a mark is being played for, he is never alone for a minute. The insideman tells the mark to watch the roper carefully so that he won't tip off the situation to any outsiders. And the mark will always guard him faithfully. That is a nice way to arrange it so you can be with the mark all the time and see that no one gets to him to queer the deal or knock him. It is a good way to keep the mark in check until his money comes from home—which may take weeks sometimes. He can think of a thousand questions—all different—to ask you. You must have answers to all of them, or you might rumble him, and that would never do."

"A mark will generally do what you tell him to do," said The General Strosnider, "once you have his con. You can talk a fink into or out of anything if you are with him all the time. Any mark will ask you hundreds of quizzes. He may wake you up in the middle of the night and ask you some damn thing about the play or the insideman. So you have to be careful that you don't get caught in a lie. That will knock a mark quicker than anything else. Marks are cute in asking questions, so you must guard yourself in all your talk."

The constant "quizzing" referred to above keeps the outsideman under a strain which, of course, he must conceal from the mark. This is the most tiresome and difficult part of his work. Over a period of days or weeks his nerves become frayed, his temper becomes short, but still he must continue to lie fluently, suavely, convincingly, and, most of all, consistently. The outsideman must pose as a stranger like the mark, but must, without appearing to know too much about the deal which is going on, be able to quiet the mark's suspicions and allay his fears. An insideman reports, practically verbatim, the following tirade which the exhausted roper slipped out of his hotel room to deliver:

"Well, I've got this savage all tied up and no place to go. He is driving me nuts with that sucker-feel-out. Night and day he tries it out. The jug where his cush is, is an eye gaff [under Pinkerton's protection], and I'm afraid of Old Poison [Postal Inspector Graham] getting the beef. He never quits and has never lost a case. You know that. And you smart gees have lost more men than there are rabbits in the state of Michigan.

"This fool is funny. He wants me to marry his daughter. He thinks he might get some of my end that way. Farseeing fool at that. I told him the girl sounded good to me, and I'd go home with him after we all got rich. Well, I'm going back to the kipper and see how the savage is. If I ever get tied with another savage like him, I'll duck. I'll take it on the lam. I'd sooner be a lamster any day than be tied up to a lop-eared mark like him.

"So please come on up and give him one more spiel. It rests his nerves when you gab to him. He thinks you are the finest man he ever met. I put you away strong. Well, tomorrow the jack will be here, then to the tall and uncut. . . ."

The roper must keep the mark tied up until his money arrives, then he is fleeced and blown off, in which operations the roper has his role to play. In spite of the anxiety and nerve-strain connected with confidence games, a good roper enjoys his work. The constant excitement of playing for high stakes gets into his blood. Once he has felt the exhilaration of big-time confidence games, he is seldom satisfied with any lesser form of crime. He is content to leave the short-con games for smaller fry and for young grifters who have yet to make their mark in the world.

Big-time ropers leave the big con only when they are forced to do so, and then only temporarily. If they run short of funds, or have a run of bad luck and do not pick up a mark for some time, or if they find themselves badly trimmed over the gaming tables, they always know that they can take off a quick, small, and relatively safe score on the short con. Most of them use the *smack,* a game based upon matching pennies, which is described in greater detail in the chapter entitled *Short-Con Games.* It is so profitable a short-con game that many a police officer, faced by a beefing mark, has scratched his puzzled head and concluded that any man who claimed to have lost $3,000 matching pennies must be an out-and-out liar. But good scores do come off, and very quickly, too. There is none of the careful build-up which goes with the big-con games. The mark is roped, fleeced and blown off all in the space of an hour or less.

There are of course hundreds of good outsidemen operating in the United States, Canada, Cuba, South America and Continental Europe. Con men differ in their estimates of individual prowess at roping, but probably there would be few dissenting votes among the good ones if we listed the following men as a kind of all-time all-American of ropers:

Bruce Upshaw, from Washington, D.C.
Frank MacSherry, from Seattle.
The Boone Kid Whitney, from California.
Limehouse Chappie, from New York City.
The Yellow Kid Weil, from Chicago.
John Henry Strosnider, from Washington C.H., Ohio.
The Jew Kid, from Omaha, Nebraska.

A good many con men feel that the Jew Kid is the best in the field. Says one, "The Jew Kid is, I think, the best outsideman in the U.S.A. He has been roping marks since he was a kid back in Omaha. He can always ride one in to be played for at any racket the Kid thinks will suit the mark. He is also a good deep-sea gambler." Says another, "I know the Jew Kid is the best of the lot. He is an excellent cheater and has card-sense—which most grifters haven't. He is a high roller at gambling, a good spender, and as witty a gee as ever you met. He never says 'No' if you want to put the bite on him. The best trait about him is that you get your end if it is coming to you. He is as right as rain. And that is a lot to say in any grifter's favor. He stands six feet tall and was at one time considered the best-looking man on the racket. . . ."

While these men listed are probably the most outstanding, there are many others who could justly claim a place in the first rank as ropers. Some of these men are adept at both inside and outside work, but most of them are or were ropers.

| | |
|---|---|
| Eddie Mines | Wildfire John |
| The Yellow Kid Weil | The Ripley Kid |
| Red Snyder | The Mormon Kid |
| The Clinic Kid | The Christ Kid |
| Big W—— | Queer-pusher Nick |
| The Boone Kid | Nigger Mike |
| Red Lager | Kid W—— |
| John Henry Strosnider | The Square Faced Kid |
| George Post and Allen | Bill Dixton |
| Little Jeff Sharum | The Painter Kid |
| The Big Alabama Kid | The Brass Kid |
| Slobbering Bob | Joe Furey |
| Kid Niles | Tom Furey |
| The Punk Kid or Plunk Drucker | Eddie Dixon |
| Little Chappie Lohr | Lee Reil |

The Hashhouse Kid
The Leatherhead Kid
The High Ass Kid
The Black Kid
Fifth Avenue Fred
The Jew Kid
The Indiana Wonder
Doc Sterling
Australian Harry
Australian Tom
Tear-off Arthur
Stewart Donnelly
Kid Barnett
The Honey Grove Kid
Lonestar Jimmy
Joe Simmons
John Singleton
The Postal Kid
Sheeny Mike
Lilly the Roper
Little Bert
Jimmy Christian
George the Greek
Devil's Island Eddie

**3**

While the outsideman goes out into the highways and byways in search of marks, the insideman waits within easy reach of the store, taking care of the marks when they come in, picking the boost for each play, giving the manager his directions, and handling the fix. He works under much more secure protection than is afforded the roper, for he has a pipeline directly into City Hall and has or can get all the money necessary to square anything that comes up. He works on a schedule with his appointments carefully made so that there will be no conflicts. He also keeps the books—such as they are—for the mob. These records include his own appointment book and an account book which lists each roper by his initials or a code-mark together with the amounts which have been advanced to him. Also, the insideman usually keeps a written record of, or knows, the address or 'phone number where he can get in touch immediately with any roper at any time. In the event of serious trouble the roper may thus be notified by the tip-off system and not only avoid the big store but be on the alert for detectives in whatever city he may be at the moment. These records and accounts are usually very sketchy and kept in code, but they are nevertheless effective and accurate. The expenses incurred for each play are entered, but the income side of the ledger is left blank, for never is the size of the touch entered in writing. The insideman is the only one who really knows how much was taken (though the roper, the manager, and even the boost may have their own ideas) and this information may be jealously guarded from other con men; however, it often leaks out and becomes a subject for gossip and speculation. The insideman deals directly with the fixer (or with the police if he does his own fixing) and they have to depend on his word for their percentage, unless the mark beefs and they have some figure to check against.

Thus, technically, the insideman is the key man of the con mob. When any roper wants to go to work, he asks the insideman; when one con man wants to get in touch with another, he writes his friend in care of the insideman, who, although he would hardly turn over a roper's address to anyone, will forward mail to the address in his little notebook. If a con man is arrested, the insideman knows how to arrange bail and may advise the con man whether to remain and face trial or jump bond. If the fix curdles and the insideman should find himself inextricably involved with the law, the safety of the whole mob is menaced; hence the insideman retains excellent legal service to be used in such an emergency. Some insidemen report at regular times each day to their attorneys, fixers or bondsmen; if they fail to call, it is assumed that they are in serious trouble and immediate steps are taken to locate them and "spring" them, for no one is so annoyed at being locked up as a con man. Meanwhile, the tip-off system goes into action among con men, their women and their friends, and all business in the store is suspended while the con men lie low or retreat to a safe hangout until the coast is clear again. Most ropers maintain some sort of contact, other than the insideman, who will communicate with them in case of trouble and get word back to the big store in a roundabout way so that steps can be taken to go to their aid. If the roper, once arrested, communicates directly with the insideman, the whole set-up will be revealed; hence, he 'phones his woman or his partner, or some good friend, at regular intervals; when he does not report, it is assumed that he needs help. Word gets back to the insideman on the very efficient "grapevine" and he does what he can to protect himself and help his roper. Sometimes fixers like Lou Blonger or Mike Haggarty would travel clear across the country to help some con man who needed assistance.

Once a roper is in trouble, the first thing needed is money to get him out. The insideman customarily raises this money, though sometimes the fixer will take care of an old and established customer on credit, knowing that he will collect every cent due him. But the insideman usually passes around a sheet of paper in the hangouts, having first himself signed his name opposite a liberal sum. Every con man who is thus approached, and has or can get money, is honor bound to subscribe, the amounts varying from $50 to $500. Each man signs his name, initials or monicker, writes the amount subscribed opposite it, and gives the cash to the insideman, who, when the fund is raised, turns over the money and the list to the con man in trouble or to his representative. Each man who puts his name on such a list knows that he will be repaid as soon as the con man can get out and take off another touch or two, for these debts are sacred. A con man might neglect to pay them—but only once. Next time there would be no subscribers. But if his name is good, even his personal enemies feel obliged to contribute; he keeps the list and checks off his debts one by one until they are paid; if his debtor should die meanwhile, he is bound to pay off his debt to his benefactor's widow or to his family. Thus the insideman is more than just a helper or partner; he is the one to whom ropers turn in time of trouble and he materially assists in building and maintaining the morale of the mob.

In playing for a mark, the insideman first sees him when the roper, having announced his arrival beforehand, arrives at the hotel with the victim. Very often this is the hotel which the mark has selected for his stay in the city. The roper and his partner have already given the mark enough of a play "against the wall" to convince him. He is usually pretty thoroughly tied up by the time he reaches the city where the store is located. It only remains for the insideman to take over his confidence and direct the big play. The insideman sees the mark only briefly, for perhaps not more than an hour or two all told, before the play. During this brief period, he must look the mark over and make his decision as to the type of play to be used; he must get the "feel" of the mark and, on the basis of this impression, plan the rest of the game. The insideman must have highly developed grift sense in order to do this accurately and instinctively; however, experience is all in his favor for, while the average roper may play only from one to four good marks a year, a good insideman probably plays more than a hundred.

As soon as these details are settled, the insideman notifies the manager to frame the store in the proper manner and goes out to the hangouts to select a boost from the con men assembled there. Then, with the time for the play set, the boost assembles and the insideman gives them their final instructions before the roper and the mark come into the store. From then on the burden of the play rests on the insideman, and though, compared to the roper, he sees relatively little of the mark, his few appearances must be sufficiently impressive to make the mark part with a large portion of his fortune. The responsibility for blowing off the mark after the play generally falls upon the insideman, with some assistance from the police.

When the temporary insideman tells the mark the "tale," the mark realizes that this man is engaged in questionable or dishonest dealings. He has been allowed to discover this very naturally through the point-out or finding the leather. The permanent insideman must take over the play where the pair of ropers dropped it, posing as a high official in the illicit syndicate and arousing both the confidence and the cupidity of the mark to a high peak. The insideman must be able to handle this work with great tact and perfect timing. If a mark feels that he is being pushed, he gets suspicious; if the play lags a bit, he may cool off and lose interest. Hence the insideman, in addition to inherent grift sense, must have a vast knowledge of human nature, a dignified and impressive manner, and a perfect sense of showmanship. His story must take effect naturally. Says one con man, "When one of those insidemen you have listed tells the tale to the roper and the mark, the roper almost believes it too, Doctor. They tell the kind of tale that would make most any man go home for his jack."

"And," said the Postal Kid, "an insideman must be intelligent enough to talk a smart businessman into losing a large amount of money to strangers within a few days. His story must ring true or he won't get any money." "He must also be an excellent judge of human nature," said John Henry Strosnider, "and he must be able to sense when his story is taking effect. He must not hesitate on any quiz that the mark puts to him. A mark can think of so many things to ask you—things you have never been asked before." An ace insideman who now ropes for a successful New York store says: "The insideman must use a method suited to the mark at hand. All good insidemen have a way with marks. Take the Yellow Kid, for instance. He had a way with marks that was unbelievable. Charley

Gondorff had about the same thing, and it enabled him to beat most of the marks who were roped for him." Said Frank Tarbo, "Insidemen play for so many different types of men and study them carefully. They abide by what they learn. They study out different angles from which to approach a mark, then experiment with them until they are perfect."

If the insideman handles the blow-off properly, the mark hardly knows that he has been fleeced. No good insideman wants any trouble with a mark. He wants him to lose his money the "easy way" rather than the "hard way" and the secret to long immunity from arrest is a properly staged blow-off, with the mark blaming the roper and feeling that the insideman is the finest man he ever knew. It is the mark who is not cooled out properly or is mishandled by a clumsy or incompetent insideman who immediately beefs; furthermore, if he is sure that he has been swindled and if the local police do not act, he may go higher up, with revenge rather than recovery of his money as his object. Marks of this type can upset the whole corrupt political machine and even land not only the con men but perhaps some of the police and the fixer as well behind bars.

Good insidemen are rare; they do not seem to occur so frequently as good ropers. And there can be only as many first-rate stores as there are first-rate insidemen. Since good ropers like to work only with expert insidemen, the natural result is that the best ropers cluster about the best insidemen, forming a kind of closed corporation, or monopoly, with the control resting in the hands of the insidemen and their fixers. Most of the really big-con touches in the country have passed through the hands of this informal corporation. This is not to imply any "organization of crime" in the sense in which certain sensational writers sometimes use that phrase, but rather only reflects the natural consequences of the best ropers seeking out the most expert insidemen, who in turn have provided the most effective fixing arrangements and as a result dominate the most favorable spots for taking wealthy suckers.

The very best insidemen who have played or are playing marks against the big store are generally conceded to be:

Charles Gondorff from New York City
102nd St. George from New York City
Fred the Florist from New York City
Christ Tracy from Toronto, Canada
Back-Bay George from Boston
John Henry Strosnider from Washington C.H., Ohio
The Yellow Kid (Joseph Weil) from Chicago
Curley Carter from New York City
Buck Boatwright from Joplin, Missouri
The Punk Kid (Charles "Plunk" Drucker) from Cleveland, Ohio

Although Buck Boatwright did not live to use the pay-off and the rag, he is generally regarded by men who have worked against the best big stores as one of the best insidemen who ever operated a store. He was a "natural." Among living con men, the Yellow Kid, another natural, is one of the best in his profession. Second to the Yellow, and in many respects quite as good, many con men would name Charley Gondorff. On the rag, Fred the Florist is reputed to be one of the best now operating. These men are all old-timers; they did not develop by slow degrees; they were good from the start. It is a peculiar fact that these men should all spring from one generation. Modern professionals who have seen the best insidemen work see little hope of replacing them from the present crop of young grifters.

This belief may only reflect the condescension with which the older men in any profession look upon the coming generation. On the other hand, partly because of the vastly changed conditions under which present-day grifters are turned out, it does seem that the old-timers have a little the best of it.

Other insidemen, some dead, some very old, and some belonging to the present generation, who deserve a place in the first rank of con men are:

| | |
|---|---|
| Fred G—— | Kent Marshall |
| Limehouse Chappie | Big Chappie L—— |
| Little Chappie Lohr | Lee Reil |
| Jack Porter | The Boone Kid (Sam) Whitney |
| Frank MacSherry | |
| The Big Alabama Kid | The Clinic Kid |
| Claude King | Joe Furey |
| Louisville Charley | Louisville Henry |

**4**

Minor members of the mob include the manager for the big store, the shills, the board-marker and clerks, and one or more tailers, one of whom serves as a lookout.

The manager, sometimes called the "bookmaker," is strictly speaking not a con man in that he does not rope or play a mark. He is more of a theatrical producer, with a minor acting part thrown in on the side. He "frames" the big store and creates the atmosphere of prosperity and swank recklessness which goes with dignified, large-scale gambling. He furnishes the rooms used for the brokerage office or the gambling club. He sees to supplying all the equipment used in either place—tickers, headphones, blackboards, etc. Also, he is responsible for all the spurious documents to be used in any kind of con game which the mob may wish to play—fake personal bonds for the con men, fake membership cards in secret or fraternal organizations, fake newspaper clippings, betting slips, stock sales and purchase orders, credit slips, ledger sheets and numerous kinds of letter-heads to be used in any sort of phony correspondence which may be necessary. He must have on hand at all times a plentiful supply of fake receiving blanks for the Western Union and Postal Telegraph Companies and a portable typewriter with type to simulate the lettering produced by teletype machines, so that a fake telegram may be received at a moment's notice from any place at any time. He has printed a great variety of membership credentials in various branch stock exchanges and gambling clubs, together with guest passes for the same. He may also have a supply of legal seals for documents, a check protector, and a variety of blank checks. A supply of membership cards in various fraternal orders is also very helpful. He keeps on hand various stock letters, copies of which can be "received" by the con men and shown to the mark when necessary. And, most important of all, he has official custody of the "B.R." or "boodle." This is the money which is used to play the mark in the store. For this purpose a minimum of about $5,000 is necessary, but the more the better; in the really big stores the boodle may contain a large sum of cash, perhaps as much as $20,000. This money is made up in bundles presumably containing $500, $1,000, $5,000, etc., but really composed of one-dollar bills for filler and having $50, $100 or $1,000 bills on the top and bottom to make the stack look real. Each bundle is stacked carefully and bound with sealed labels like those used in banks for marking bundles of bills. A rubber band around each end holds the pack together. When a skillful manager makes up his boodle, he can make $10,000 in real cash look like several hundred thousand dollars. This money is used over and over again by the shills in placing bets and is paid out again to them when they win. The idea is to keep as much money circulating before the eyes of the mark as possible.

This money, like the other props which are necessary, usually belongs to the insideman, but is always in the custody of the manager. As soon as the insideman notifies him, he sets up the store for play, and when the play is over, he takes everything down and packs it away in suitcases or trunks, ready for use again, but hidden away somewhere so that, if the mark returns, he will find nothing but an empty room. His part in the game is a small one, with routine lines and routine action.

One of the most competent American managers is William H. Loftus (the Sleepy Kid) from St. Paul. He started as a pickpocket and had quite a reputation as a "tool" or "wire," but never liked that form of the grift. He is always set apart in the minds of professionals because of his burning ambition to become a con man himself. He could not resist the atmosphere of the big store and traveled over the country, hanging around all the important stores and hobnobbing with the big-timers. For years he managed Lou Blonger's stores in Denver. At one time or another, he worked for many of the big and successful stores. However, it appears that he never progressed beyond this post (when Van Cise raided the Blonger stores in Denver, Loftus was charged with being a steerer; however, I can find no verification for this from his contemporaries. The charge against Kid Duff in Denver named him as the "manager" for Blonger; according to my information, he was the ace insideman, while Loftus was the manager). "He was always hanging around the outsidemen," reminisced one of the ropers who knew him well, "trying to learn how to rope a mark and become an Upshaw. God, how you could burn him up when you called him the 'manager'! That is just as far as he ever got in the grifting line, just a manager."

Willie Loftus always took great pride in his boodle. When the play reached its height, he would have money all over everything, the counter, the shelves, and the floor. Finally, he would call to a clerk, "Hey, George, get this stuff out of my way."

"What shall I do with it?" asks the clerk.

"I don't give a damn what you do with it," Loftus would say, "sweep it out if you have to, but get it out from under my feet." Loftus liked a boodle with quantities of new crisp bills in it. "I like to hear them squeech under foot," he said. This boodle, properly handled, is what really rouses the larceny in the mark and makes him want to get some for himself. When the manager goes to pay the mark off, and stacks pile after pile of bills before him, it makes an impression which no mark ever forgets.

The shills or "sticks," known collectively as "the boost," vary somewhat with each type of confidence game and often with different types of mark. They add the final touch of authenticity to the big store. Most of the big-time stores use full-fledged professional ropers for shills; these ropers happen to be in town when the play is going on and are picked up at the hangouts by the insideman. They collect one per cent of the touch, or a liberal "consideration," which is easy money, but many of them participate as much for the fun of seeing the mark given a lively play as for the commission. Each stick has one or more types of character which he can represent to perfection. From ten to fifteen are used on each play; they are selected just a few hours before the play by the manager or insideman, who instructs them how they are to dress and act. "We use mostly old ropers and professional grifters, with just a few young men thrown in," says one insideman. "They win and lose big chunks of money like nothing at all. It makes a big impression on a mark to see some distinguished-looking egg lay down $100,000."

The boost, generally speaking, is not permanent, but changes somewhat with each mark—though Charley Gondorff at one time maintained an almost permanent boost for his New York store. At the height of the big-con games—1914–1925—New York was the center for much of the swindling activity which stripped thousands of marks of millions of dollars. At this time, the social and unofficial headquarters for big-con men was Dan the Dude's saloon. "In New York City you could always get the best boost," said John Henry Strosnider, who had a store there at that time. "All the con men hung out there. In the morning the managers would come in and pick out what they wanted. They would give the sticks the address of the store, tell them what to wear, and give instructions of what kind of boost they wanted. You could get any kind of a stick you needed in Dan's scatter. Many of them made up like millionaires and some wore morning clothes and top hats. Old Man Eaton always wore a silk hat on the boost. He had a beautiful set of whiskers like Justice Hughes of the Supreme Court and was always in demand as a stick. A good boost is everything to a store."

The board-marker, sheet-writer, caller and other clerical help are usually young grifters who are learning the game. They have little or nothing to say and go through the motions of working for whatever the manager chooses to pay them, sometimes straight one per cent like the rest of the boost. When they feel that they are good enough to try their hands at roping a mark, they get the permission of the insideman to play their victim and go forth on the road. Some, fortunate in having some big-time roper for a friend, are given special instructions by their friend and "turned out" by the big-timer. However, this is about all the training a youngster gets and this is perhaps the place to deny sensational statements often made by careless writers—and sometimes credited by those who should know better—to the effect that con men, pickpockets and others maintain "schools" where young grifters are turned out. Such institutions have long been the delight of fictioneers, but there is no reliable evidence to indicate that they ever functioned in the American underworld.

The tailer may serve as a lookout or doorman, and thus fulfill a double function. When he sees the roper approaching with the mark, he gives the office and the store starts operating. While the play is on, he keeps an eagle eye on the street in both directions to see that no one disturbs the play, that no traps are being laid to catch the con men in action. Most mobs use one or more tailers—men who follow the mark when one of the con men is not with him to see that he does not communicate with some wrong copper. In cities where the heavy-rackets flourish and where it may not be safe to let an unescorted mark carry a large amount of cash around, he follows at a discreet distance behind when the mark brings his money from the bank just to be sure that no one robs the victim. Also, where competition is keen, other ropers are wise and will spot a mark who has been tied up. If the con men who have him in tow leave him alone for long, another roper may slip in, tell the mark that he has been sent to take him somewhere else for the deal, then switch him over to another store. So the tailer must be on the alert to see that no harm befalls the mark. He is really a sort of bodyguard and is usually the only man around the store who is armed.

## 5

The big store functions only while the mark is in play. At all other times, it is "cleaned and stashed" and no con men are to be seen there. Only an empty suite of offices remains. The mob gathers there only by appointment. At all other times, it is scattered in as many directions as there are members, and each goes about his own business or pleasure. The mob is held together by loose but effective bonds; it has little formal organization.

When a con man arrives in a strange town, he knows or can find out where the "right spots" are. These are hangouts in the form of cigar stores, hotels, restaurants, bar rooms or brothels where con men know they can congregate free from molestation. Some hangouts specialize in one type of criminals, others cater to all types. Usually the heavy-rackets keep pretty well to themselves, while all types of grifters tend to congregate. Con men know where they will find their kind, and when they are not in the store, they usually keep to the company in the hangout, for it is not good for them to know too many legitimate citizens who might speak to them on the street when they have a mark in tow. Furthermore, con men know that if they visit the hangouts regularly they will eventually meet any other con men whom they may wish to see. Most hangouts of this type have a proprietor who is well aware of the fact that his place is a rendezvous for criminals.

If one con man wishes to locate another, he goes into a hangout and asks the bartender or the proprietor if, say, Harry Brown has been in recently. If the proprietor knows the questioner, he will tell him that Brown comes in and out, and that he will probably find him in later in the evening. If the proprietor does not know the newcomer, he says, "No. If he comes in, I'll tell him you are looking for him. Who shall I tell him wants to see him?" The newcomer then gives his name and departs. When Brown comes in, the proprietor tells him that so-and-so has been in and Brown indicates whether or not he wants to see him. If he does, he makes an appointment through the proprietor so that when the newcomer returns he may find out when they can meet. If he does not, the proprietor discourages the newcomer. If Brown does not know the man who is hunting him, he gets a description of him and may sit in the back room so that he may get a look at him if he comes in again. If he distrusts him the newcomer never knows that he is there. If, on the other hand, the stranger asked for the Big Alabama, the proprietor might assume that he knew Brown rather well and would be less cautious. But most big-con men know one another on sight and have no trouble finding one another when they want to get together.

The hangouts are often run directly or indirectly by a fixer, and thus they provide protection to grifters who are in a strange town. There is usually a private back room in connection with the place where only established professionals and "right" people are encouraged to congregate, and from which the general public is excluded. In this connection an old-timer recalls: "There were always thieves in Dan the Dude's scatter, but no suckers [legitimate people] and no dicks. If a sucker came in and started to go back into the big room, some gee would stop him and say, 'This is a private club. Are you a member?' And if he went over to the bar to buy a drink, the beer glass would be about the size of a thimble and the whisky terrible. And the Mickey Finns were always ready for some punk grifting kid who thought he would crash the joint. They gave him one, then sloughed the donicker on him, and you should see him cop a heel out of that scatter."

Dan the Dude was an unusually helpful fixer. He kept a large ledger in which a record of all touches was kept, as well as a list of promising prospects for all sorts of thievery and con rackets. Professionals in good standing were given information from this book whenever they needed it. So far as I have been able to determine, this was the only document of its kind ever kept by a fixer in a hangout.

In these hangouts the grifters "punch the guff" and "cut up old scores," gamble, drink, carouse and mingle together socially. Here news is relayed rapidly and accurately, for each of these hangouts is a post in the so-called "grapevine" system of communication, and here con men are sure to meet their colleagues if they are in town. Almost every town in the United States has one or more of these hangouts, and in the larger cities there are many. Most famous among old-timers in New York were Dan the Dude's place at 28 W. 28th St., and Bob Nelson's place on 8th Avenue. On the West Coast the hangouts were and are legion. In the middle West and South there are many places—impossible to name here because they masquerade under very respectable fronts—into which thieves from all over the world come for sociability and sanctuary.

Among those notorious places which can be named, John Ullman's saloon in St. Joseph, Missouri, and Mike Haggarty's place in Memphis stand out, as well as the two places maintained by a prominent Chicago fixer. In Toledo, Ohio, since the days of Brand Whitlock known among thieves and grifters as a "right" city, there were many hangouts, but the most popular one was run by John Singer, an old heavy-man. Modern big-con men also have their hangouts in hotel bars, cafés, and good restaurants in Miami, Daytona, New York City, Hot Springs, Reno, New Orleans and in all cities where the big stores are located. The hangout is becoming more and more high-toned while the old saloon is waning in popularity.

Individual con men live at the best hotels and travel first-class. Often they are known to the managers of the hotels where they stop, and these managers see that their mail is forwarded to them and that their friends get in touch with them. The managers who are friendly with the con men can rest assured that, in return for their courtesy, all bills will be paid and no patrons of the hotel will be molested. Con men are good spenders and their steady patronage is very advantageous to the hotel; furthermore, they all associate with celebrities and wealthy persons, and bring to the hotel quite a volume of profitable business. A high-class con man is careful not to be seen publicly in the company of small-time thieves or hoodlums, not because he is unduly snobbish, but because he feels that it hurts his professional reputation. Hence the hotel manager knows that he will not bring into the hotel an undesirable class of criminals; he can meet these at the hangouts.

All mobs have certain systems of communication among themselves, including their professional argot which is more or less unintelligible to the outsider, and a system of signs and signals (called "offices") which are somewhat standardized. For instance, if one con man sees another on the street and does not want to be recognized, he will give the office in the form of a slight, high-pitched cough or a signal made by tapping the closed hand casually against his mouth. That means "Don't rap to me" and his friend will pass on without giving any sign of recognition. If one con man sees another with a stranger, of course he would not accost his friend without ascertaining if possible who the stranger is, for it is likely that his friend has a mark in tow. If one con man wishes to speak to another, or if he has a stranger with him and meets a friend whom he wants to join them, he "raises for him"—that is, he catches his friend's eye and raises his hat slightly. In some con stores (monte and mitt stores, for instance) a member of the mob watches for a roper to come down the street with a victim, and if the roper "raises" as he approaches, the mob knows that he is going to bring the mark in. However, with the big con these appointments are usually well worked out in advance. In a city where there is a large tourist trade, the ropers may pick up marks right on the streets, strike up an acquaintance with them, and walk them around past the store. As they pass, they will "raise" for the insideman to meet them at a prearranged place to play the point-out for the victim. The lookout or doorman will report this fact immediately to the insideman. However, most big-timers prefer to work more cautiously and with greater preparation.

The tailer who follows the victim when he is not in the custody of one of the mob also has a set of signals by which he communicates with the mob. Suppose, for instance, that he has followed the mark home for his money and the mark has telegraphed the insideman by a prearranged code that he will arrive at such and such an hour. The insideman waits for him safely outside the station where he can see the tailer, who has been on the train, but who passes the mark in the crowd and slips past the insideman, giving him the office as he does so. If the mark has the money all safe and has not been tampered with, the tailer presses his hand over his heart as he passes by. Then the insideman approaches the mark and greets him. However, if the tailer knows that the mark has been "rumbled" or that he has brought back a detective, or that there is a detective awaiting him ready to arrest the insideman as soon as the mark identifies him, the tailer pulls casually at his nose. That means "Don't contact the mark" and the insideman melts away without meeting his victim. These signals are standard and are used by most mobs, while of course there are other private ones which each mob may agree upon for its own members.

Thus mobs are organized. Even though their members are loosely held together and the functioning units are often flung far afield, there is a remarkable sense of professional unity. A highly developed group solidarity keeps intact a very strong morale. However, these mobs are not consciously "anti-social" groups set up to make war on legitimate society; they are the informal results of certain technical demands and certain very potent social pressures; they probably would not exist at all if confidence men could function as individuals instead of as groups. Although there are channels of communication from mob to mob, and, on occasion, even co-operation of a professional nature, these inter-relationships are casual and personal. It should not be assumed that there is anything like an organization of mobs on a wide or even a national scale under the direction of "super criminals" so dear to the minds of a gullible public nourished since childhood on flamboyant film and fiction.

# 6

# Birds of a Feather

## I

Confidence men are the elite of the underworld. They have reached the top in the grift* (which includes crimes depending upon lightness of touch and quickness of wit, as contrasted to the *heavy-rackets* which involve violence); they have arrived at the ultimate in success and achievement; they have gone as far as any professional thief can go.

* If we arranged the major criminal professions (each comprising a great number of separate rackets) within the *grift* into their respective categories, we would have something like this:

I. Confidence men
   1. Big-con men
   2. Short-con men
II. Pickpockets and professional thieves of all types
III. Professional gamblers
IV. Circus grifters
V. Railroad grifters and other minor professionals.

Other grifters recognize this fact; they look upon the confidence man with envy for his position, admiration for his success, or desire to emulate his feats, according to their individual inclinations. Some, with the predatory instincts almost universal in the underworld, have a very personal interest in the confidence man; they see in him a fat mark to be trimmed like any other sucker.

Confidence men are not unaware of their social preeminence. The underworld is shot through with numerous class lines. It is stratified very much like the upperworld, each social level being bounded by rather rigid lines determined largely by three factors: professional standing, income, and personal integrity. While, as in the upperworld, income has much to do with social position, professional excellence and personal "rightness" appear to play an even greater part among con men than they do in the upperworld.

There are rigidly observed class distinctions in the underworld. In a society where one's reputation depends solely upon his individual exploits, and where one is judged by his peers or his superiors, social status is not easily attained. There is no public as a court of last appeal. If, for instance, a country physician is unknown to his confrères, he may find solace in the fact that he is regarded as an important person by the patients he serves. If a writer is panned by the critics and his colleagues, he may still be a hero to his public. But a con man—with the exception of that rare individual who seeks newspaper notoriety—has no public. He is judged by his colleagues alone. And the underworld has a very keen sense of professional values.

A confidence man must have plenty of ego. Once he loses his self-confidence, he is a failure; without the knowledge that he can trim a mark, he is incapable of trimming one. As a consequence, he sustains that self-confidence at all costs—or degenerates to some other form of the grift where he can function more successfully. But he cannot fool his associates for long. Either he takes off the scores or he doesn't, and he stands or falls in his profession by the record he makes for himself. Good confidence men take their standing for granted; they recognize the ability of others casually; they treat their own professional excellence lightly.

Professional jealousy is, however, rife; there is a widespread tendency to "knock" other con men; real or fancied wrongs lead to strong and bitter personal criticism; it is not difficult to find a confidence man who classes half the men he has worked with as tear-off rats. However, the smooth professionals know the tear-off rats for what they are and have little to say about their associates except among intimate friends. If a con man is really a tear-off rat—as all too many of them are—the news circulates rapidly and it is soon a widely accepted fact; if he is not, the "knocking" of a few cheap grifters will never seriously menace his professional standing. Some con men have worked for a lifetime with never a serious black mark against them. They know that a clean professional record is a most valuable asset.

Hence, confidence men on the whole are wont to look with some condescension upon their lesser brethren in crime, especially grifters lower in the social categories and lesser professionals on the heavy-rackets. Pickpockets, because of the widespread reputation they bear as stool pigeons, are often shunned, though once a pickpocket has turned con man and established himself in that profession, he is accepted as a social equal provided he conducts himself according to the established code for con men. Small-time thieves, pimps, touts, traffickers in narcotics, hoodlums, some types of professional gamblers and all the numerous riffraff of the underworld are commonly excluded from the company of con men, who prefer association with their own kind, with higher-ups from the heavy-rackets, or with the political bigwigs, criminal lawyers and fixers who, in one way or another, derive revenue in return for protection.

But it must not be assumed that con men confine their personal associations to underworld channels. The American underworld shades off almost imperceptibly into the upperworld. Many socially respectable citizens have useful underworld connections while, on the other hand, many criminals have equally useful or desirable connections with the upperworld. Furthermore, many good folk who would resent being classed with criminals wink at the violation of the law as long as it is to their political or financial advantage to do so; while the law on occasion might consider these persons criminals, the underworld would not accept them as such because they do not practice a recognized criminal profession. Practically all con men make friends in this area, and many establish themselves among folk who are both reasonably honest and quite legitimate, preferring association there to mingling with their own kind. How widely this type of association extends it is difficult to say for, from a desire for mutual protection, both the legitimate persons and the con men prefer not to reveal these friendships. On reading this manuscript, one con man makes this note: "You'd be surprised at the number of good businessmen who make friends with con men, loan them bank rolls, and entertain them at home. All con men have good legitimate friends in the cities where they live. They always play square with these friends, as they consider them 'folks.' " The fact remains that con men are the most cosmopolitan of all thieves, for they travel widely and cultivate associations on a rather high cultural level. Some of them enjoy the friendship of celebrities, sportsmen and socially prominent persons from legitimate society who may consider it "smart" to be seen in the company of a confidence man.

Because of the advantages which accrue to his profession, a confidence man, once he has established himself, seldom changes it for another in the underworld. He may "pack the racket in" and go into legitimate business (where some have notable success), but as long as he remains "on the grift" he prefers to play the confidence games. To step back down the scale permanently, returning to thievery or professional gambling, would be to lose professional status; more than that, there is a thrill about big-con work which no other branch of the grift can duplicate. The confidence man extends himself fully while he works; all his faculties and abilities are called into play; each mark is a new challenge to his ingenuity; and, perhaps most important, the stakes for which he plays are very high. "Once a heavy-gee [safeblower] always a heavy," said the Postal Kid. "And it's the same with the con. When the mark is being played for a big chunk, there is a kick in it just like there is to the heavy when a big peter [safe] is being knocked off."

Consequently, once a con man "arrives" in his profession, he usually remains a con man until he dies or until he quits the rackets. There is a constant feverish social climbing among grifters desirous of attaining the rank of confidence men; relatively few of them succeed. Sometimes they resort to all sorts of subterfuges to get to work with the big-timers. For instance, the Sanctimonious Kid, well beloved for his inexhaustible stock of quotable poetry, always thought the way to the big-con games lay in the "smack"; he constantly hounded good smack players, showing them a bank roll he claimed to have taken on the smack, and begging to "cut them in" on the score. But whatever other professions the con man may have mastered during his lifetime (and some are indeed versatile) he always likes to be known as a con man because that assures his place among the smartest, merriest and most effective thieves who ever trimmed a sucker.

## 2

When we think of cheese, it's Wisconsin; when we speak of oil, it's Pennsylvania; but with grifters, it's Indiana. Many a first-rate con man has hailed from that state, and many, many more second- and third-raters. Heading the list are the Indiana Wonder and Stewart Donnelly, two of the finest ropers who ever rode a fool in. Other top-notch grifters would include Jerry Mugivan, the Harmony Kid and many others whose names cannot be listed here.

Con men look puzzled and scratch their heads when you ask them why this should be so. A former insideman for the Wonder says, "I don't know why, but the state of Indiana is out in front in turning out grifters of all kinds. At one time you could go to almost any county fair and some farmer would take you aside and show you some new kind of flat-joint [crooked gambling device] that he had invented." Another con man who got his start on the grift playing the short con with circuses adds: "It's an old saying among grifters that any Hoosier farmer would come up to you and ask you where the squeeze [controlling device] was on your joint, and then show you that he had figured out a better one. So I guess the farmer boys thought flat-jointing was better than looking at a horse's tail all day for about a buck."

Perhaps the fact that for many years it was customary for circuses to winter in Indiana may help to explain the number of grifters who come from that state. The American circus was a grifter's paradise on wheels. Until very recently, most circuses carried grifters and confidence men as a matter of course, for the grift was a source of great profit—as men like old Ben Wallace and Jerry Mugivan could testify. Circuses carried their own private *menders* (fixers) who cooled out any irate citizens who might cause trouble for the show; the grifters, who paid the show management a fixed percentage of their takings, shared with the management the "privilege-car" (which not a few circuses lined with sheet-iron to stop bullets fired by trimmed marks with a primitive sense of vengeance), took their food with the owners and their chief henchmen. Many of the best big-con men operating today learned how to handle marks with some form of circus grift, notably flat-jointing; many more first-rate short-con men were developed there. Hence it would seem no more than natural for grifters of all types to congregate in Indiana.

Although New York was for years—and still is—a center for all kinds of confidence men, few outstanding ones hail from that area, and relatively few from the East. The West appears to have produced more good grifters than the East, with Texas heading the list, while the Deep South, like the East, trails behind. "That's about right," comments an old-timer. "New York doesn't turn out many good con men—but there are a few. In olden times [around 1910–1915] in Dan the Dude's place, you could see a hundred con men there at once, and not one of them would be a native New Yorker. Indiana, I think, has turned out more good grifters than any other state." Since the 1920's, Australia has contributed a number of prominent professionals to the racket, among whom we should mention Pretty Sid, Australian Harry, Snowy T——, Snowy P——, Kangaroo John, and Melbourne Murray. So much, then, for the geographical derivation of con men.

Their social origins stand out much more clearly. Most of the best ones grew up with the rackets, especially with the short con, before they were turned out on the big con. A large proportion of the outstanding early con men were developed on the gold brick, the spud and the smack. Some started passing counterfeit money. The short-change rackets, the circus grift with all its numerous rackets, flat-jointing, and railroad grift all account for a considerable number. But the best ones had their early training with the short-con games in which the fundamental set-up for the big con was used in a small way and in which the forces employed in the big con were latent, or already emerging in forms which obviously presaged the big con. These games, the tip, the mitt, monte involving the use of a store, and others were really fine training for big-con men-to-be, and con men who had experience with playing the double-cross with foot races and fight stores graduated easily to the big con when it developed.* It has been estimated by one informant that in Chicago alone in 1898 there were, to his personal knowledge, more than two hundred ropers working for five permanent and protected monte stores alone; there were hundreds more roping against unprotected stores which ran "on the sneak," while the railroad lines running into Chicago were infested with mitt mobs. And similar conditions prevailed in New Orleans, San Francisco, New York City—in fact, in any city which was a railroad center. Most of these ropers were youngsters who played against older and more experienced insidemen. From these ropers, as they matured, sprang a generation of big-con men who have never been surpassed. These men got into the rackets young, had the benefit of training under the best con men then operating, and were fortunate in that they lived in an era when every man believed himself a potential millionaire. When, shortly after the turn of the century, the big con developed, they were still young men, but seasoned, experienced, with a heart for anything.

Next to the short-con workers and related grifters

* Representative con men who got their start on the short con include: Post and Allen (the spud and the gold brick), Pretty Duffy (roper for mitt stores), Curley Carter (the lemon), Jimmy the Rooter (flat-jointer), Kid Barnett (three-card monte), Swinging Sammy (the hype), the Leatherhead Kid (8 dice player), Sheeny Mike (three-card monte), John Singleton, the Painter Kid, Wildfire John (the tip), Honey Grove Kid (foot-race store), Johnny Taylor (the hype).

whose rackets prepare youngsters admirably for the big con, provided of course they are sufficiently talented, professional gamblers and pickpockets most frequently turn con men. Gamblers, because of their natural grift sense and their wide knowledge of people, fall naturally into the routine of the big con. And the good professionals all have their own bag of tricks for fleecing a mark.* More important still, they have learned how to handle victims from a somewhat higher social level than those which the average short-con worker encounters; they have the manners and the suavity necessary on the big con. Says John Henry Strosnider, "When a professional gambler turns roper, he is good or will make good. He knows how to cut into a mark and how to talk to him. Once he gets his con, he knows what to do with it." Because of their natural instincts and grifting experience, most gamblers play the outside when they turn out on the confidence games.

Pickpockets who turn out on the big con† have a fair chance of success. They already have thieving sense, but often lack the ability to rope a mark which short-con workers have cultivated. It is significant that pickpockets, in contrast to gamblers, usually find that the post of insideman is best suited to their talents. Perhaps this is because pickpockets are not very talkative, except among themselves; a roper must be able to open up a conversation with anyone. Pickpockets are frequently too secretive and suspicious to approach strangers in the most effective manner. The Postal Kid, who was himself a pickpocket before he turned out on the big con, explains this trait

* In addition to those men already mentioned who worked for the mitt stores, the following are representative of those who left the ranks of professional gamblers to join the confidence men: Big Bill Keely (card cheater), Plunk Drucker (the Punk Kid) and Nigger Mike (deep-sea gambler), Queer-pusher Nick (deep-sea gambler and smack player) and Slobbering Bob (mitt player).

† A few of the typical pickpockets who turned con men include: John Snarley, the Postal Kid, Jerry Daley, the Ripley Kid, Parkersburg Eddie and Little Jeff Sharum. There were many others.

among pickpockets by saying, semi-facetiously, that "they hate a mark so much that they don't like to talk to one." When they work the inside, the roper has laid down the preliminary groundwork, and handles the mark most of the time, which is a most satisfactory arrangement to an insideman with light-fingered antecedents.

Race-track touts sometimes turn out on the big con, especially on the pay-off, but they constitute a very small proportion of successful big-con men. Perhaps this is partly due to the peculiar type of men who take up touting, for as a class they lack backbone and courage. However, the good ones learn how to handle marks successfully and from the ranks of touts come such top-notch con men as Glouster Jack, 102nd St. George, Frank MacSherry, Claude King and others of high professional reputation. And the fact must not be overlooked that the pay-off had its inception in the minds of two touts, Hazel and Abbot.

Not all con men have underworld backgrounds. Training in some other branch of the grift is very helpful, but is not always essential. Some men like Lee Reil and Buck Boatwright step directly from legitimate life into the big con and make a success of it. Reil's transition from legitimate employment to con work was abrupt but natural, for his instincts were those of a confidence man, but he had simply not been in a situation where he could give these instincts free play. He worked for many years as a railroad conductor and made the acquaintance of con men through "copping the short." He also made the acquaintance of a thief-girl in New Orleans who served as an entrée to underworld circles in that city. When he lost his job as conductor he went to New Orleans and turned out on the big con with professionals. His grifting career has been long and successful. Buck Boatwright, formerly a railroad engineer, was fleeced by con men. He suddenly realized that he could play that little game too, and opened up a store. He seemed to have been born a good all-around con man, but played the inside with excellent success. Other con men with legitimate backgrounds range from N—— Q—— (engineer and contractor) to the Square Faced Kid (mule-skinner) and from Charley Gondorff (bar-tending) to the Hashhouse Kid (waiter). The Yellow Kid, at the top of the list, was born a con man and never in his life had time for any other occupation.

## 3

So much sensational material has been printed about confidence men and, generally speaking, the public entertains such romantic and even fantastic ideas regarding them, that a chapter like this would not be complete without a few modest but realistic notes regarding their personal lives.

There is nothing superhuman about confidence men, nor is there anything mysterious or occult about the methods they use. Although they sometimes perform sensational crimes, they are not the super criminals of fiction. They are neither violent, blood-thirsty, nor thieving, in the ordinary sense of that word. They are not anti-social—whatever that term really means. They hold no especial hatred or antipathy toward the individuals they fleece, nor toward society as a whole. They are not, on the one hand, the romantic and sentimental crooks of the movies, nor, on the other, the sinister, plotting, cold-blooded criminals of the crime-story magazine. They are human beings, manifesting salt-and-pepper mixtures of all the vices and virtues to which mankind is heir. If fifty of them were selected and mixed indiscriminately with a group of successful business and professional men, all the correlations and statistics of a Hooton or a Lombroso would not set them apart; and, if a census of opinions upon politics, ethics, religion, or what-not were taken from the entire group, not even a Solomon could separate the sheep from the goats on the basis of their social views. If confidence men operate outside the law, it must be remembered that they are not much further outside than many of our pillars of society who go under names less sinister. They only carry to an ultimate and very logical conclusion certain trends which are often inherent in various forms of legitimate business.

However, since all confidence men live in much the same environment, have something of the same training and background, live by a loose but nevertheless real code, are all of high intelligence, have similar attitudes toward their victims, toward the law, and one another, and run somewhat true to form in their amusements and recreations, it follows naturally that they develop certain traits in common. While these traits can hardly be said to be earmarks of the profession, and certainly they could not be used to identify a confidence man, they are, regardless of individual variations, characteristic of the group.

As we have seen, most con men have a criminal or semi-criminal background, though some, like the Yenshee Kid for instance, come from good family stock and a high middle-class background, but fall early into criminal company. Most of them have a wide variety of thieving experience before they become confidence men. They have grown up in a tradition of cheating, grifting, stealing; their habits and attitudes are fixed, sometimes from boyhood. "You are shaped by the company you keep as a youngster," said the Postal Kid. "You tangle up early with guys who cheat for a living. Then you meet other grifters through them and get hardened to their ways. You lose your dough and that hardens you up to the other side of the picture. You become hungry for dough to gamble with. Then you go out looking for a mark you can trim. You take the chances and the gamblers take the dough away from you. They are very nice to you when you are flush, but when you are chick, boy, they give you the chill. They think you might put the bite on, and gamesters don't like to associate with grifters who are chicane. So out you go for another mark. . . ."

Thus is begun a cycle which is likely to continue, with minor variations, throughout a lifetime, for most con men gamble heavily with the money for which they work so hard and take such chances to secure. In a word, most of them are suckers for some other branch of the grift. Among the old-timers, it was twisting the tiger's tail; among the present generation, it is cards, dice, roulette or stocks. It is indeed strange that men who know so much about the percentage which operates in favor of the professional gambler will risk their freedom for the highly synthetic thrill of bucking the tiger. Yet a big score is hardly cut up until all the mob are plunging heavily at their favorite game; within a few weeks, or even a few days, a $100,000 touch has gone glimmering and the con men are living on borrowed money, or are out on the tip or the smack to make expenses.

Con men are well aware of this weakness, yet few of them, it seems, are able to curb their gambling instincts and gear their lives down to the speed at which the ordinary citizen lives. Many amusing stories are told about this tendency, each con man laughing at the mote in his neighbor's eye while he ignores the beam in his own. One of these stories concerns Little Chappie Lohr and Plunk Drucker. Plunk had an insatiable lust for faro-bank and played it at every opportunity, even though he lost with distressing regularity. The two men started out on the road with a bank roll between them. Plunk promptly lost it all at faro. They borrowed from an accommodating saloon-keeper in Chicago. At Council Bluffs Plunk disappeared. Little Chappie, fearing the worst, sought him out in the den of the tiger.

"You can't do this," remonstrated Chappie. "You'll lose our bank roll again."

"Oh, no, Chappie," said Plunk, confidently, "don't worry. Back in Chicago, they were only dealing it out at $5 and $10. Here they are dealing it out at $12.50 and $25."

(For the benefit of those who do not understand faro-bank—strictly a grifter's game nowadays—the point of the story lies in the fact that Plunk felt confident that he could win just twice as fast because the cards were dealt for double the former price in Council Bluffs; in reality, of course, he was losing at more than double the rate he did in Chicago.)

Another, which is now almost legendary in the underworld, illustrates how Kid McGinley's lust for poker consumed all of his income from the grift. One time he and his partner stopped for a time in Rochester, New York, just after taking off a big touch. Every night the Kid played poker in a brace-game and lost heavily. He was rapidly going broke. His partner, who had been a professional gambler, tried to warn the Kid.

"Kid," he said, "that stud-horse poker game is Mill's lock. All those starters are subway dealers. If you play any longer, you'll be behind the six."

"What the hell can I do?" asked the Kid. "It's the only game in town."

This indulgence of the gaming instincts becomes more than relaxation; their gratification is the only motive which many con men have for grifting. With many, especially old-timers, faro-bank is an obsession. As soon as they have taken off a score and cut it up, away they go to a faro-bank to try out the systems which they hope will beat the bank in this most fascinating of all card games. They win and lose, win and lose, always losing more than they win, until they come away broke and full of reasons why their "systems" didn't work that time. The only way con men can come away substantially and consistently richer is to use the same methods the gambling house uses and beat the house from the outside. Kid S—— and Jerry Daley, for instance, claim credit for inventing a crooked system (probably much older) which they called "copper on and copper off." At any rate, they perfected it to a high degree and several con men and gamblers formed a mob which traveled over the country taking scores of from $7,000 to $10,000 from each gambling house; but work as hard as they could, all the con men in the country, using the "copper on and copper off" system, could never win back all the money that the faro-dealers have taken from con men. Old-timers have lost heavily at this game, but many young grifters have never seen it played.

While no con men ever play for such high stakes as did some of the multimillionaire plungers of the Canfield era, many of them throw money over the gaming board at a rate that seems impressive to us in these degenerate days. Kid McGinley, who was infinitely more successful at making money legitimately than he was at grifting, always bet high on sporting events, especially prize fights and baseball games. It was common for him to bet as much as $2,000 per race when he was at the track. The Indiana Wonder likes horse-racing, but plunges on longshots only. The Jew Kid gambles on anything, but likes horses and craps best; there are rumors that he has a hand in fixed races. 102nd St. George concentrates on horses, while the Postal Kid, on the contrary, never liked horses but gambled away sizable fortunes on faro and craps. The High Ass Kid likes blackjack; Limehouse Chappie, Curley Carter, and the Boone Kid gamble on anything. Chappie Moran, who had himself been a bookie and should have known better, always aspired to beat the horses. So did the Honey Grove Kid. Fifth Avenue Fred is a high-rolling gambler, sometimes rolling as high as $5,000 at a pop on the crap table. Lee Reil enjoyed a little faro. The Ripley Kid loves gambling, especially bridge, but his enthusiasm exceeds his card sense and he never wins. The handsome Kid W—— does likewise. Queer-pusher Nick gambles heavily. The Square Faced Kid, himself a fine card cheater, and one of the best bridge players anywhere, is a sucker for stocks and loses his winnings in speculation. Little Bert, although an excellent bridge player, put the interests of his family first, and seldom gambled for high stakes. Wildfire John, a heavy gambler during his entire life, now in his old age lives practically in the gutter.

Naturally those confidence men who gamble heavily seldom profit much from the large sums they take from gullible marks. Others spend their cut of each score rapidly as soon as they get it, or give it to their women, who put it promptly into clothes, furs or diamonds.

In this connection, there is a tale told of E—— S——, who for years shepherded the S——s' assets, buying diamonds as fast as her husband turned over to her his end of a touch. These she carefully hoarded in a little chamois bag which fitted snugly inside her stocking above the knee. Ironically, for all her thrift, the S—— fortune came to grief in a most plebeian fashion. Several con men and their wives were crossing the southwestern desert by train; E—— retired to the ladies' room where, in the course of certain solemn rites enthroned, she let slip the little chamois bag and it skittered through to the ties beneath. She leaped for the bell cord and gave it a lusty pull. The train stopped long enough for E—— and her friends to pile out onto the blistering sands. For long hours they paraded back and forth over the right-of-way, but the winds arose and the sands shifted, and for all I know, E——'s diamonds still lie buried there.

But some eschewed gambling and bad investments, salted away their money, and became well-to-do. These would include the Narrow Gage Kid, Doc Sterling,

Glouster Jack, Little Chappie Lohr, George Ryan, John Henry Strosnider, the Clinic Kid, Joe Furey (who was broken by the Norfleet case), the Black Kid of quiet demean and refined manners, Nigger Mike and the Big Alabama Kid. Christ Tracy did not gamble but gave away most of the money he made during a prosperous lifetime. The notorious Yellow Kid doesn't gamble, but indulges a vast and expensive taste for women.

Although many confidence men lose heavily to professional gamblers, a few of them are themselves first-rate gamblers with both grift sense and card sense—a rare and fortunate combination. These men are wise enough to protect their winnings from braced gambling houses, carefully hoarding them up to lose on stocks, horses, women or whatever they are suckers for. "Grifters who are gamble-wise can make a braced gambling house right away," said Tom Furey, who evaded them with enough success to leave a comfortable fortune at his death. "Why? Because when they step into a house, they look around for a short time at all the shills who are boosting. Then they'll notice from the way the sticks handle the chips that they're not interested in the play. They are professionals and handle the chips like no mark could ever handle them. They just shuffle them like cards. I think that within one hour I could pick out every shill in the gaff. But there is no gambling game invented that you can't beat either from the inside or the outside, so what the hell. . . ."

The money which a con man does not throw away over the gaming table is rapidly used up in maintaining a very high standard of living. Because he must appear at an advantage in a highly respectable world, he lives on a high and even luxurious plane. Most con men dress well, carrying with them on the road an extensive wardrobe which provides for any sort of social situation in which they may find themselves. They wear their clothes well, for most of them are well-built, substantial-looking men; this build seems to occur with remarkable frequency, though one immediately thinks of exceptions in John Singleton, short, heavy-set, portly; in the Brass Kid, short, rosy-cheeked, jolly; and in Little Bert, and the Little Alabama Kid. Probably natural selection explains the fact that most of them are well set-up and attractive physically; some of them are distinguished-looking. Their manners are excellent, their behavior during professional appearances beyond reproach.

There is at least one ill-mannered exception to this generalization who deserves a bit of space because he is widely known among con men as the prime example of everything a con man shouldn't do or be. He is the prosperous Red Lager. Ignorant and repulsive-looking, freckled to the point of blotchiness, with the nasty shade of blue eyes which often accompanies a certain cast of red hair, awkward and slew-footed, Red Lager is certainly the acme of unattractiveness among con men. He is everything and does everything which, theoretically, a good con man shouldn't. He has never heard of Dale Carnegie and is unaware of the barest rudiments of the science of "influencing" people; yet he has made a fortune on the pay-off. And he has a son, the exact replica of his father down to the duck-like walk, who, despite his addiction to drugs—one vice which the old man shunned—is today a successful confidence man.

First-class accommodations on railways and steamships are necessary if con men are to meet well-to-do people. Many of them now travel in their own chauffeured cars. Their hotels are always the best and their suites imposing. Their work takes them into swank clubs and resorts. Naturally, their personalities and their manners must not betray them. Consequently, they have cultivated the social side more than any other criminal group. They are able to fit in unobtrusively on any social level.

Although their culture is not very deep, it is surprisingly wide and versatile. They must be well informed in business and financial matters, have a glib knowledge of society gossip, and enough of an acquaintance with art, literature and music to give an illusion of culture. I have observed that many of them read widely, and that it is an almost universal habit to run through ten or a dozen newspapers daily in order to keep constantly informed on topics which may come up in conversation. Newspapers also furnish a wide variety of news vital to grifters who want to thrive in their profession and keep out of jail. A few go deeper than casual browsing among the periodicals and haunt libraries when they have time, reading books omnivorously. One con man of my acquaintance buys a great many books, reads them, and promptly gives them away.

Among those who pursue learning for its own sake, I might cite three examples. One, a man of about forty-five, has his own special interests, largely sociological, and sits in sporadically on classes in a large mid-western university. Another, a man of some sixty years of age, has never sought any formal education, but delights in literature, has read widely and indiscriminately from Shakespeare to the moderns, and has his critical views which compensate in originality for what they lack in orthodoxy. A phenomenal memory enables him to quote at will from almost anything he has read. Another has made a hobby of history, with especial emphasis on Napoleon, and has, at one time or another, acquainted himself with most of the documents in English, both here and abroad, which touch upon the career of that general.

But most confidence men read for mercenary rather than cultural reasons, seeking only information which they can use in their profession. "All grifters [con men] try to educate themselves by reading a lot," says one con man, who might well speak for the entire profession. "I read to learn something, so when I bump into Mr. Bates I can hold my own with him on most any subject. If you are posing as a banker, for instance, you must know enough about banking to get away with it. I read the financial pages and the investment journals so I won't slip up and rumble the mark. The same is true for any business I claim to be engaged in. Of course, I pick up a lot of it from just talking to people, but I have to read a lot too."

Often one encounters a creative spark in con men; if given the opportunity and the incentive, they might write quite well. Their wide experience with people, their keen powers of observation, and their fluent command of picturesque language would all stand them in good stead if they chose to record the colorful world about them. Certain of them have a genuine love of poetry and rather apologetically exhibit their own efforts at verse; I have in my files numerous manuscripts, some of which rise decidedly above the level of doggerel.

In general, however, the culture of con men is no more than a superficial veneer which, combined with attractive personalities and a ready mother-wit, gives the illusion of polish. Once a con man is thrown back on his own resources and into his own society, he relapses into the ways and the tastes of the common grifter. He has no real interests to sustain him. "A few of the boys have something they like to play around with when they have the leisure," says an old-timer, "but for most of them, I guess it is only faro, craps or just the gals. When a con man hits a new town, he can smell a faro-bank just the same as he can smell a policeman."

Almost all con men live irregular sex-lives, because they are away from their women so much of the time; much of their money is squandered in fancy brothels of one sort or another. And most con men drink when they are at leisure, some, like Roy Brooks (the Major) probably to excess. However, no competent con man drinks on the job, and drinking with the mark is always frowned upon. Certainly no con man who used alcohol continuously to excess long maintains his standing in his profession.

With the increased use of narcotics among underworld folk, it is inevitable that some con men should become addicted, though most modern big-time criminals shun narcotics like poison. Some of the old-timers took up opium around 1900 when it was considered no more dangerous than smoking cigarettes—when many citizens on the West Coast placidly puffed the pipe on their own front porches, and an opium lay-out was standard equipment for most prostitutes whose Pekes and Pomeranians often acquired a "lamp habit" from breathing the smoke while their mistresses puffed. But the Harrison Act changed all that. As opium became more difficult to buy and to take, many addicts turned to morphine and heroin. However, confidence men have always felt that there was something disgraceful about addiction, the present generation being particularly sensitive about it. Consequently, once a con man becomes addicted, he carefully conceals the fact as well as he can and only his intimate associates are aware of his misfortune. How many of the more prominent grifters are addicted it is impossible to say, but it is rumored that Kid Duff, Jack Hardaway, Charley Dixon, Pretty Willy (better known as a thief), Kid Niles, the Yenshee Kid, Claude King, Kent Marshall, Red Lager (the Younger), Jimmy the Rooter, the Sanctimonious Kid and Jackie French are, or have been, addicted. There must be many others who have successfully concealed their addiction. As one goes down the social scale among grifters, addiction becomes increasingly common.

Some con men have pleasures which are less deleterious. Many now play golf for sport, while old-timers like

Wildfire John, the Honey Grove Kid, the Indiana Wonder and the High Ass Kid played it largely for business reasons. Some fancy horses and, like the Clinic Kid and Big Kentuck, maintain their own racing or saddle stables. But mostly their interests stop with gambling and girls.

On the other hand, it must not be assumed that all con men live fast, dissipated lives. Some are temperate or even ascetic. Stewart Donnelly, for instance, has a reputation among his colleagues for being exceedingly abstemious and far more decent in his living habits than many legitimate citizens. He is reputed to refuse all kinds of liquor, even beer and wine, does not use tobacco or narcotics; and, at past fifty, has the physique of a boxer. Many of his associates feel that it is to his credit that he does not gamble, that he scrupulously pays his debts, and that he has been married to the same woman for twenty years.

Confidence men, like legitimate citizens, mate once or more (usually more) during their lives. But, unlike the legitimate citizens, they seldom get divorces, probably because of the publicity which would attend such an event. If they separate, they do it quietly and without benefit of legal papers. Some con men marry into higher social levels and acquire property and status through marriage. Others associate themselves with wealthy women; Kid McGinley, who once short-changed Anita Baldwin on the circus lot and soon found himself in possession of a fortune, is a happy example of this. Some, like Cockroach Gary, scion of a wealthy family who acquired four hundred pounds, more or less, of thief in Big Cad, reverse the process. Some marry waitresses, some prostitutes. But most of them marry girls who are in one way or another connected with the grift, although few women ever work into the confidence rackets with their husbands.

Grifters differ in their opinions about the extent to which women are able to help their husbands in the business of trimming marks. "Grifters," observes one cynic, "are always marrying some squaw who is a bum and who will never make a grifter. I never knew one who married anybody who knew much, or who wanted to learn. They just never seem to meet the right sort." Another con man, an expert on the pay-off, says, "Grifters use girls and women for contacting marks around high-class resorts. If a grifter has his girl or wife with him, and if she is smart enough, why then he uses her. But few are smart enough." Another, who has himself used women as part of his roping technique, says, "Some women are smart to grifting if they have a chance to grift. A clever girl can certainly lead a mark around. She knows how to keep him on the line while he is being played, too. Sometimes she promises the mark that, after he makes all his money, they will take a little trip to Europe together. Marks like that kind of goings-on. . . ." An old-timer who remembers the genesis of big-time confidence games adds, "A long time ago I knew many women, like Ollie Roberts in St. Louis, who were roping for panel stores, and some of them were good. But most of them have passed on. Some of them should have been on the pay-off. They were natural ropers. There are plenty of women today who would make good, too, but they haven't the chance because they don't know any good grifters." The majority of con men, however, want their women safely at home while a mark is being played; then they know that a woman won't do something impulsive and ruin the play. Furthermore, some con men feel that it is beneath the dignity of their wives to work on the grift.

Other branches of the grift are peopled with women aplenty; some of the best pickpockets are women, women have been dealers in gaming houses from western frontier days on down, and have been professional gamblers since long before the Civil War. As big-time professional thieves, some of them are unsurpassed, and the small-time thieving rackets are overrun with them. They are well represented in flat-jointing and in some other branches of the short con. But the only full-fledged con woman whom I have been able to turn up, who is recognized by male colleagues everywhere as a competent professional, is Lilly the Roper, who is now over fifty and has spent her entire life on the grift. Early in life she made a reputation as a pickpocket and had her own mob. She was first married to a heavy man named Harrington. Following his death, she married a thief whom she divorced to marry her present husband, a pickpocket turned con man. "Lilly can rope a mark for the big con and trim one, too," commented one professional who has known her for many years.

The fact that there are few marriages among con folk and even fewer divorces need not imply that there is no code governing relations between the sexes. The men provide for the material needs of their women very liberally; they have good living quarters, fine clothes, servants and all the comforts that money can buy. Most of them do not discard their women when they grow old, even though there is no legal tie binding them. One con man seldom steals another's woman unless she deliberately throws herself at him, or has already left her man. However, if one does steal another's girl, the only resultant social criticism is a little good-natured ribbing directed at the loser. If he takes his loss very seriously, he may kill or try to kill his rival; usually, he takes his kidding graciously and consoles himself with another woman. And, in all justice to the women, it should be said that, in spite of the fact that they know that their husbands live free-and-easy love lives on the road, they usually remain faithful to their men. As long as they live in wedlock, they carefully observe the double standard. Probably there is no more infidelity on their parts than there is among legitimate middle-class wives. A woman who is unfaithful to her man is not regarded very highly; this is especially true when she is living or staying with friends while her husband is in prison or away. Her indiscretions are her own business, but she should not bring them into the homes of her friends. If she regards herself as still belonging to her man, she should conduct herself properly; if not, she should stay on her own, or get another man. In other words, as long as she permits her husband's friends to support her, she is obligated to maintain a respectable demeanor and behavior. And she usually does. Kid Duff's wife, for instance, held in her possession all the Kid's assets—amounting to several hundred thousand dollars—until he finished his last bit in prison, then, after his release, returned them to him and secured a divorce. She could have very easily run out on him while he was helpless, but she dealt fairly with him.

Con men get out of life little more than they can buy with money; in addition, they are beset on all sides by dangers which the legitimate citizen never has to cope with. They like to believe that their women will be the last to let them down—despite many examples to the contrary. There is sometimes a deep and somewhat pathetic attachment between the pair which may be life-long. Charley Gondorff, for instance, has always stuck to his Maude, even though wealth and wide social contacts made it possible for him to have had a choice of many clever and more handsome women. Many of the older generation have done the same thing. And Farmer Brown, king of the monte players, frequently and vociferously proclaimed in public that he was "married to the most beautiful woman who ever straddled a chamber-pot," expert testimony to the contrary notwithstanding.

The women do not always have an easy time of it, even though their wants are liberally supplied. If they are aware of their husband's occupation—and few of them are not—they live in constant fear of a "fall" with disastrous consequences. They see little of their men for weeks on end, while, at the same time, correspondence may be both difficult and dangerous. They are usually incapable of helping their men or of sharing any common interest with them. But many of them do try to do their part as well as they can. Perhaps the most pathetic case in point is that of the schoolteacher who married the illiterate Sheeny Mike. John Singleton swears that when he once visited the pair, he overheard her teaching her husband the alphabet. "I could hear Mike droning, 'Aaa, Bee, Cee,' then starting all over again, 'Aaa, Bee, Cee. . . .' His wife said that was as far as he was ever able to get." But Singleton was having his sarcastic little joke; the teacher did make Mike literate and he became a prosperous roper.

In spite of the fact that con men live on the road almost continuously, they try to maintain more or less permanent homes, most of them in or about Chicago or New York, some of the fine ones on Long Island. The location of these homes is always carefully guarded and kept secret from all but very close friends. Grifters frequently know one another well, and even work together professionally, without revealing their addresses to one another. In fact, it is rigidly observed underworld etiquette to refrain from asking a professional where he lives; if he volunteers the information it is a mark of trust and esteem. Some con men, like Joe Furey, maintain two homes with a separate family in each; but, on the whole, con folk appear to be hardly less monogamous than legitimate middle-class society.

However, marital life on the grift is by no means always calm and unruffled, the relationship mutually faithful and felicitous. Far from it. "Storm-and-strife" is a common argot word for wife, a coinage which is probably rooted rather deeply in bitter experience. Some con men marry "sucker-broads" who trim them and run out on them; others marry "gun-molls" who are themselves "on the lam" most of the time; and not a few find themselves harboring a "rat" who only awaits an opportunity to turn stool pigeon for the police. "My boy," old John Henry Strosnider once said, "the best way to avoid the big house is not to tell your twist how clever you are. Broads have been known to put the finger on smart young apples. So cop my advice, and last longer on the outside than on the inside. . . ."

All too often the home life of the grifter, especially the small-time grifter, is like that of the famous Cheerful Charley and his girl, the Cheerful Chicken. Charley had fallen upon lean days as steerer for a mitt store in Minneapolis and had done what small-timers frequently do—"joined out the odds"—that is, he had put the Chicken on the market for all and sundry who would buy. One wintry Saturday night the Chicken came into the room, weary and stiff from pounding the pavements in her worn-out shoes. She gave Charley all her money, then showed him her toes sticking out of the wet leather.

"I have to have some new shoes, Charley," she said.

"No, by God," roared Charley, "not with my money."

Obviously, the home life of grifters does not make a desirable background against which to raise children. Yet some do raise families; and some of the children grow up without suspecting that their father is a confidence man. However, when the mother is also involved in the rackets, the offspring almost inevitably follow in their parents' footsteps, for they meet thieves at home, hear thievery discussed from their earliest recollection, and grow up in an environment which they cannot escape. There are, however, some notable exceptions like John Singleton's son—who has a legitimate profession in New York—whose name, for obvious reasons, cannot be given here.

An ironical little anecdote illustrates the relation between grifters and their children. One successful grifter had three sons, none of whom suspected his father's occupation. He determined to send them to college so that they need never know the rigors of the grift. When the first two were old enough, he bundled them off. Very shortly, and somewhat to their father's embarrassment, they were apprehended in some thievery. Said the grifter, "If they are going to be thieves, they might as well learn right." So he took them all on the road and thus ended his experiment in higher education.

## 4

Although con men live prosperous lives, they are constantly harried either by federal officers who threaten to put them in prison, or by local officers who demand a cut of their profits. They are continually on the move and ever on the alert, for they have many predatory enemies who prey on them, even as they prey upon legitimate society. Some thrive on this sort of anxious life, refusing to worry about the future, and successfully rationalizing their own criminal acts away. Others find that the strain gets on their nerves to such an extent that they "pack in the racket" and go straight. Almost never do professionals "reform" for purely moral reasons; they simply go off the rackets because they cannot stand the worry and uncertainty, the feeling of being hunted, the threat of prison, which always hangs over them. "If a man had any sense in the first place," runs an old saying among grifters, "he'd never be a thief."

The external pressures which are applied to con mobs help to foster a professional morale which is very high—perhaps the highest among all underworld folk, and certainly the highest on the grift. It is not this writer's intention to attempt to answer the old, old question about honor among thieves. Because of the diverse personalities which are to be found among confidence men, it is hardly sound to generalize; obviously, some con men have a highly developed sense of loyalty and honor, others do not. By carefully selecting his evidence, one could easily establish a strong case for either side of the question. While it would be fruitless to include here numerous anecdotes which might tend to support one side or the other of the controversy, it might be interesting to see how confidence men generalize upon this subject.

"They have plenty of honor," said old Christ Tracy. "If they hadn't they wouldn't last long with the better kind of grifters. I've received money due me from paper that I had forgotten about for years. Only a rat refuses to pay his honest debts."

Says the Postal Kid, "Con men don't hold out on their pals. Only rats do that. And news travels fast. Of course, some heels will tear you off if you turn around to spit. But it is seldom done. I know the old saying is that there is no honor among thieves, but I've seen plenty of it. And I've seen thousands of marks who claimed to be square paper, but had all the corners torn off."

"Yes," comments John Henry Strosnider, "con men try to be square with one another and are trustworthy among themselves. But you'll find finks in any racket. If you are known as a finger-egg for some dick, it gets around in a hurry. Even so, a lot of those rats seem to prosper." (Strosnider's testimony can probably not be taken at its face value, as many of his ropers represent him as being expert at the tear-off himself.)

Notes another con man: "Lots of con men pride themselves on being great ropers or fine insidemen, and are proud that they are on the square with the men they do business with. Lots of grifters, like Post and Allen, stay put with their partners for years and wouldn't have anyone else."

In spite of evidence of a well-developed sense of professional honor among con men, there are equally impressive indications that they sometimes step over the line—dangerous as that may be—and tear off their partners for a part of the score. Usually the insideman does this, for he is the only member of the mob who is alone with the mark's money for any length of time; the only opportunity that the roper has for cheating on the score is to "pad the nut" (falsify expense accounts), which is not often done. The Yellow Kid, one of the best insidemen in the country, has the reputation of cheating his ropers if he thinks he can get away with it. Many ropers curse him for this trait, but still gladly work with him because of his ability. Some ropers, sure that they have been torn off, have protested, only to be taken gently in hand and convinced that they are wrong; others, knowing that they have no chance against that silver tongue and winning personality, are said to have visited him privately at his home to collect what is due them at the point of a pistol. "That Yellow Kid would tear himself off if he could," said one of his ropers.

There is still the mystery of who robbed the famous Buck Boatwright on his deathbed. He was known to have carried about $200,000 in a money belt, but he was found dead in his hotel room without a trace of the money. Underworld gossip fastened the blame upon Conk Jones, who was reputed to have been with Buck when he died; but no one ever knew certainly that Conk had "rolled" his friend.

Fifth Avenue Fred, high in the ranks of insidemen, still carries across his belly the scar from Bill Caldwell's pistol-bullet, a wound inflicted by the Kentuckian in a personal dispute on Twenty-first Street in Chicago. John Henry Strosnider wore to his grave the knife-scars inflicted by Post and Allen as a reminder that he should not tear them off in the future; characteristically, Strosnider turned this disfigurement to an asset by claiming a Heidelberg education and showing his "sabre-cuts" to prove it. Elmer Meade was disfigured for life by a shot in the face received in a dispute over gambling spoils. And sometimes a con man is not lucky enough to survive a tear-off, even with scars. Australian Harry is quoted as complaining that he and his partner lost $84,000, which they took from a mark in Paris, through the connivance of Tear-off Arthur, who knew about the play and arranged with the Paris police to raid the store, confiscate the money, then divide it. Big Bill Keeley also bore the reputation of a "tear-off rat"; one of the men whom he tore off for $2,000 once told me apologetically that "Big Bill wouldn't have done it on his own accord. His wife made a rat out of him."

Many grifters who would not tear off a partner or beat what they consider an honest debt, would, at the same time consider other grifters as fair game for any sort of swindle; gamblers, of course, prey on all other grifters, including gamblers, without conscience. The Harmony Kid once double-crossed the High Ass Kid for a reputed $20,000 at chuck-a-luck. Two con men whose names cannot be used here once stole a faro-dealer's tell box (crooked dealing box) from Little Dan in Minneapolis, planted it in the lobby of a Chicago hotel, and allowed Wildfire John to find it there. Wildfire, himself a con man and professional gambler, had a mighty weakness for faro. They skinned him just as they would any other mark and took him for $2,000. Joe Flaherty once put up a mark to be trimmed by a con mob of his acquaintance. The "mark" was a train-robber named Estelle, who had plotted with Flaherty to rob the grifters of a large sum of money they were carrying. However, just as Estelle was robbing his victims in a hotel room, a bellhop entered, spread the alarm, and Estelle fled with only about $100. Be it said to Flaherty's credit that, once he became a con man himself, he repaid the $100 out of his own pocket. On the whole, I think we might say that con men are generally on the square with men they consider "right guys," but are not so particular about the "wrong ones." And a stool pigeon or rat merits their undying contempt and hatred.

While it is hardly necessary to explain that a stool pigeon or police informer is hunted down and killed by professional criminals, the following anecdote illustrates very clearly the attitude of con men toward these criminal pariahs; it concerns a saloonkeeper and notorious Chicago fixer and stool pigeon: ". . . What a rat Andy was. He had to have two Central dicks take him home every night. He never left the Village, as he knew he would be knocked off. Billy Reynolds once took two shots at him, but missed. I asked him why he shot at Andy, as Andy was not a grifter, and Billy had never worked for him. Billy was a right egg, and he said, 'I always get a hard-on [reach for a pistol] when I see a rat, and I want to do him in.' "

## 5

Whatever personal philosophies a grifter may work out for himself, he usually makes no outward show of religion—unless he is a Roman Catholic—and as a rule does not attend church or maintain a church membership. A notable exception to this was Rebel George, who was an itinerant preacher on Sundays and a con man during the week. "All Irish con men," says one professional, "are, generally speaking, Catholics, and go to church the same as guns. Then they come right out and rob a chump." Says another: "All grifters who are papes go to the kirk regularly; the other half never go." He adds an anecdote which implies something of the grifter's attitude toward the church:

"One Sunday morning Maxie F—— and Greenie G—— were out in New York looking for a score on the dip. They wandered into a church, and while they were waiting for the crowd, began to study the frescoes on the walls. They came to a familiar scene showing the Last Supper. Greenie pretended to be greatly puzzled.

" 'Maxie,' he said, 'who are all those old bald-headed pappies?'

" 'Oh,' said Maxie, 'those are just some old cannons that were mugged in Jerusalem!' "

Though con men may be non-committal regarding their theological beliefs, there is one creed on which most of them agree—and that is: never pay for anything that can be had free; and if it must be paid for at all, get it at a reduced price. They buy everything that can be bought from thieves—clothing, jewelry, automobiles, etc. In the larger hangouts, professional thieves take orders and steal to order much of the fine personal furnishings which are a part of every good con man's stock in trade. Color, size and quality are agreed upon in advance. When the goods are delivered, they are paid for at a specified price. On the other hand, some few do not like to have stolen goods in their possession; they buy and pay for quantities of custom-tailored clothes, hand-made shoes, and exclusive haberdashery from well-known merchants. At current retail prices, a good con man's wardrobe will cost him about $5,000 a year.

Con men always stay at first-class hotels. Many of them are extremely adept at beating the hotels for large bills; others believe that it hurts their business to beat hotels and pay as they go. I once heard several con men arguing this rather fine point in professional ethics with some heat. They were preparing to leave an expensive hotel where a large bill had been run up. The question was raised as to whether or not they should pay. "What the hell," interrupted a practical soul, "we're supposed to be out on the road robbing people, aren't we?"

A good grifter never misses a chance to get something for nothing, which is one of the reasons why a good grifter is often also a good mark. Indiana Harry, the Hashhouse Kid, Scotty, and Hoosier Harry were returning to America on the *Titanic* when it sank. They were all saved. After the rescue, they all not only put in maximum claims for lost baggage, but collected the names of dead passengers for their friends, so that they too could put in claims.

This tendency to want something for nothing extends to all branches of the grift. A tale is told of Johnny Tolbert and a team of pickpockets, one of whom, Kansas City Boze, was killed in a fight in El Paso. Johnny Tolbert, fixer for the city, went with the surviving partner to an undertaker's establishment to arrange for laying Boze away. While Johnny stalled the undertaker, Boze's partner changed the tag from a $500 casket to a $1,000 one, and placed the $1,000 tag on a cheaper casket. Johnny then bought the $1,000 job for $500 and paid for it in cash. As they left the funeral home, Boze's partner turned to Tolbert and said, "You know, Boze would like that."

Grifters, especially those in the lower brackets, often cheat one another quite merrily. And sometimes such dealings have humorous repercussions. A tale is told about Ella B——, wife of a well-known grifter, and her friend Sofa L——. Ella stole a set of what she thought was sterling silver, but, on examining it carefully at home, she discovered that it was only cheap plate. So she gave the set to her friend Sofa for Christmas. Sofa was delighted with it until a friend examined it and told her it was a fake. Several days after Christmas, Ella visited Sofa, who had a story all ready for her.

"Ella," she said, "you are a cheap skate to send me a phony like that silver set."

"Why," asked Ella innocently, "what is wrong with it?"

"Wrong with it?" echoed Sofa. "It's a crow if there ever was one. Why, my little niece took one look at it and spotted it."

"How can that kid tell the pure quill when it comes to silver?" asked Ella, surprised.

"That's what I asked her," snapped Sofa, "and she said, 'I can't, but I know Ella B——, Aunt Sofa.' "

A pickpocket, whom we shall call Frenchy, tells this anecdote regarding tear-off tendencies in his branch of the grift. He had been a partner of Spot B—— for years. Spot had been cheating Frenchy by surreptitiously removing a few dollars from each pocketbook they lifted.

"You know that old Spot B——," said Frenchy. "That old gun had been putting me in the hole for years and had burned me for plenty. He had been putting his hump up for me, and when I weeded him the leathers, he weeded them of a few push-notes before we counted the score. I decided to break him of the habit, so I gave him a Mickey Finn. Believe me, it worked on him. He thought he was going to croak, and he called me in and said, 'Frenchy, I've burned you for thousands of bucks. Can you forgive me?' "

" 'That's O.K., Spot,' I said, 'don't worry about it. I'm the gee who poisoned you.' "

Once a con man always a con man; never does he resort to common thievery or pocket-picking unless he is very hard pressed. He always prefers to play the con for his victims. Only as a last resort does he revert to thievery or take the last downward and degrading step—join out the odds.

The Wise Cracking Kid of Chicago tells how a bit of quick thinking and an impromptu short-con game got him fare to New York. "I was broke and had to get to New York," he said, "so I went down on the levee to see a bartender who was a friend, but he was broke. Then a funny thing happened. A fool walked in and bought drinks for the house and laid down a C-note. Jack took a good look at the bill, then gave the chump his change. Then he saw me looking at it and said in an undertone, 'Kid, this note looks like it might be counterfeit.' I looked at the note and told Jack it looked queer. He said, 'Take it out, Kid, and see if it is O.K.' So I grabbed the note and beat it to the shed and bought my ticket. When I got to the City, I wired Jack: 'C-note all O.K. The Wise Cracking Kid.' "

But whether a con man has money or not, he is always playing the con for someone, for merchants, for hotel men, for prostitutes, brothel-madams, thieves and even for other con men. He loves his work and is constantly experimenting to see what new angle he may develop, what technical point he can improve upon. He is only half-serious in this merry foolery but nevertheless he always profits from each new situation, from each new type of person he approaches.

Nothing pleases him more than to *tish* a lady—that is, to place a fifty-dollar bill in her stocking with the solemn assurance that if she takes it out before morning, it will turn into tissue paper. Being a woman, she removes it at the earliest opportunity, only to find that it *has* turned to tissue paper, often with a bit of ribald verse inscribed upon it.

Sometimes a grifter will meet a gun-moll who craves the *cold poke.* So he plays "roper" while an older con-man friend will play the "inside." He steers the girl to a night club where the point-out is played. She is pleased to meet this elderly gentleman who is dispensing his money freely from a very fat wallet. The "roper" connives with the thief to steal the old man's pocketbook. Covering her movements with the aid of a feint to the flank, she slips in through the postern gate and takes the wallet. Just as she is stealing out of the club, the old man "beefs gun" and the chase is on after the girl. She dashes down an alley, clutching the wallet. When she stops to "weed" it, she is disconcerted to find that it is bulging with paper, frequently garnished with indelicate sentiments and ribald suggestions.

When a con man has taken off a big touch or two and allows his good opinion of himself to become obnoxious, he may be given *the engineer's daughter* by his friends and acquaintances. The point-out is used with such skill that he falls all unsuspecting into the trap where a woman is bait. Soon he finds himself in hot amorous pursuit of "the engineer's daughter" (acted by some grifter's sultry dame). His program for seduction is somewhat complicated by the fact that the girl's father has a high temper and a wholesome distrust of men. She can receive callers only when he is on his night run. But obstacles like this only make the little affair more zestful for the con man. He sneaks in and out of her apartment with great secrecy. One night, just as he is about to be favored with the lady's surrender, the lights go on and there stands the engineer in overalls and goggles, brandishing a businesslike pistol. The victim takes one look at the pistol, collects such of his wardrobe as he can, and looks about for a way of retreat. But the engineer blocks the door, so the retreat turns into a rout. Over the porch roof or down the fire escape he goes, with the pistol blasting behind him. In resort cities like Hot Springs where grifters habitually congregate, he will find a reception committee outside composed of all his friends and acquaintances. This mock con game, or one of its numerous variations, is reputed to have a most salutary effect on an inflated ego.

Horse-play among con men really knows no bounds except the limits of their ingenuity; while it would be pointless to cite numerous illustrations of mock con games, it might be of some interest to include the rather grotesque account of how the Postal Kid discouraged Snotter Jack from becoming a con man.

The Kid had a pay-off store in Hot Springs, Arkansas. Snotter Jack, a cheap grifter who fancied himself a big-timer, made himself a nuisance by hanging around the hangouts and begging the Kid to let him try his hand at roping for the big store. Finally the Kid and some other members of the mob cooked up a scheme to take Jack down a peg. The Kid called Jack in and told him, "Jack, I believe you have the makings of a great roper. So I'm going to put you on the street and I want you to work double with the Honey Grove Kid. You rope the mark and play the point-out with the Honey Grove Kid, then he will take the mark off your hands and you can play him in the store. That way you can sting the first time."

Jack was highly pleased.

The next day a prosperous businessman (played by a roper whom Jack didn't know) began to talk to Jack in the hotel lobby. He told how much money his business was making and how he had come to Hot Springs for a little vacation. For two hours he held forth, then made a luncheon date for the next day and left. Jack, swollen with importance, hurriedly sought out Jimmy to tell him that he had roped a mark who would be good for at least a hundred grand.

"It sounds good to me," said the Postal Kid. "I believe you have something there."

The next day, according to schedule, Jack pointed out the Honey Grove Kid to the mark. From here on the con men enacted the entire play backward, with the "mark" taking the part that Jack should have played. The mark took Jack in tow, bet the bank roll in the store, and made the mistake which ruined them. Then the Honey Grove tried to change the bet, but the bookmaker stood pat. Then the Honey Grove came back and began cursing the mark. "You are the bastard who caused my friend and me to lose all this money," he snarled, "and now I'm going to fix you." With that he produced a tremendous revolver and shot the mark right in the belly. The mark fell to the floor, groaning and spitting blood all over Jack. The Honey Grove then stepped up and handed the gun to Jack, who dropped it like a hot coal. Befuddled and frightened half to death, Jack took it on the lam and decided that the big con was not for him.

Con men are always fixing, conniving and finagling. It is in their blood. They are always talking themselves into and out of all kinds of complications. Once Jerry Daley made a little side trip to La Salle, Illinois. To kill time there he dropped in on a beauty contest. There on the platform was a little raven-haired Irish girl who immediately caught his fancy. He began to circulate about the crowd and sound out sentiment for her. She didn't seem to be very popular. The fact that the odds were against her aroused Jerry's sporting blood to the extent that he began to buy votes for her. Whenever he encountered opposition, he called into play all his ability as a fixer with excellent success. When all the votes were counted afterward, his little protégée led by an overwhelming number. That night Jerry married her.

On more than one occasion con men have saved their lives with their smooth tongues. One time the Honey Grove Kid was arrested with his partner on a con charge. They were put in jail in a western city in the same cell with a "heavy-gee" who had the name for being bad. For some time the heavy-gee plotted his escape but just as he was poised for flight, news of his break reached the sheriff and he was forced to delay his departure. According to the creed of the heavy-men, all grifters are to be distrusted, so he blamed his two cell-mates for turning stool pigeon. Since the situation called for direct action, he promptly turned on the Honey Grove's partner, slit his throat, and left him weltering in his gore. Then he moved in on the Honey Grove, who realized that his end was near. However, he began to plead with such convincing sincerity that the heavy-gee paused in his grisly work. Such fluency—an attribute notably lacking in heavy-gees—fascinated him. He listened. The Honey Grove pulled out all the stops and gave himself over wholeheartedly to oratory. Finally the heavy-gee wiped off his knife and sat down, convinced that he had made a mistake, and spared the perspiring Honey Grove the fate of a stool pigeon.

According to press accounts, the Yellow Kid recently talked the judge into materially reducing a sentence which the court had just meted out. This was not the first time that the Kid has talked himself out of a difficult situation.

When con men go to prison, they naturally exploit their position as fully as they can. They are model prisoners but before they have been there a day they are "shooting the curves" (conniving for privileges). They live off the fat of the land, enjoy a diet of their own choosing, and sometimes manage a business of some sort which makes them a very good profit. One con man of my acquaintance, at the end of a year in a northern prison, had managed to gain control of the commissary and was actually selling and reselling foodstuffs to the state which had imprisoned him.

Perhaps we should make one more point regarding the way con men live. Many of them are superstitious, and there is quite a body of thieves' folklore which most of them know and many observe with varying degrees of seriousness, though none of them like to admit a belief in anything supernatural. "Con men are superstitious the same as anyone else," says one grifter. "They are just as superstitious as some mudkickers who believe in any kind of signs. Most all thieves are that way. I was always told that if my left hand itched, I should rub it on the seat of my pants and I'd win at faro-bank. But I tried it out hundreds of times and something always went wrong with the gaff. But when it itched again, I'd always give it a break and try it again. I always think it may work the next time. Then, meeting a cross-eyed mark is bad luck. Professional thieves don't work on rainy days. I always avoid a harelipped Bates. Redheaded girls are poison to some thieves. Giving money to a plinger is always good luck. I always spit over my left shoulder when I see a dick, so he won't shake me down. If your train is late, you'll get a touch sure. There are many more, but I don't recall them, as I was never superstitious."

"What becomes of con men?" I once asked an old-timer.

"They just dry up and blow away," he answered laconically.

But they don't. Whatever happens to them during the course of their lives, it is a notable fact that, as their years increase, they remain young in spirit. They do not become "dated" as many men do who are marked indelibly with the characteristics of a particular generation. In attitudes, in dress and manners, in tastes and language, they live always, like theatrical folk, in the present. Their interests do not lag. They do not live in the past; perhaps they prefer not to do so.

I have asked many con men about their attitude toward their victims, and I feel sure that they do not admit any pangs of conscience at having swindled a victim. One professional thought carefully back over his life and surprised me by saying, "Yes, I can remember once when I felt terribly sorry for a mark. We had taken a man and his wife for $35,000 in the Miami store. I was taking them back to the hotel in my car. When the chauffeur went to let them out, he accidentally slammed the door on the woman's hand and mashed it. It was terrible. . . ." He then launched into a graphic account of his own emotions at the sight of the poor woman's suffering. But the fact that he had just swindled her and her husband of $35,000 had nothing to do with his remorse. Con men are, in a hundred ways, soft-hearted and sentimental;

they love dogs and little children; but no big-timer can afford to feel sorry for his victims. It never occurs to him that a mark is deserving of any consideration and hence he feels no remorse at taking his money.

As con men grow older they grow rich in experience and mellow in the wisdom of the grift. When they grow too old to play the outside any longer, they play the inside of some racket for a younger generation of ropers. But that is about the only change. They move forward with the times, adapting themselves easily to social and economic change, and improving their professional technique so that they are always at least one jump ahead of the mark and the law.

Old John Henry Strosnider said, "I think the reason that a con man never dies is that, like the Wandering Jew, he is always on the go. He is always traveling somewhere and seeing and doing new things. If he is in California, he looks forward to going to Florida, from there to Cuba, and so on. Then, too, he is always with young people. He dresses and acts like a young man, even when he is seventy. His talk and manners are up to date. I never saw an old pappy con man. Besides, con men never loaf around much. They are always active rooting out a mark. Much of their time is spent in the open air. Nowadays you will find the old-timers on any golf links where they can get by."

Age is apparently no deterrent to old con men who want to remain on the rackets. For instance, old Chappie Moran, one of the first really big-time grifters, is still working. He started as a nut-player and was one of the first to use the "electric saddle" in con games. When the wire came out, he became very successful, and still has a heart for anything in the line of grifting. Old Man Millsap also grifted well past the mark of three score and ten; to his dying day he pugnaciously resented anyone who called him "Uncle." John Russell roped to a ripe old age, and passed on much of his technical skill to the Yenshee Kid, whom he "turned out." For many years he was a partner to Larry King, who began his grifting career as a pickpocket during the Civil War, worked up through the short-con rackets, and steered for the big con until he was past ninety. All the grifters who knew him regret the passing of this distinguished-looking Southerner who knew so well how to tell fine stories and how to ingratiate himself with the ladies. He made many marriages, not to mention the fact that he was simultaneously on very intimate terms with at least one lady in every large city on the American continent. Just after turning ninety he bedded his last bride—a young girl from Salt Lake City. It is sad, but hardly surprising, that he died quietly and peacefully soon afterward.

Some con men marry money or save their earnings and retire from the rackets to live in comfort and ease. Good investments sometimes increase their original nest egg appreciably, as, for instance, they did for Kid McGinley, who died leaving an estate of over four million dollars, made largely in oil. The Postal Kid increased the proceeds of his confidence games by investments in stocks. The Big Alabama Kid made and laid away a sizable fortune on the pay-off. Dan the Dude made money as a professional gambler and as a fixer for con men, and later profited from his investments in securities. The Judge laid away a fortune made largely through professional gambling. Eddie Mines became wealthy on the grift, especially on the proceeds of con games, big and little. Nibs Callahan retired comfortably from confidence work and has further increased his fortune in later years by acting as a professional fixer in Toledo, Ohio. Jerry Mugivan, Bert Bowers, and old Ben Wallace laid away large fortunes taken on the circus grift. Joe Frog, Bill Bennett, Tom Furey, and Ben Marks all retired wealthy from the fruits of the grift, principally con games. Big Mucks rose from a pickpocket to a big-time grifter, then used the proceeds of the grift to finance his book-selling activities and eventually retired wealthy. Martin Downs, Joe McMann and Crazy Horse Thompson all acquired small fortunes on the grift. George Ryan used his profits from con work and other grifting to finance his gambling establishment, from which he made and saved a handsome sum. Lou Blonger, for long a power in the western underworld, amassed his wealth through applying the chain-store principle to big-time confidence games. Many others died wealthy, while of course many more gambled away their profits, or made bad investments. And many are now in the higher financial brackets, maintaining a place in highly respectable society and sometimes building up convenient local political connections until they become powers in city or state governments.

During prohibition days a great number of grifters sensed the big profits to be made, became bootleggers and either dealt wholesale or opened up speakeasies, some of which have survived as legitimate saloons, night clubs or cafés. Others have entered legitimate business on a higher plane, and some of them, whose names in justice can hardly be given here, have succeeded. But most of those who aspire to become legitimate successes go broke in short order. "Con men set up in all kinds of business," said one professional, "but, as a general rule, they are poor businessmen. They just don't know the value of jack."

"A good businessman," says the Postal Kid, "knows money and its value. He knows what it is for. He knows that it takes money to make money. But the grifter doesn't know what it is for. He thinks it is for playing the bank or the ponies, or for shooting craps. He never gives up the idea that he can win, and nothing can knock him. He is the same kind of a sucker for certain rackets as the legitimate businessman is for a sure-thing game."

"Many con men and dips go into business," says another con man. "But they seldom make a success of it. For instance, a gun saves up ten grand and opens a scatter. It turns out to be a dud. Then he saves up more and tries it again, but that venture curdles too. Then he gets disgusted and says, 'I'm going out on the dip with a stiff upper lip and get myself some dough with my mitt.' It is the same with con men. They can't make it stick, somehow."

Relatively few confidence men end their lives as wealthy men. Either they lose their money to professional gamblers, make bad investments or squander it in one way or another. A few make the mistake of becoming involved with the federal law, which is well-nigh impossible to fix; they spend their substance trying to beat the rap, but generally end broke, in Atlanta or Leavenworth. Some of them lose their nerve and degenerate into pimps in order to live. Some grifters turn stool pigeon and work as informants for the law, but very few full-fledged con men can stomach that work. Some, like the Waco Kid, shot in the back by Big Alabama, and Brickyard Jimmy, stabbed to death, die at the hands of their confrères in quarrels over women or money; others, like Bill Larson who jumped from a Jacksonville hotel, Red Snyder, or Kid Duff who inhaled monoxide gas, commit suicide. Some, like Plunk Drucker, succumb under the weight of accumulated venereal decorations received in a thousand bouts at illicit love. Several, like Big Bill Keeley, the Brass Kid, the Little Alabama Kid and Grove Sullivan suffer mental derangement and find their way to institutions. A few, like Little Jeff Sharum, who died last summer in Michigan City, and Kent Marshall, who recently died in Sing Sing, pass their last days behind bars. Most of them, when they die, pass gently away, as did old Larry King, as old men at home.

Although most con men grift right up to the end, I know of only one who actually died with his boots on. Pete Nugent, a fine big-con roper, dropped dead not long ago—much to the dismay of his insideman—right in the midst of a play in the big store.

# 7

# Tin-Mittens

## I

The public is not only apathetic but naïve toward the relationship between confidence men and the law. The man in the street sees crime something like this: if a confidence man trims someone, he should be indicted and punished; first he must be caught; then he must be tried; then, if convicted, he should be sent to prison to serve his full term. The average citizen—if we ignore his tendency to wax sentimental about all criminals—can be generally counted upon to adopt the following assumptions: that the victim of the swindle is both honest and unfortunate; that the officers of the law want to catch the con men; that the court wishes to convict the criminals; that if the court frees the con men, they are *ipso facto* innocent; that if they are convicted, they will be put in the penitentiary where they belong to serve out their time at hard labor. If these assumptions even approximated fact, confidence men would have long ago found it impossible to operate.

Confidence men have a problem which does not perplex small-time criminals who steal a little here and a little there. Since con touches must be big in order to make the play profitable, the bigger the touch, the more "heat" develops and, as a result, the more of a hue and cry is raised after the con men. However, this works both ways. The bigger the touch, the more money the confidence men have to pay their way out or to fight the case if it gets into court. The con man knows that if he does not have money he will go to prison, and no con man likes to contemplate the drab and monotonous life behind bars. So the con men as a group have solved this problem by what is known as the "fix."

The fix, like insurance, is protection bought and paid for. It is an institution among all professional criminals, but perhaps no other professionals use it so continuously nor rely on it so implicitly as con men. When it is "in" con men know that certain powerful representatives of law and order will not only wink at the operation of con games, but will actually co-operate if necessary. All this is accomplished by paying a percentage of each touch for stipulated protection. As long as the con man has the money to meet his obligations and as long as he knows that the fix is reliable, he has every reason to feel secure. When he is broke or when the fix "curdles," he knows that his days at liberty are numbered.

All habitual and professional criminals employ the fix in one form or another. The legitimate citizen is often aware of the process involved, for any motorist who has had a traffic ticket fixed for him has invoked the same principles that the professional criminals use—except that he usually pays for the small favor he receives with a cigar, political support, or simple good will. But the legitimate citizen seldom if ever does business through the fixer. The fix for professionals is administered through a more or less permanent fixer who is a part of the underworld-political set-up in every city which harbors any sort of organized crime—and that means every city of any size in the United States. It is not implied that a fixer is necessarily a part of any party political machine—a good fixer can weather many a change in administration—but he usually pays off to that machine, directly or indirectly, in cash. This fixer is sometimes a respectable and legitimate citizen, often an attorney, but in some places he has a hand in the rackets. His underworld connections are legion.

Different types of professional criminals employ different types of fixers, not all of whom operate in the same manner. Heavy-men, for instance, approach the problem of the fix quite differently from pickpockets, gamblers or circus grifters. Here we are mainly interested in the ways and means which confidence men employ to keep out of the penitentiary.

A good con mob would no more think of setting up a big store until the fix had been investigated and found effective than Mr. Chamberlain would think of setting out without his umbrella. Con men have long ago established the value of "appeasement" and they have developed the proper machinery for distributing it in an equitable manner. They well know that a "fitted mitt" is the best—in fact the only—insurance against paying the penalty for their acts.

Sometimes con mobs operate through one fixer who buys protection wholesale, so to speak, for all types of criminals. This is likely to be the case in cities under 30,000 in population, where one man handles all types of protection for a price. More often, however, they locate the big store in a community as permanently, say, as a merchant might locate a dry-goods store there. This means that they must have sound connections with the forces of law and order—connections which can be depended upon to withstand stormy times. It also means that often the fixer must have a specialized technique for this type of work—fixing con touches. Hence, con men sometimes depend upon one powerful fixer who works constantly in their interests for a stipulated percentage—usually fifty per cent of the insideman's share after he has paid off the necessary expenses incidental to playing the mark. Thus, from a $100,000 touch, the fixer would receive something like $17,500 (though this might vary slightly one way or another) from which he would "fit" as many "mitts" as he found necessary—sometimes only one, if it is high enough up in the politico-criminal syndicate. The remainder—perhaps $5,000 or $10,000—he puts in his own pocket. In a city where the big store does a thriving business, the fixer has an exceedingly satisfactory and steady source of income.

Because of the close and powerful political connections which a fixer must of necessity cultivate, he frequently becomes a very important person in his community and is very often recognized by legitimate citizens as a "political boss," although it is not implied that all bosses are fixers. Because he controls police officers, judges, prosecutors and other public officers, he is highly respected by underworld folk, who know that he can "break" them at will, or at least banish them permanently from any particular city, as Frenchy B——, a con man from Chicago, discovered when he borrowed a $500 bank roll from a prominent Chicago fixer and did not repay it; the powerful fixer banned him for life from Chicago as an example of what could happen to grifters who do not pay their just debts. Con men are very careful to pay off the fixer and to protect him from publicity on all occasions; in return, the fixer serves the con men faithfully and well. It is significant that American criminals do not, as a rule, fear the law; they fear the fixer, whose displeasure can follow them anywhere and whose word can put them behind bars more effectively than any local enforcement agency.

Con mobs, however, differ somewhat from other professional criminals in that the insideman is often capable of taking care of the fix himself—in short, he is the local fixer and usually a good one too. When this is the case, of course the proceeds from the touch are kept right in the family and the insideman is not required to split his share of the profit with a fixer; he "fits" the "mitts" of the law directly and saves the difference.

Confidence men normally have occasion to fix the following persons and institutions: a bank in the city where the store is located; the chief of police or the chief of detectives—usually the latter; prosecuting attorneys or district attorneys; judges; juries; sheriffs; and, on occasion, the mark himself in the form of a portion of his money returned. Also, where mitt men operate on trains, the conductor is usually fixed. Federal officials are much more difficult to fix than local men, and only rarely can it be done directly; only in extreme cases can direct political pressure be brought to bear through someone high in government circles, and in these cases there is usually no cash price paid. However, the recent conviction of Judge Manton may be indicative of fixing among federal officials which has not yet come to light. It must not be assumed that all these officers named are fixed in any one case. Usually one or two of them is enough, and those are most often connected with the enforcement arm of the law. Thus the most desirable plan is to forestall any complaint the mark may make and prevent the arrest of the con men. This is handled through the police department. Sometimes the fix here "curdles"—that is, something goes wrong within the department, or, more commonly, the mark goes over the heads of the local detectives in pressing his prosecution. Then the fix must go up, and usually becomes progressively expensive. The fixer sees the sheriff of the county. The next move is to forestall prosecution through preventing an indictment, or through the prosecutor's office. This failing, if the mark has sufficient endurance to see the case to trial, the fix is put into the judge, or more commonly the jury. This seldom fails, and, if the federal officials can be kept off the scene, the con men go free. But most con touches never reach the stage of prosecution.

## 2

The first thing a big store must have is the protection and co-operation of a bank. In the early days of the wire, just after the turn of the century, con men did not know that they could fix banks and encountered a good many knotty problems as a result. But it was soon discovered that, if they could get to one bank official, their troubles connected with getting the mark's money into town and quieting his suspicions dissolved into thin air. "The first time I ever heard of fixing banks," says an old-timer, "was in Memphis in 1902. Mike Haggarty there had his banker collect the tear-up checks that were won in the mitt store. Then in Colorado Springs Byron Haynes had the jug right for his fight store there starting in 1903. Boatwright had big stores in Webb City and Joplin, Missouri, and he fixed a bank there starting in 1902. From then on, jugs were righted up all over the country."

On reading this, another con man adds: "I've seen bankers that you could go to cold turkey and put the proposition to them on a ten-per-cent basis and they'd cop a mile a minute. Then there are some bankers who, after you have made a large deposit at their bank, will stop you and get acquainted. All bankers like percentage." But it must not be assumed that the con men ordinarily go into a bank, tell the president that they have a pay-off store, and ask how much he will charge to become a party to a swindling racket. It is customary to handle the matter in this way:

The professional fixer (often the insideman) goes to a bank official, usually the president, and says, "Now this establishment which I represent handles a number of out-of-town checks, accepted in the natural course of bookmaking. It is, of course, perfectly legitimate business. Many of the gamblers who bet large sums on horses are strangers, and, while most of the checks which they give are good, some of them bounce. Now our firm has to have some way of collecting these checks immediately, and they must all have your personal attention. All you have to do is to get this paper away fast and see that our clients have every consideration shown them in transferring their accounts to this bank. We can't wait for the usual delays for identification and all that. We will vouch for the client, and you see that his account is properly taken care of. Of course we don't expect you to perform this service for nothing. It is worth something to us. Our firm will pay you five per cent of the face value of all the checks you handle in this manner."

"How large are these checks?" asks the banker.

"They will run fairly large. From $10,000 on up. Sometimes they will run pretty high."

The banker calculates rapidly, and sees a neat little commission. He says that they will try that arrangement. Within a few days the first check comes through. The roper brings the mark to the bank and the matter is handled with all the dispatch which can be desired. The mark meets the president and is made to feel that every courtesy is being shown him; he is flattered and impressed by the manner in which he is received. The account is transferred, the check is paid, and the following day the fixer calls on the bank president with an envelope containing five per cent of the amount of the check. The banker likes this easy money; he hopes it will happen again. It does. Before long, if the big store is receiving heavy play, the bank is doing a land-office business in checks. The commission for the president amounts to a rather handsome figure.

Perhaps he never inquires further into how and why these checks must be rushed through. Perhaps he believes the fixer's original story and thinks that the whole matter is legitimate; perhaps he prefers not to question too closely into the situation. He is making his five per cent and no questions asked. He never admits to anyone that he has been fixed; he might not even acknowledge it to himself. However, if he reads the newspapers and has his ear to the ground, he cannot help eventually knowing that a pay-off store is being operated in his locality; that often the amounts lost by the victims coincide exactly with the value of the checks which have been passing through his hands. This bit of correlation is almost inevitable. And he realizes that he is indirectly a party to these swindles.

He may be very honest and immediately refuse to have any further dealings with the con men, either directly or through the fixer. He may be that honest. But, once a banker has agreed to co-operate and has tasted these easy profits, he seldom quits unless he thinks there is some chance of his being caught. Most often when he realizes what is happening, he longs for a larger share of the spoils. So he hints delicately that he may have to discontinue handling the paper unless his commission is increased. Some mobs will drop him and get another banker for five per cent; most of them will raise him as high as ten per cent—but that is the limit.

Fixing the bank has many obvious advantages to the con men. It provides that the mark's property can be liquidated and his assets transferred without delay. It enables the insideman to time his plays perfectly, for if he has a number of marks in play at once, his friend the banker will arrange to delay any account until it is convenient for the insideman to handle the transaction. Then, too, the psychological effect on the mark is soothing. He feels that he is dealing with responsible persons. He cannot help noting the sound connections which the insideman has with the bank. And most important of all is something the banker does *not* do. He does not knock the mark. Any honest and conscientious banker would feel obliged to make some inquiry into the nature of the transactions the mark is making, and warn him that he might be swindled. A fixed banker will never do this. The fact that he does not has a very salutary effect upon the mark.

But there is one serious disadvantage to working through a fixed banker. At first, it was a perfect set-up. But as the Federal Government has become increasingly touchy regarding the use of the mails to defraud, connivance with the fixed banker has become more and more dangerous. For the law is now so interpreted that if the mark's check passes through the mails, the government can step in and prosecute the case—which is the last thing the con men want. However, many big stores still take that risk, counting on the fix to forestall all attempt at prosecution on the mark's part. Others, more cautious, put the mark on the send for his money and "tighten him up" so effectively that he goes home, draws out his own money, and returns. This arrangement technically evades the dreaded mails-to-defraud law, and, in case the mark gets out of hand and prosecutes, keeps the case within local jurisdiction where the local fixer can get his work in.

## 3

Most con cases are fixed with the police officers or detectives in the city where the touch is made. If the insideman does not do the fixing himself, he goes to the professional fixer in the city where he plans to open up a store and has a chat with him. He finds out what his connections are and how effectively he can cope with local law-enforcement agencies. He checks on the fixer's reputation through his underworld connections. If the insideman is satisfied with the fixer's credentials, he makes an agreement to work with him on a percentage basis. No fixed amount is paid, but the percentage is always about the same—in the big con fifty per cent of the insideman's share after the manager, the bank and shills are paid off. Once the preliminaries are out of the way, the insideman gives the fixer instructions on how to handle the mark if he goes to the police. If the sheriff is of the same political party as the city administration, little trouble is anticipated because the sheriff's office can be counted to line up with the city police; if not, or if there are city-county factions, some arrangement will have to be made to take care of the sheriff in case the mark goes over the heads of the local police. The insideman agrees that the store will not play for local citizens or "short-riders." The fixer tells the insideman which coppers and detectives can be counted upon to co-operate, and which ones to stay away from. The fixer agrees to pay off public officials as he sees fit—the con men neither know nor care whom he pays or how much so long as he gets results. The insideman agrees that, if some mark threatens to cause serious trouble or cannot be handled by the local officials, part or all of his money will be returned. These arrangements completed, the insideman wires his staff of ropers to this effect: MULE MARKET OPEN. SHIP THEM AT YOUR CONVENIENCE. And immediately the outsidemen start rooting for marks and riding them in on the trains.

For the short con, the operators pay the fixer as much as ten per cent of the score, sometimes a flat fee. And often they do not bother to fix at all. Usually if short-con men want to play, say the *tip* in a certain city, they might go to the fixer in advance, tell him what they were doing, and arrange a settlement on a percentage basis. This would be the probable procedure if they knew the fixer well. If not, they would go right ahead and play the mark, then consult the fixer if they were arrested. If the mark beefed too hard, they might "kick back" some of his money, or give some directly to the police.

If a city provides complete and exclusive protection for one or more favored con mobs, it is known as "airtight." This means that the fix is very strong, that the con men are quite secure, and that all competition will be discouraged by vigorous non-fixable prosecution. If this is the case, the con touches are cut up immediately after they are taken and all parties are paid off in cash. This is the usual situation. If the town is "shaky"—that is, if the fix is not very strong, or if there is trouble between political factions which might backfire—the touch may be held for a week or ten days until the insideman feels sure that the mark will not prosecute. Then it is cut up and the fix is paid for at the agreed price. But no fix, even in an airtight city, is impregnable. There is always a chance that it will curdle and not only the con mob, but the fixer and the police as well, may be caught in a trap laid by some ambitious district attorney. Very good recent examples of a curdled fix may be seen in the developments in New York City, Kansas City, Buffalo, New Orleans and Detroit.

On a police force there are two kinds of officers—"right" and "wrong." A right copper is susceptible to the fix, whether it comes from above, or directly from a criminal. A right copper really has larceny in his blood and, in many respects, is an underworld character, a kind of racketeer who takes profits from crime because he has the authority of the law to back up his demands. He differs from the professional criminal only in that he aligns himself with legitimate society, then uses his position to protect the thief and to betray the legitimate citizen. A con man is what he is; he is at least sincere and straightforward in his dishonesty. However, the con men do not hate or despise a right copper; they simply regard him as wise enough to take his share of the profits, knowing full well that if he doesn't, some other copper will. So, in a sense, the con man looks upon the right copper as a businessman who is smart enough to sell his wares at a price which the criminal can afford.

The con man also knows that, if a right copper can be bought by one man, he can be bought by another. It is only a question of the amount of money involved. So the con men never completely trust a copper whom they have bought. His reactions are never completely predictable and on the witness stand his performance may be disappointing or even dismaying. On the other hand, the wrong copper—that rare and admirable officer who cannot be bought—is something to be reckoned with. He is usually avoided, if possible, and business is transacted through right coppers. But the con man can always be sure of this much—if a wrong copper arrests him and refuses a bribe, that copper will take the stand to tell the truth as he sees it, and nothing on earth can stop him—except perhaps irresistible pressure from above. If the copper has damaging evidence to present, he will give it; if not, he will make no effort to frame the con men or give them a "bum rap." Con men universally agree that the bum raps always come from right coppers and not from wrong ones. In other words, the maxim of the big con works both ways—if you can't cheat an honest man, neither will an honest man cheat you.

In the city where the store is located, the police officers and detectives have little to do to collect their "end." If the mark can be cooled out properly by the insideman, they may never be called upon. If the mark beefs and goes to the police, he is treated very well, asked to tell his story, gives a description of the con men, and may even be asked to look through a rogues' gallery (from which the local boys' portraits have been carefully removed) in the hope that he can identify his malefactors. In other words, the police and detectives make a rather elaborate show of going through the same process they would use if they were really trying to catch someone. The swindling detail from the detective force may accompany the mark to the hotel in an effort to check up on the registry, and of course the mark will lead the detectives to the big store—which is now a vacant room. Usually the detectives explain to the mark that he has been swindled—which he already strongly suspects or he wouldn't have visited the police—by some notorious swindlers whom the detectives pretend to have recognized from the description given them. The mark is assured that every effort will be made to apprehend the criminals; as soon as they are caught, he will be brought back to the city to identify them. Meanwhile, he is told, the less publicity which the affair is given, the better. A city detective takes him to the station and puts him on the train for home. The chances are that he never causes any further trouble. At first he inquires frequently by mail or even visits the police to see if they have found anything; by and by he tires of this and inertia sets in. He is too weary of the whole matter to pursue it further.

Sometimes a mark turns up who shows the capacity to think for himself. He realizes that he has been swindled. Immediately he consults the police. He notices that he is not receiving any very active aid. He has some powerful financial or political connections in the locality. He goes to them with his story. They are interested in discrediting the administration in power, or have some other reason for wishing to "get" someone on the police force. The heat immediately goes on. The state and county police may be called into the case. The federal men may have a look at it. The newspapers publish the story; there is quite a furor. The con men may have to "lam" for a while, or cease operations in that city until the thing is blown over. However, there is always the chance that the identity of the con men becomes known or that the mark identifies them from some rogues' gallery elsewhere. Then some wrong copper may spot one of them on the street somewhere or be tipped off as to their hide-out by a stool pigeon (the usual method), whereupon one or more of the con men is taken into custody. "When a wrong copper makes a pinch," says one con man, "it usually sticks. He really takes you in." Once a con man is apprehended, he may be identified by the mark, but even then matters are not beyond repair. Let us look a little further into the relationship between the con man and the minions of the law.

The assistance rendered the con men by the fixer is just what the con men pay for, no more, no less. They pay for the protection of the police, and they are entitled to it. But what about the con men who are not paying protection locally? The right coppers habitually look upon all grifters as a source of revenue; a con man who is not paying, even though he is not working in that city, represents undeveloped opportunity. And so the right coppers proceed to develop it. Once a con man is recognized, he is picked up on the street and shaken down. He pays to remain free, even though there may be no immediate order for his apprehension. This is known as "stem-court," the implication being that the con man is arrested, tried, convicted and fined, all on the "stem" or street. "All big cities have coppers on the grift out looking for con men," said one professional. "The con men know whether they are right or wrong." This fact is emphasized by every con man who comments on the fix.

The reaction of con men toward this type of shakedown is philosophical. They believe that, if one doesn't have sense enough to avoid right coppers, he gets only what he deserves. Furthermore, he may need the services of that officer sometime, so he usually decides that it is better to pay. This is especially true if he is picked up in the morning, when he is working; con men—especially those on the short con—often work hard all morning, lie around in the afternoon, and work again at night—though of course circumstances alter cases. But, as a rule, if the detective picks up the con man when he is working, the grifter knows that the easiest way out is to pay the detective ten or perhaps twenty dollars. If he is not working, he may say, "Well, I guess you'll have to take me in," and the detective usually takes him in, just for the moral effect. He knows that he will be released as soon as he gets to the station, so he doesn't worry. He can easily make bond if necessary—that implies that charges will be made against him, which is not likely—or he can get a lawyer to sue for his freedom on a writ of *habeas corpus*. But usually he accepts the fact of the shakedown and pays, then is careful to avoid that detective in the future. If he has a charge filed against him somewhere else, or if he knows that he is wanted, he is very glad to pay and pay well. The detectives know this and some of them, with an eye to business, keep very close tab on those con men who are wanted and on those who have recently taken off big touches. Then when they meet one of these men, they say, "Come along with me, Jack. I've got an order to pick you up for that touch in Memphis." The con man isn't sure how much the detective knows, or whether or not he is really wanted, but he has just taken off a touch in Memphis and he can't afford to take any chances. He is still flush with his end of the touch (as the detective has surmised) so he pays and pays handsomely. But if a wrong copper picks him up, he knows it is serious and immediately goes over the officer's head and tries to put the machinery of the fix into operation. He is usually successful.

Occasionally if con men do not pay off, detectives

become abusive or slug them, but the latter seldom happens. The feelings are not often that personal. Furthermore, the detective knows that, if the fix is in, the con men can easily revenge themselves upon the detective from above. An old-timer says, "In the old days in Chicago, if the fuzz got smart with a con man, Mike would let him smell the stockyards for a while." The same procedure is used in many cities. Two detectives on the con-detail in Chicago once stopped a well-known con man, whom we shall call Eddie, and tried to shake him down. He declined to pay. They beat him up and took a large diamond from him. Like much of con men's equipment, it was stolen. Eddie happened to know where it came from, took the stand against the detectives and they paid dearly for their little shakedown.

The Waco Kid did not fare so well in a similar situation. He roped a man for Barney the Patch's store in Chicago and played him for $25,000. He had the mark in a cab preparing to put him on the send again when two shakedown detectives stopped the cab. They told the mark that Waco was a con man, but he refused to admit it. They took him to the central station and gave him "the works," during which they broke both his legs and he spent some months in a hospital. But cops do not often use con men roughly; in fact, once arrested, a con man is likely to receive better treatment than any other criminal, with the possible exception of big gang-lords or powerful fixers.

In the old days (1898–1910) Chicago was swarming with grifters and the detectives were kept busy with the shakedown. Since the grifters knew the detectives on sight, they would always run for a saloon or other "right" hangout so that they could not be picked up without a warrant. Since many con men are tall and long-legged, the detectives often pursued their game without success. Some genius in the police department saw to it that Norton Johnson, an exceptionally good runner, was transferred to the con detail and for a time it went hard with the con men. However, Johnson met his match when he tried to pick up the professional foot-racer who was used with one of the foot-race stores. The professional just made it to Andy's saloon and sanctuary. Gone, alas, are those hurly-burly days before the teletype and the squad car, when the boys played cops and robbers for all they were worth.

A few detectives throughout the country have photographic memories which enable them to carry a whole rogues' gallery right under their hats. Such a man is Frank (Camera-Eye) McCarthy, very recently sent to prison because of his activities on the fix in Buffalo. These men are greatly respected by con men because they can be counted upon to pick out a known grifter anywhere, though there is nothing serious to be feared, for they frequently "take their end" with monotonous regularity. They are always on the lookout for con men because they know con men have money and they know how to cause trouble for them if they do not pay up. But there are very few such smart detectives. Many others, hopeful of gaining such a reputation and eager to get credit (and the shakedown money too, perhaps), learn through stool pigeons where con men habitually hang out, then wait outside and follow any stranger who emerges. Some distance down the street they stop him and, once they feel sure he is a grifter, put the shake on him.

Perhaps this is the place to indicate the falsity of the popular belief, fostered by film and fiction, that some detectives can spot a criminal by looking him over. Unless the criminal gives himself away by some slip of speech or attitude, there is no detective who can pick him out for a professional—without a keen memory for the photographs in the rogues' gallery.

However, it must not be assumed, on the whole, that

there is anything like the traditional enmity portrayed in film and fiction as existing between grifters and detectives. The wrong coppers are usually too fair-minded to hate con men; they know only too well that con-game victims are fleeced while trying to profit by a dishonest deal; furthermore, they see arresting a con man and giving honest testimony against him only as a part of their sworn duty. But the wrong copper is a very rare bird. The right coppers who have been on duty for many years know all the important con men in the country and con men know all the detectives. They do not hate each other any more than a merchant hates his customers; they co-operate for their mutual well-being; it is a part of the system. On the other hand, they seldom become very good friends, because the quickest way for a con man to acquire an unsavory reputation among his colleagues is for him to associate with detectives. And a smart detective does not encourage personal friendship with con men, for he understands the situation perfectly. The wise detective causes a con man as little trouble as possible, never asks him embarrassing questions, and takes his end quietly and unostentatiously. He knows which side his bread is buttered on; he may go out of his way to do favors for those con men who pay regularly and generously, but there is nothing very personal about this action. Con men reciprocate, not only to protect themselves, but also in the interests of their friends, and are very careful to protect certain detectives, especially if they are in court and giving testimony which might reflect upon the officers. This is in general true; in exceptional cases, grifters turn state's evidence against detectives, or in other ways reveal their connivance with crime. Then, especially if a "reform" administration is in power, the officers are liable to indictment and trial. When these conditions are revealed, as they are in every city from time to time, the public is momentarily scandalized, then lapses back into the complete apathy which characterizes it. Certain public officials profit politically from the hullabaloo which is raised and, when the reform administration goes out, things go on much as before.

In some places the fix is so strong and the grifters so well organized that hangouts for grifters like Dan the Dude's place and Mike Haggarty's saloon in Memphis in the old days are completely immune from police interference and even from police visits. This protects the con men from shakedowns and provides them with privacy for their leisure and recreation. Haggarty himself saw to it that all coppers and detectives stayed clear of his place. When they disobeyed his order, they were "broken." When Stuttering Conway, a Pinkerton detective who thought he was immune from local pressures, defied Haggarty's order, Haggarty himself delivered a roundhouse right which felled the detective like a slaughtered ox, then vented what remained of his rage on Conway's derby hat, which he literally kicked to pieces. A year later another Pinkerton man named Humphries tried to come in and Haggarty whipped him and sent him home. After that they stayed away.

Confidence men sometimes have to fix agents for Pinkerton, Burns and other private agencies. This is a difficult task, at least as it applies to Pinkerton and Burns, though some con men report that they have done it. Many other agencies do not have such proud records. Any con man can testify that, next to agents for the Federal Government, detectives from these two agencies are hardest to bribe. Perhaps part of the answer lies in the high morale which these organizations have built up, part of it in the fact that they pay their good men good salaries and fire those who show any weaknesses. Furthermore these men, like federal agents, work largely through stool pigeons; they collect their evidence very carefully and plan their case before they make an arrest. And very often their cases stick. Con men, knowing this, do the sensible thing—try to avoid any entanglements with them.

There are some towns in the United States known as "sucker towns." Here there is no fix, or at least no fix of which con men can avail themselves. Really first-rate con men would hardly take chances by grifting these places, but some mobs will. "There are sucker towns where a mob sneaks in and tears off a touch now and then," comments one professional. "A mob might be in one of those sucker towns for a long time and never get made, but they are asking for it. If they get caught, of course they would try to fix their way out." In towns like this, the con men sometimes approach the "fly cop" directly and fix him in advance, because the mark will probably beef to him if he beefs at all. Sometimes, when there is only one touch to be made, the mob does not fix at all, but takes off the score and leaves immediately; but it is dangerous to leave any loose end like that about.

Small towns which are not right are often very difficult to fix. Public officials have not grown up in a corrupt political machine and are likely to have very simple but very obdurate views on honesty and dishonesty. So if con men have to fix in such a place, they face difficulties which do not beset them in larger cities where the fix is an established institution. First, they try to get a good lawyer working on the case, and, if he cannot straighten matters out, they approach some prominent person in the town and, if they can persuade him to help, he is paid liberally for his trouble.

International con men working in Europe, Mexico and South America report that the fix abroad works much the same as it does in the United States, and, because of the highly centralized police systems, is reputed to be even more secure than it is here. I was somewhat surprised when a former international con man told me that he had fixed a representative of Scotland Yard while he had a store in London, and freely named names and amounts paid. The fix in Europe, however, seems to apply only to non-violent crimes; it is almost impossible to fix for crimes of violence as is done almost universally in this country.

So much, then, for the fix as it applies to enforcement officers. In towns which are right for con men, they do not pay off to the officers directly, but leave the disbursement of illicit profits to the professional fixer. In towns which are not right, or where there is no professional fixer for con men, they may settle directly with individual officers, police chiefs or heads of detective departments. And in the large majority of con touches, the fix stops here, for the case is never allowed to come to trial.

## 4

If the local police, working under the fixer's instructions, find it impossible to cool out the mark successfully, they may, as a last resort, refund part or all of his money. However, con men report that the police do not favor this mode of settlement—if there is any other way out—because they must "kick back" the money which the fixer has already distributed. Often they compromise on a settlement whereby the mark is given back a part of his loss and convinced that he is very fortunate to have regained even that much. Thus the mark is satisfied, the con men and the coppers make something from the deal, and the police get the credit for obtaining and returning part of the stolen money.

Refunding the mark's money is sometimes done directly through the insideman without benefit of intermediary action by the police. This type of settlement is made only when the mark, sure that he has been swindled and threatening to be dangerous, returns and finds the insideman or the roper whom he accuses. If there is no other way out, and all persuasion fails, the insideman may admit the accusation and agree to refund his share of the score (though of course he does not kick back his full share) provided the mark will not prosecute, or take any vengeful action. He explains to the mark that the rest of the money has already been divided up and the other participants have fled with their shares, so that the mark loses all hope of recovering more. Sometimes the fixer may also arrange this type of settlement.

Some con men, once the mark insists on prosecuting, offer him his money back in installments. Says the roper, "I'm sorry I swindled you because you are such a fine fellow. You can bring me to trial if you want to, but that will cost you money and you will never get any of your losses back. But if you will settle this with me personally, you will get your money back. I have spent most of your money, but I'll make more. So I'll have my lawyer draw up a contract which we will both sign. I'll pay you $750 now and $200 a week from now on until we are square." If the mark signs this contract, the con man pays him the $750 and laughs in his face, for when the victim accepts the down payment, he forfeits all right to proceed with criminal prosecution and of course he never receives any further reimbursement.

If the con man is arrested and identified by the mark, the situation is easy to handle. The fixer immediately arranges for the con man's release on a writ or bond. The police then explain to the mark that they are going to delay this man's trial until they catch the other members of the mob. So the mark is to go home and take up the threads of his business, for it may take some time to catch the others; however, he is assured that he will be notified so that he can identify his swindlers when they come to trial. Since, however vigorously he may wish to prosecute the case, he cannot remain indefinitely in a strange city away from his family and business, he goes home. Shortly after this the con man is brought to trial; the case is dismissed because the prosecuting witness does not appear. If the victim becomes too dangerous at this stage, the con man may simply jump his bond and disappear.

Occasionally when the fix fails, the case goes to the grand jury where an indictment is returned. This usually means that some powerful outside forces have entered the case and must be reckoned with when the case comes to trial. Even so, the con men do not feel discouraged for they are reassured by the fact that only a small proportion of con men ever go to prison. Those cases in which conviction is obtained are prosecuted very, very hard.

As soon as the con men see that a case is likely to go to trial, they engage the best criminal lawyer available, usually one who has represented them or their friends before. Men like Erbstein and Bachrach in Chicago could be counted upon to secure acquittals in most of the cases they handled. The fees paid lawyers of this caliber are naturally very large, but the con man either has or can raise any amount of money necessary to take care of legal counsel. A roper for the Yellow Kid tells this story about him and his lawyer, Erbstein. The Yellow Kid had swindled a mark for $10,000, found the fix inadequate, was brought to trial where, through the efforts of his attorney, he was acquitted. After the trial Erbstein said, "Kid, you owe me $7,500."

"Oh, no I don't," protested the Kid. "Why I fixed the jury myself and I couldn't lose."

"That's what you always say," said Erbstein, "but it was really my legal skill and experience that got you off. And my services are worth $7,500."

"You're taking advantage of me," wailed the Kid. "You're victimizing me."

"Bosh," retorted Erbstein, "anybody can swindle a sucker."

Many con men, like most other professional criminals,

deposit a large sum of money with some legitimate person whom they can trust and with whom they can get in touch immediately should they be arrested. This is known as "fall money" and is used only in emergency. Some con men can get all the credit they need but most of them feel more secure if they are able to lay the cash on the line. No one knows better than they how eloquently money talks.

Some itinerant grifters, especially pickpockets, carry their fall money sewed up in their seams. Detectives know this and sometimes shake them down for a considerable amount simply because they have it on their persons. In one town in Iowa, this procedure has become an institution known to thieves as the "hurdy-gurdy." Pickpockets report that they are run in there and their clothes literally cut to pieces for the cash they contain.

When a con man is in distress, his lawyer plays for delay, hoping for any sort of "break" which may favor his client. The prosecuting witness may become ill or die; since the victims of big-con games are very frequently elderly men, delays and continuances work materially in favor of the con men. Then, once the mark has had time to cool off, he may be more amenable to fixing than he was immediately after being swindled; the fixer or his representative may be able to persuade him that it would be better to get part of his money back than to prosecute and get nothing. Also public opinion becomes less critical with the passage of time. The continuances which a good lawyer can always get often postpone a trial long enough to undermine the endurance of the most determined prosecution.

If and when trial becomes inevitable, the con man resigns himself. Circumstances will determine whether or not he will sign a jury-waiver. If he has some assurance from the fixer that some politician can get to the judge, he may prefer not to have a jury trial. A con man would never approach a judge directly as he might a detective or even a police chief. He must depend upon the fixer or some other intermediary to take care of that. Judges, like coppers, are known as right and wrong. A right judge can, of course, be handled, just like a right copper—but it costs more, often up in the thousands of dollars if the con man is well-known and prosperous. A wise right judge knows how to keep his accounts with the public balanced by going easy on the professional criminal and administering stiff sentences to the amateur or unprotected criminal. If he does this carefully and covers up his tracks with sufficient fireworks in court, only those who see behind the scenes suspect that his decisions have been influenced. A con man was shown a newspaper account of the recent trial of another prominent con man in the East. The con man had been acquitted and the judge had given the jury a very severe lecture for acquitting him. "That's how you can tell when the fix is into the judge," commented the professional.

A judge naturally cannot guarantee an out-and-out acquittal. The evidence which gets to court in a con case is always very strong and the prosecution thoroughly embattled. But, if things look too bad for the con man, the judge can always follow the standard procedure of a St. Louis judge ("the rightest judge in the U.S.A.") who, when the con man pleaded guilty and threw himself on the mercy of the court, gave him a sentence of one year, then probated it.

"There was one judge in Hot Springs," says an old-timer, "who always wore a slick Prince Albert coat. He was a terror. There was a judge for you. He'd drink all night with thieves, then in the morning fine them ten dollars apiece for being drunk. Then there was Judge ——— in Chicago. He would turn out any thief for two dollars—one dollar for himself and one dollar for the bondsman. But there was Judge Dunn in Frisco. He was the squarest judge in the whole United States—the dirty bastard."

There are other dodges, like vacated court orders, which a judge may employ on occasion to save the con man from a prison sentence while at the same time he preserves his judicial integrity apparently intact. There are cases on record in which the fixed judge went easy on the accused con man, then, by way of compensation gave the mark (who had embezzled the funds with which to play the game) all that the law would allow.

Most con men who fix never come to trial by jury, but those who find themselves in court continue to pay their way. In view of the unpredictability of jury decisions, con men feel much safer if they have at least one champion in the jury-box to hang that august body in case things look dark. This champion can be bought, as a rule, much more cheaply than a judge; he is an obscure person and suffers no danger of political repercussions; and the con men have a twelve-to-one chance of buying him. A hung jury will throw the case out of court, the only recourse being a retrial. Delays and continuances will intervene even if the prosecution decides to follow up the case, and the same methods which worked on one jury are likely to work on another. So for the price of one measly juryman the con men go free.

There are several methods used in buying juries. For the professional criminal, the police, a court official, a bailiff or a clerk performs the office. And it is not uncommon, if the lawyer for the defense can get away with it, to plant a friend or someone who has previously been bought in the list of veniremen, then succeed in placing him without challenge on the jury. But the con man, in contrast to the run of professional criminals, is a supersalesman; he buys and sells people for a living; so it is not uncommon for him to buy his own jury.

Erbstein, who won most of his own cases by fixing,

affected a dislike for the Yellow Kid personally, but admired him professionally. He has been said to declare, "The Yellow is a rascal and he'll get you if he can. If he were going to the penitentiary for life, I wouldn't contribute a nickel to get him out. But he certainly can pick a jury." The Yellow Kid, with his shrewd knowledge of human nature, could pick the jurymen whom he thought he could influence when they came up for examination, give his lawyer the high sign, and, once they were placed on the jury, proceed to buy them as he would a new hat. One con man says of him: "The Yellow always chose his own jury, and he'd discard the tough babies."

The Yellow Kid is reputed to have bought juries right in the courtroom. Says one of his colleagues: "The Kid would pick out a soft guy in the jury and smile at him. If he smiled back, he'd be the guy. Then Yellow would wink at the juror and pass some money to another grifter so that the juror could see it. Then he'd wink again, and if the juror winked or nodded, the fix would be in. He has been known to stop Attorney Erbstein in the midst of an impassioned plea or a vicious cross-examination and say quietly, 'Don't level so hard on them, Erpy. It's in the bag.' And the lawyer would know that from then on he just had to go through the motions, for the Yellow had bought the jury." Almost as notorious as the Yellow Kid for their singular ability to buy juries were Charley Gondorff and John Henry Strosnider.

Most of the time the jury is bought outside the courtroom. The con men are free on bail and one of them follows the jury when it goes out to dinner; he stalls the bailiff who has the jury in charge while another singles out a previously selected juryman and puts the fix in in the flick of an eye. Sometimes one man does the whole trick. It is also common to "tail" the jury when it goes to lunch until the right man steps into the washroom, then to speak with him there. "When a good insideman like the

Yellow Kid speaks to a juryman," comments a professional, "that juryman is hooked." But few con men who know how to fix properly ever come to trial.

## 5

When all fixing is in vain and the con man receives a prison sentence, he fails to "beat the rap." Those who do time on confidence charges are prosecuted very hard; most of them are convicted as a result of interference by the Federal Government; federal officers, agents, juries and judges are generally looked upon by con men as almost incorruptible, though most con men will wave a large bill under their noses on the chance that they may like the looks of money; conviction in federal court means a sentence in federal prison where local pressures are not so strongly felt and where the con man is almost sure to serve more of his time than he would in a state institution. About the best a con man can expect in a federal court is a relatively light sentence. While quite a number of confidence men have been indicted and convicted since the advent of the big-con games, the small number of convictions balanced against the very large number of touches during the last thirty-five or forty years indicates a very low correlation between confidence crimes and conviction therefor. This low correlation gives con men a feeling of security because they know that the odds are overwhelmingly against their doing time for any given offense.

Some professionals go through an entire life of grifting without doing time. But these are the exception rather than the rule. Many of them do several "bits" and most of them do at least one stretch, almost always brought on through succumbing to the temptation of using the mails and consequently inviting "that bad Graham man" into the case. The Brass Kid and Eddie Spears were, so far as I can determine, the first big-timers to be "lagged" for using the mails. Jack Porter was involved in the case also, but escaped temporarily. The three of them trimmed a mark from Indiana at the store in Hot Springs. The Brass Kid and Eddie Spears were picked up and held temporarily in the Cook County jail in Chicago; from there they were spirited out of Chicago into Indiana, and from there sent to Hot Springs, and after a hard fight, were convicted. The case was carried to the United States Supreme Court, but to no avail. Later Porter was captured and convicted. This case made quite an impression on confidence men, who now realized that the Federal Government was a force which, free from local political entanglements and untouched by the blandishments of the fixer, could and would exact a penalty whenever con men violated the federal law. However, many continued to use the mails—and still do—depending on expert "cooling out" by the insideman and the strength of the local fix to keep the case from getting into court.

If the confidence men thought that the Hot Springs case was only an isolated example of federal power, that, like the reform waves which periodically occur in all cities, federal ardor would cool and the public would forget, they were mistaken. The public rapidly forgot, as it always does, but federal ardor only burned the brighter. At Council Bluffs, Iowa (as well as at Webb City near by), Ben Marks, a powerful fixer himself, and owner, at one time or another, of many, many big stores, had an ideal set-up for confidence men. Here were several stores, including fight stores, foot-race stores and wrestle stores. Old Ben had some of the best young grifters in the country working for him and, the fix being what it was, everyone was happy—except the marks who were being trimmed. The Honey Grove Kid, Crazy Horse Thompson, George Ryan and other first-raters were roping. An ex-champion of the prize ring and his brother were being used in the fight store. The government stepped in, the fix "soured," and the government indicted all the ropers, who were listed in a fatal little black book. Five or six of the lot were "lagged," and again the Federal Government had scored.

However, Hot Springs and Council Bluffs were small places; the big political machines in the larger cities did a good job of protecting the con men along with most other forms of organized professional crime; as long as the government could be kept out the con men prospered. But shortly after the Council Bluffs trouble, the fix curdled in Chicago, where Barney the Patch, in front of the Sherman Hotel, engaged in a shooting fray with detectives who appeared to be trying to protect someone higher up, the final score being one slug in Barney and one copper down.

There was no doubt that the government meant business. From this time on, con men concentrated about certain focal points where the local fix was strong as it could be made, perfected further their "cooling-out" systems, and hoped for the best. Probably the greatest single round-up of con men occurred not under the Federal Government, but under the direction of Colonel Philip Van Cise, District Attorney in Denver, who, financed by a citizens' fund and backed by State Troopers who were not involved in the local fix, engineered a series of raids in March, 1923. Although Federal Inspector Graham assisted in collecting evidence, the government did not prosecute. Moving with great secrecy so as to avoid tipping off his plans, Van Cise's Rangers closed in on the big stores controlled and operated by Lou Blonger and corraled more than thirty big-con men, some of them first-raters, including Blonger's ace insideman, A. W. (Kid) Duff. The raids were so carefully organized that not a single local police officer nor any member of the city or county machines knew about them; the Rangers, as a preventive against escape of the con men, kept them out of the city and county jails, and herded them into a church basement where they were held under armed guard. Because of the strength of the local fix, special prosecutors, S. Harrison White and H. C. Riddle, were brought in to try the cases. This time there were no delays and continuances, no bribing of the judge or buying of the jury. By the end of March more than a score of them had been convicted and sentenced.

While in the meantime many con men have been sent to prison, some of the outstanding big-timers who have served sentences since the inception of the big-con games would include the Yellow Kid, John Henry Strosnider, Charley Gondorff, Lee Reil and several others. The Yellow Kid has done five or six stretches, all very short, and is now in the midst of the latest one. He seems to have captured the public imagination and likes the publicity which attends all his exploits. "When the Yellow falls," said one of his best ropers, "there is always a lot of notoriety connected with the case. He seems to play for it. Well, he surely gets it—in the neck." Charley Gondorff was sent up from New York City, in spite of the fix. Joe Furey and Goldie Gerber, partners with others in the Norfleet case, went up in the 1920's, Furey for twenty years (an unusually stiff sentence which he did not live to finish) and Goldie for ten (which he reduced greatly by good behavior). The fix, which had always heretofore been "airtight" for Lee Reil, went sour and Lee, with his partner—one of the few con men reputed to be stool pigeons—were sent up from Los Angeles. Mickey Shea and his mob from Toledo, Ohio, were sent up for five years (in spite of all the powerful Nibs Callahan could do to fix for them) for beating a Michigan farmer on the pay-off; there were two exceptions in this mob; Jack Arthur was, in some mysterious manner, released from prison and packed the racket in, while Eddie Mines, wanted with the same mob, fled to Canada, fought extradition, and has remained a lamster ever since. John Henry Strosnider beat a banker from the stockyards district in Chicago, fought the case bitterly to the Supreme Court of the United States, but lost and drew a one-to-ten year bit, of which he served one year. Prominent men who were imprisoned for taking off large touches on the short-con would include Eddie Schultz and Joe Simmons from Coney Island, both first-rate big-con ropers, who, in spite of all the fixing they could do, got ten years for a smack-touch. A curdled fix in Philadelphia brought Fred Manning and Curley Carter each five years on the same sort of short-con touch. The High Ass Kid, a first-rater who escaped the penalty for many a big-con touch, received a short term in New York for a short-con touch in the summer of 1939. Many other big-timers have served time—some of them under false names. Most recent of the really big-time fixers to be sentenced are perhaps William Graham and James McKay, Reno, Nevada, vice lords who have for years protected both rag and pay-off stores where some of the largest single scores in recent years have been taken off. In February, 1938, they were convicted in federal court, but their nine-year sentences were delayed until August, 1939, in order to give them time to raise the $30,000 in fines and court costs which the government assessed.

The more prominent a con man is in his profession, the harder he "falls" when he does get into trouble. Obscure professionals, even if they are convicted, get off rather easy. But the big-timers, with scores of big touches back of them, a horde of beefing marks at their heels, and a court disposed to take an unsympathetic view of their long and habitual record, are likely to find little mercy at the hands of a federal judge. Also, because of their known prosperity, they find fixing expensive and the shakedown constantly stares them in the face. Then, too, some big-con men seem to be just naturally unlucky, like Little Jeff

Sharum, a partner of the Postal Kid, who has done a dozen stretches in prison and recently died behind bars; his bad luck with the law was paralleled—and equaled—by his sad fortune with women. Other con men like Post and Allen seem to be watched over by a lucky star, for they grift away for a lifetime without a single fall to discourage them. But all con men know that, ninety per cent of the time, the panacea for all legal troubles is the fix.

Once a con man is sent to prison, the odds are heavily against his serving much time. If he has exhausted his personal funds during the trials, his friends—and his enemies—in the underworld will raise any sum necessary to alleviate his incarceration. This means that while he is in prison, pressure will be put directly upon prison officials by politicians and fixers so that he will receive favored treatment, get easy work, have luxuries which are ordinarily denied prisoners, and even, as a trusty, be permitted outside prison walls where he can have access to liquor, women and friends on certain occasions. Con men are notably adaptable to any sort of existence and adjust to prison life much better than other types of professional criminals; but, above all, they miss the excitement, the tension, the high pressure under which they live; they love their freedom, and they are not long in getting it. They seldom do more than two or three years at most for any big-con touch.

Back in 1919 a group of con men, five in all, swindled a Texas rancher, Frank Norfleet, on the rag. First they played him for $20,000, then almost immediately gave him a second play for $25,000. He was a prime example of a mark who could not be cooled out. He determined to catch and convict all the swindlers. Hampered by the fix in almost every city where con men operated, he devoted two years of his life and more than $80,000 to catching these men and returning them for prosecution. He was, on several occasions, offered all his money back, but he seems to have developed a complex; nothing would satisfy him but conviction and imprisonment. Con men seriously discussed having him taken for a ride. This case was prosecuted with great vigor. Finally in 1922–1923, all the men had been caught and one had committed suicide. They fought the case bitterly, but all went to prison. The case received so much publicity that it might appear that politicians would hesitate to intervene in an effort to reduce their sentences. Yet, four years later, Norfleet was disillusioned and somewhat discouraged to find that not a single one of the confidence men he had hounded with such determination remained behind bars. Such is the tale of the fix.

# 8

# Short-Con Games

## I

The short-con games are, theoretically, any confidence games in which the mark is trimmed for only the amount he has with him at the time—in short, those games which do not employ the send. However, big-con operators do sometimes put the send into short-con games with excellent results, so, perhaps it is more accurate to say that, from the big-con man's point of view, short-con games are any con games except the rag, the wire and the payoff. Before the advent of the big-con games (including the wrestle, foot-race, and fight send stores, and other obsolete forms which were, in principle, big con) everything was short con. Generally speaking, we might say that the short con went out with the horse and buggy; of the scores of short-con games* which were widely and ex-

* In addition to the short-con games discussed in this chapter (the smack, the tat, the hot-seat, the tip, the money box, the last turn, the huge duke, the wipe)

pertly played in 1900, only a few remain in the hands of competent professionals. Here we are concerned only with those short-con games which are regularly used by big-con men to tide them over between touches on the big con. Meanwhile the older con games have passed into the hands of short-con men, who still use them with surprising success. Just as this is being written (November 21, 1939) the newspapers carry headlines telling of several Texas bankers who were swindled for $300,000 on the old gold brick game, a chestnut, if ever there was one. The games grow old but the marks are always new.

The touch from the big-con games is usually gone with the wind; it is spent or squandered or lost at gambling in a remarkably short time. To the ordinary citizen, $50,000 seems like a great deal of money; if he had it, he would invest it and live from the income for a lifetime; he would, probably, adjust his wants to his income. But not so the con man. Much of his $50,000 is spent before he makes it, for he owes many debts. His living is geared to high speed. He has no sense of the value of money and seems to see how rapidly he can empty his pockets. Within a few weeks, or, sometimes, within a few days after he has taken off a touch, he is broke and living on borrowed money.

One doesn't pick up a mark for the big con every day, but suckers for the short con are much easier to find.

---

the following were once very popular with con men and are still played by short-con men. Each large fair or exposition brings a revival of these short-con games and an accompanying chorus of "beefs" from marks who have been fleeced with them: the spud, the bat, the send store, the green-goods game, the rocks, the tale, the lemon, the tickets or the ducats, the fight send store, the wrestle send store, the strap, the short-deck, the pigeon, the poke, the shiv, the sloughs, the broads, the autograph, the tear-up, the big-mitt, the big joint, T.B., the single-hand con, the dollar store, the high pitch or the give-away, the slick box, the penny-box, the double-trays, the cross, the slide, the boodle, the count and read, the electric bar, the transpire, three-card monte. There are many others, including the old Spanish prisoner, which is now being revived by con men in Mexico City.

And, since most good big-con men cut their teeth on the short-con games, it is only natural for them to fall back on some short-con game when they need money. As they travel over the world, their expenses mount up and they feel the necessity for some other source of income. "The only way to keep the nut down," says one con man, "is to make a rule with yourself to get a hype touch every day for a sawbuck by laying the double-saw." The hype is a form of short-change racket with a clever line of con talk which accompanies it. It is always good for a ten-dollar bill.

Of the several short-con games regularly used by big-con men perhaps the smack is the most popular and the most lucrative. It requires a minimum of equipment, no store, and two men only are necessary. A mark can always be found in any metropolitan railway station. Each smack mob has its own particular variation of the game, but the following version should make the principle clear.

The roper waits in the "shed" or railway station, in, let us say, Indianapolis, while the insideman "plants" himself at a pre-arranged spot a short distance from the station. The roper watches for a prospect—preferably a country man or a small-town merchant who is waiting for a train. He cuts into him and finds out where he is going. The mark says he is waiting for a connection to, shall we say, Marion, Indiana. "I'm going out on that same train," says the roper. "It doesn't pull out for an hour. Let's walk up town and look over the city a little." The mark sees no harm in this, so the two stroll out of the station, the roper meanwhile asking the mark all kinds of questions about Marion, Indiana, which is to be his destination also.

A short distance down the street they are accosted by the insideman, who has a marked Southern accent. "I beg your pardon," he says, "but could you tell me where the Merchants' Bank Building is?" The roper turns to him rather rudely and says, "No, we can't."

The stranger takes offense at the roper's curt manner. "You wouldn't tell me if you did know," he sneers.

"What's that?" says the roper, annoyed.

"I said you wouldn't help me if you could, you damned cheap Yankees," says the Southerner with a good deal of heat.

"What do you mean, cheap?" demands the roper. "We've got just as much money as you have. You can't insult us just because we're strangers here. I said we don't know where the Merchants' Bank is, and we don't. Do we?" he asks, turning to the mark.

"No, we don't," says the mark.

"I beg your pardon," says the Southerner politely, "I thought you gentlemen lived here. Down in Alabama where I come from folks try to help each other out. I'm sorry I bothered you."

"I'll tell you what," says the roper. "We don't want you to think we're cheap. We just didn't realize you were a stranger here, too. I'd like to buy a round of drinks. Come on, and I'll set 'em up."

"No, thanks," says the Southerner. "I don't drink with Yankees. I don't trust 'em."

"Well, then, let me buy smokes all around," says the roper.

"I've got plenty of money and can buy my own cigars," says the Southerner.

"I don't doubt that," says the roper. "I just wanted to be sociable. Well, if you won't let me buy them, I'll match you for them."

"All right," agrees the Southerner, "I'll match you for them." He starts fishing for a coin.

The roper turns to the mark and whispers, "You call heads and I'll call tails every time and we'll have some fun with him."

"Are you ready?" asks the Southerner, poising his coin.

"O.K.," say the other two.

They match and of course the odd man wins the smokes and the Southerner, whatever he turns up, loses to one or the other of his opponents. He grows testy at this and proposes that he will match them for a whole box of cigars, punctuating his proposal with pungent remarks about cheap Yankees who want to gamble for the price of a cigar.

"I can't use a whole box of cigars," says the roper.

"Well, how much does a box of cigars cost, four dollars? All right. I'll match you for the price of a box."

The roper gives the mark a wink and they match again. Naturally the insideman loses, this time to the mark, who begins to see possibilities in this game. Then the roper begins to kid the touchy Southerner, whose temperature mounts perceptibly.

"We could take every cent you've got the same way," he says.

"I don't see how you could," says the Southerner, heatedly. "I'll just show you. I'll match you dollar for dollar for all the money you have on you." The roper and the mark get out their wallets, and they smack the coins on the back of their hands. (A smack-player, on reading this, comments: "Marks carry their money in the funniest places. They get it out of their shoes, their socks, their hat bands, and out of their seams. Some carry it all sewed in and have to cut it out before they can play.") The roper whispers to the mark that they will divide up the winnings later. Again they match. Since the mark has called heads, the insideman throws heads also, which leaves the roper the odd man. The Southerner fumes and frets, but pays the roper all his money. The mark then pays the roper all his money, and the insideman takes his leave, cursing his luck.

The roper and the mark pass on down the street, stopping just around the corner. The roper begins to sort out the wallets and divide the money. Just as he is paying the mark off, the old Southerner pops around the corner.

"By God!" he says, "I might have known this was a trick. What are you men doing with that money? You are dividing it, aren't you?"

"Why, no," says the roper. "We were just talking."

"It doesn't look that way to me," says the insideman. "It looks to me as if you two are in cahoots to swindle me."

"Why," says the roper, "we are total strangers. I never saw this man in my life before I met him just now in the station. I won and won fairly, and I intend to keep the money."

"That's right," says the mark. "This man is telling you the truth. I never met him before I got off the train in the station there."

The insideman is still suspicious, but finally agrees not to have them arrested. "Now," he says, "to show me that you two are not together, and that there is no conspiracy here, you separate, and you go that way, and you go that way. Then I can watch you and see that you don't get together."

The two men agree, and the roper whispers to the mark, "I'll see you on the train." Then each goes his way, the mark to the station and the roper toward the city. The Southerner watches them angrily until they are out of sight.

The mark arrives at the station in time to board his train. He fully expects that his friend will get on and divide the profits with him, but the roper is at that moment dividing the touch with the Southerner. The train pulls out and the mark is disillusioned. The roper plants the old Southerner again and returns to the station for another mark.

Touches from this game run from fifty dollars to several hundreds of dollars. Marks have been found with several thousands of dollars in cash, but touches over $3,000 are indeed rare. The blow-off is simple, for the mark has his ticket and is scheduled to leave immediately after the score. The con men usually make sure that he has boarded the train before they pick up another mark; also, the roper always makes sure that the victim has his fare or his ticket, and that he has enough money to buy his meals until he gets to his destination. This keeps him from getting panicky and going immediately to the police. Sometimes marks do go immediately to the police, but if the fix is in, the detectives cool him out just as they would on a big-con touch and the fixer settles for the whole thing.

Smack mobs work mostly in the early morning, take the afternoon off and work again at night. They know that strangers in a large city cannot sleep and that they are likely to arise early and wander about the streets until train time, or go early to the railway station. Hence, a good smack mob can usually stop work by noon with one or two good touches. At night, the same game, with some variations, is worked in night clubs and hotel bars where the roper and the mark start matching the insideman for drinks. There are many variations to the game, but the principle and the essential elements are always the same.

The send can be applied to the smack, and sometimes is, but it takes expert con men to do it. Briefly, the insideman becomes very earnest about this game. It develops that he has a very large sum of money with him, and wants to match for large stakes. They match for a while, with all of them winning and losing, but with most of the money going to the roper. The insideman insists on playing for very high stakes, so the roper and the mark agree to go home and get more cash so that they can trim this fellow. They return with the money and again both the mark and the insideman lose to the roper. Then the roper is split out from the mark, with an agreement to meet and divide the profits. But they never meet.

The smack is most convenient for big-con men because of the relative simplicity and speed—the whole play may come off in ten or fifteen minutes—with which a touch can be taken off. Some con men believe that it has taken off as much money, all told, as the pay-off. The scores, while never so large as those on the pay-off, come faster and as a rule the overhead is almost nil. It requires very little working capital; in fact, the story is told of Tommy Fells of Toledo, probably the best of the old-time smack players, that he once came out of prison broke. He picked up a partner and sent him to the station to rope a mark. He filled his handkerchief with green grass, made this pass for a bank roll, and took off a score. Most con men use the smack sporadically, and some mobs subsist almost entirely on its proceeds.

2

Next to the smack, the short-con game most used by big-con men is the *tat*, also known as "up and down Broadway" because it is much used in the night clubs and cafés along Broadway. "Mark it down and mark it well," says a man who has taken off thousands with this game, "that a New Yorker is the best sucker that ever was born. He is made to order for anything. You can't knock him. He loves to be taken because he's wise. When you are on Broadway this little tat gets the jack, and how!"

That tat is a crooked die with fives on four sides and sixes on two sides. It has a mate which is an exact replica in size and weight, but which is numbered in the usual manner, from one to six. Tats are made of ivory, bone or some synthetic substance. Others are made of sugar-cubes; con men find that the sugar-cube tat is more effective because it does not arouse the mark's suspicions as quickly as a commercially manufactured one.

The mob consists of two players whom we might designate as roper and insideman for purposes of distinguishing them, although these terms hardly apply in the strict sense to a tat mob. The roper moves into a night club where he selects a party of men at a table; he is careful to avoid parties with women. He hangs around closely for a short time until he gets the drift of their conversation. He finds that they are part of a delegation attending a convention; they are from Chicago. The roper cuts into them, saying, "Aren't you boys from Chicago?" The party has been drinking and is feeling convivial. They admit that they are from Chicago. The roper starts a conversation with them, pretends to be slightly tipsy, and orders a round of drinks for them. The roper is witty and amusing; he establishes himself solidly with the party. More drinks follow. Then his partner enters and passes the table. He looks quizzically at the roper, then greets him with a handshake. "Why, Mr. Swift," he says, "what are you doing here in New York?" Mr. Swift mumbles something about business and introduces his partner to the party. His partner orders drinks for everyone and joins the group. Meanwhile, the square die has been placed on the floor where one of the party is likely to see it. If no one notices it, one of the con men says, "Look there. Somebody has lost a watch charm."

The man looks on the floor and there is the die. He picks it up and examines it. Then the other con man reaches over and takes it away from him. "Why," says he, "this is a part of somebody's game. Here, let me show you a little game I saw in West Baden last summer. It goes like this. You give me a dollar. And you, and you, and you, and you." He collects a dollar bill from everyone. "Now," he continues, "we'll put this one die in a hat and we'll each shake it three times. We'll add up the number of spots each one gets, and the one who gets the highest number wins and has to buy the next round of drinks for all seven of us."

He drops the die into the hat and starts the game, appointing one of the party to keep score. The derby passes around the table and each one gives his score. The natural law of averages takes care of the first couple of rounds; in other words, the con men "cop and blow" so that no one will suspect them. Interest in the game increases. The roper suggests that they put in enough money to make it interesting, so the stakes are doubled. He puts the tat in for his partner who "cops" that round. And so it goes, until they have "cleaned" the party. One of the pair always holds the tat in his hand except when his partner shakes, at which time the tat is momentarily substituted for the square die, the numbers are shown to anyone who wishes to see, the tat removed, and the square die replaced. The die is always kept in the hat so that the players will not notice that the tat has all fives and sixes on it. Naturally when the tat is in, the con men cannot help running up a higher score than anyone else in the game. When the con men depart, they leave the square die on the table for anyone who wishes to examine it. They do not both leave at once, but the partner who has won the money leaves first, then the roper takes a friendly leave; only after the con men have gone do the marks, rather tipsy by this time, suspect that they have been swindled. And, since the square die still remains there, they do not know of the existence of the duplicate tat. They may attribute their misfortune to a run of luck on the part of their visitors and go on with their party.

The con men may take off a fifty-dollar score by this method. As soon as the roper leaves, he enters another night club, selects another party, and the game starts all over again. The mob may visit three or even four places during the night and take off a score in each one. All they need is a highly developed technique for conviviality, stomachs strong enough to stand the large amounts of liquor they must consume, the necessary sleight of hand for handling the dice, and the nerve to cheat strangers for money. "The clip-joints are filled every night with marks who crave the tat," said one con man. "If you gave one of them an even break, it would spoil his evening."

## 3

The *tip* is a game for con men who are also gamblers, for it requires some dexterity in the manipulation of the cards. It is really no more than a crooked poker game with the confidence element added. However, the confidence element is the thing that hooks the mark and makes a good score possible, while at the same time it reduces the possibility of trouble resulting from the swindle. There are many different versions of the tip, and many different approaches used to hook the mark, but fundamentally the game differs little from time to time and place to place. Each mob works out the method which is best adapted to its needs, its abilities, and to the mark at hand. It is essential that the insideman have some experience at dishonest gambling and that he can successfully manipulate cards.

The mark is usually selected through someone who "puts him up"—that is, gives the con men his name and some details about him in advance. One expert tip player now operating gets his "sucker lists" from a girl friend connected with a large Chicago firm which supplies all kinds of crooked gambling equipment—marked cards, loaded dice, shiners, card holdouts, etc.—to would-be sure-thing gamblers. Few real professional gamblers buy these devices, and when anyone places an order, it is practically certain that he likes "the best of it." This tip player organizes his lists geographically and visits all those in one section at a time.

The roper approaches a mark in Harrisburg, Pennsylvania. Says he, "Mr. Jones, when I was in Scranton last week, I was making inquiries for an honest and trustworthy man in Harrisburg. Mr. White, who is a friend of yours there, said that you could be trusted in anything, and said I couldn't find a better person for the deal I have in mind."

"What's on your mind?" asks Jones.

"This is the situation," explains the roper. "But first, have you any scruples against making some sure money in a poker game?"

"Suppose I haven't?" asks Jones tentatively.

"Well," continues the roper, "this man I want to take the money away from has just inherited nearly half a million dollars. He loves to gamble and likes the best of it. He has cheated with me in several games."

"Yes," says Jones. "Go on."

"I met him in Pittsburgh this last week and he told me that he was coming to Harrisburg to look at some property. He is here in the city now. I told him that I was coming here to play in a little businessman's game, and he was all ears. He wants to be in with my play, for he knows that I can cheat any card game anywhere. I told him that I played here quite often and that I would see that he got into the game. He always carries a big bank roll on him and tries to make his money win for him. He is a sucker for gambling and is bound to lose his money. We might as well get a little of it. He will have at least $10,000 with him when he comes.

"Now I have figured out a way to beat this man. You don't have to have any money. I'll furnish you with all the money you need. You just do as I tell you and you will win this man's money. Then after the game we will divide the profits."

Mr. Jones agrees that he would like to be counted in on the deal. So the roper tells him to report at the hotel in the afternoon, and he will give him the final instructions for the play.

That afternoon the two men meet in the hotel lobby.

The roper asks the mark to buy the cards at the cigar counter. This is done to allay any suspicions he may have regarding marked cards. The roper provides himself with a large box of matches. They go up to the room to set a trap for their victim. The roper pulls the table to the center of the room and spreads the bedspread over it so as to have a good surface on which to shuffle the cards. He seats the mark at the proper place, gives him $100, and keeps $100 for himself.

"Now play carefully with that," he admonishes the mark, "for it is all I have. At first we will play 'percy pots' and you won't have to show your hand until it is called. You can open a jackpot on anything, just the five cards you hold in your hand. You understand?"

"Yes," says Jones.

"All right. Now I'll play along for a while and then I'll lose my money to you. That will give you $200 to play with. And you never show your hand unless it is called. Just as soon as I lose my money to you, I'll get out of the game and sit behind the man. I can see his hand from there and I'll tip his hand off to you so you'll always know what he has."

"But," says Jones, "how will I know? How will you signal me?"

"It's easy, and you can learn it in five minutes," says the roper. "Here I'll show you." Then he shows the mark how he will signal with his fingers to indicate the contents of his opponent's hand. The mark has hardly memorized the signals when the insideman calls from the lobby. They tell him to come right up.

"Where is everybody?" he asks. "I thought there was a game going on here."

"The boys will be here any minute," says the roper. "Let's get things going."

So they start to play, the matches selling for a dollar apiece. The insideman displays large quantities of money and bluffs heavily. The roper throws off his money to the mark, as arranged, then takes his place behind the insideman, who is betting from $100 a hand up. The insideman asks the roper, "Do you want to be in with my play?"

"No," says the roper, "I'm broke and if you should lose, I couldn't make my end of it good. I'll just stay out now. You go it alone until the other boys come up."

The game goes on, with the insideman using a shiner so that he can see what he deals the mark, and signaling the roper what to tell the mark. The mark gets the roper's signals perfectly. The stakes go up until there are large jackpots every hand. Then comes the "spring hand." The insideman sees that he has dealt the mark two pairs. He gives the roper the office to tip the mark that he, the insideman, has one pair in his hand. The mark bets fifty dollars on his hand. The insideman raises him $200. The mark stays with him. The mark has the best of it. They draw cards, but neither helps his hand.

"What will you bet on that good hand you are holding?" asks the insideman. "I'm going to make you lay it down."

The mark, feeling sure of his ground, bets all he has in front of him, perhaps $150. The insideman pulls out his bank roll and says, "That's all right. I'll take you and raise you $500 more."

The mark has only a few bills in his pocket, say twenty dollars, and he puts that up. The insideman starts to beef about a showdown. The mark sees his winnings slipping away. Then the roper gives the mark the wink and says, "You can get it, can't you? Here we'll put the cards in an envelope and I'll hold them until you come back."

"O.K.," says the mark. "I have it in the bank. You hold the cards and I'll be right back."

The insideman says, "O.K.," and the mark starts for the door.

"While he's gone, I'll try to round up the boys," says the roper, and starts for the door also.

"Here, here," says the insideman, "I doubt that either one of you will be back. So just pay me for the chips you have before you leave."

"Oh, we'll be back," says the mark. "At least I will," and hurries out.

In the hall the roper shows the mark the hands he has in the envelope. There can be no mistake. The mark holds the winning hand. The roper goes with him to the bank and urges him to get enough money to raise the insideman and force a showdown. The mark gets all he can, for he knows that the insideman has enough money with him to raise again. He draws, say $1,000. The two return, the hands are laid out, and the mark wins the pot.

Another hand is dealt and the process of "faro-banking" begins. The mark knows that the insideman has a large bank roll with him, and lusts for more of it. The signaling process goes on, and the mark wins and loses, while the stakes mount up. To the mark it looks like a repetition of the first play, so he raises his bets as fast as he dares. Finally in the excitement of the play the mark bets his hand before the draw. The insideman draws out on him, thus winning the pot. There are many variations in the method of "putting in the sting," but the principle remains the same.

Sometimes the roper blows the mark off immediately. However, if he feels that the mark has more money in the bank and if he still has the mark's confidence, he may send him back to the bank again with the assurance that this time there will be no slips and the promise that they can recoup their losses—$200 of which apparently has been sustained by the roper.

To cool the mark out, the roper may use any one of a number of tricks. A favorite one is to take him to the telegraph office and wire for a friend of the roper's to come immediately on the next train and bring plenty of money and a hold-out machine. This leads the mark to believe that it is only a matter of hours until they will take the insideman for his bank roll. Meanwhile, the roper may give his personal note (worthless, of course) for the amount the mark has lost, since the roper claims to feel some responsibility for the mark's losses.

A thousand dollars is a good average score on the tip. Often the mark yields less, and sometimes of course he is good for more. A score of $3,000 is considered very good, while one of $5,000 is phenomenal.

One of the earliest con men to specialize on the tip was Old Man Jennings. Later came Bill Bennett, Scotty, Wildfire John and others. Today any of the con men who gamble proficiently are likely to fall back on it for a touch.

**4**

Another short-con game popular with con men who gamble is *the last turn*. The build-up for the mark is somewhat similar to that used in the tip. The roper locates a mark with some money and larceny in his soul. He tells him this story: "I have come to you because you are an honest man and I know you can be trusted in a deal which will make you some money, but which must be handled by a man with both discretion and integrity. If you will finance this matter, you can make yourself a handsome profit, with no chance of losing. It is a sure thing."

The mark is naturally curious about this deal and asks for details.

"It is like this," says the roper. "An old friend of mine has dealt faro for a rich old gambler in Buffalo for nearly fifty years. The gambler has made a fortune with his gambling house, and my friend has helped him build up his fortune but has nothing to show for his life's work. My friend has made a pretty good salary during his lifetime, but put all his savings in stocks and lost it. Now he is an old man, and broke. The gambler has promised to cut him in on the business, but he has put it off and put it off, and now he is about to retire and leave my friend out in the cold. That is pretty tough on him, and you can't blame him for wanting to make enough to keep him on for the rest of his life, can you?"

The mark admits that he can't.

"Here is what he intends to do," continues the roper. "Do you understand how faro is played?"

If the mark says, "No," the roper explains what a faro lay-out is, how the players bet against the bank, how the dealer pulls the cards from a dealing box, etc. The roper explains that many wealthy gamblers and playboys come to the gambling house and play for heavy stakes against the bank. The betting always grows progressively heavier throughout the game, the bets being placed on the order in which the dealer will draw cards from a dealer's box. The odds are always greater on the last turn, and anyone who wins on that play may make a young fortune. The gambler is well heeled and the bank is always able to pay off. If the mark plays faro, so much the better, for he sees his own advantage all the more quickly.

"Now," says the roper, "this friend came to me with this idea. He wants me to come into the gambling place and bet a little on certain turns that he will indicate. That is so no one will become suspicious. Then he will tip off the last turn, and I can make a sure-thing bet which will put us both on easy street. That is the proposition he made me. But I don't have the money to finance it. That is why I came to you. You put up the money, I will handle the betting, he will tip off the last turn, and we will split the profits three ways. You and my friend will take eighty per cent and I will take twenty per cent."

"How much would I have to put up?" asks the mark.

"The more the better," says the roper. "How much can you raise? Fifteen thousand dollars?"

The mark considers and thinks he can get $10,000. It is agreed. The most important thing, the roper explains, is to have someone finance the deal who can be trusted not to run off with the profits once they are made.

The mark is taken to Buffalo to meet the old faro-dealer who shows him a faro lay-out and dealing box, explaining in detail how the game is played. He instructs the mark which turns to bet on and rehearses the play carefully with the mark and the roper so that the whole thing will come off without the old millionaire's suspecting that there is collusion between his dealer and the two patrons. A date is set for the play and the two go to the gambling house where the other patrons are playing at various games.

Immediately the roper takes charge of the mark's money, for faro is an intricate game and the mark has probably never seen it played. They bet on a number of turns before the last one, winning on the turns previously indicated by the dealer, but losing large sums on all the rest. The losses are also according to a pre-arranged agreement between the dealer and the roper, but the mark does not suspect this. He is somewhat alarmed to see the roper betting his money like so much lettuce, but the game moves so rapidly and is so complicated that he hardly realizes what is happening. The last turn falls as predicted, but it is impossible for the mark to recoup his losses on the last turn. He is lucky if he has railroad fare home as his share of the winnings.

If the mark thinks his losses were due to a run of bad luck and does not suspect a swindle, he may then be sent for more money and the play repeated. If he suspects foul play, or if he has no more money, the millionaire gambler accuses his dealer of turning traitor and fires him. The old dealer cries and bewails his fate, and may even try to borrow money from the roper and the mark. The mark cannot stand this for long and soon goes back home.

The last turn may require the co-operation of a gambling house, for which a percentage of the score is paid. In the old days when faro-bank was more widely played than at present, this was a common swindle. However, in recent years, with the decline of faro since the World War days, it is not so extensively used. But in the hands of big-con men it is still a very effective swindle, for it eliminates the need for the send and produces very respectable scores. When good big-con men tell the tale to the mark, he is thoroughly convinced before the game is begun and moves to the city where the play is to take place prepared to put a given amount of money into the game. Occasionally big-con men get scores which rival those taken off on the pay-off or the rag in size, as, for instance, the $50,000 touch which was referred to in an earlier chapter. Old-timers who were rated the best at this game were old Hugh Brady, Sam Roberts, Charlie Stebbins (Ben Mark's one-handed faro-dealer), Martin Fisher and Doc Middleton. The one essential which may be difficult to provide these days is an expert faro-dealer to play the inside.

## 5

The *huge duke* is a short-con game widely used by big-con men. It is played extensively on the trains, coastwise steamers and transatlantic liners. It is one of the easiest, quickest and least obnoxious methods for big-con ropers to make expenses while they are traveling. But it requires good card sense and an expert knowledge of crooked gambling techniques, assets which all con men do not have.

The mob usually consists of three men, all expert card players. On a train, each will rope a mark and two by two they collect in the club car. One of the con men suggests a card game, inviting the other two members of the mob and the most promising of the three marks. They call for a card table and the four of them settle down to play.

At first it may be any card game, probably euchre, played for cigars. Finally one of the mob says, "I surely wish this was a poker game, for I have a swell poker hand."

"I'll bet you a cigar my hand is a better poker hand than yours," says another.

And so they lay down their hands and deal again. From now on, they jokingly bet on their hands as poker hands, even though theoretically they are supposed to be playing euchre.

Says one of the mob, "I've got a fine poker hand this time."

"I'll bet you a box of cigars that mine is better," says another.

"How much is a box of cigars worth?" asks the first.

"Oh, four dollars," answers the second.

"O.K.," says the first, and they put down their hands.

Next deal they give the mark three aces. The third member of the mob says, "I've got some poker this time myself," and he gives the mark a "flash" of his three queens. The mark knows that he can beat the queens with his aces, so he says, "I've got some poker, too," and they bet a few dollars. The mark wins.

The plays have been so timed that the following deal falls to the mark. If he deals the cards himself, he knows that there has been no manipulation. He shuffles the cards and as one of the mob cuts them, he is "cold-decked"—that is, a duplicate deck is introduced into the game. It has previously been "chilled" or stacked in preparation for this play; the cards are so arranged that the mark will deal himself four aces, the hands of the other three members of the game being also prearranged.

The mark deals out the hands. He is elated to find the

four aces in his hand. The betting starts and they run him up as high as he will go; usually several hundred dollars is the limit. Let us say that this mark stops at $350. They get him to write a check if he does not have the cash on hand. The check goes into the pot and the hands go down. The mark sees his four aces lose to a straight flush. One of the mob is the winner and rakes in the pot.

Many con men who play the huge duke prefer the mark to use a check, for it provides a perfect blow-off. Just as soon as the mark loses, he may beef a little; if he doesn't, the man who roped the mark speaks up and says, "Here, this man isn't a very good player and he doesn't know much about this game. I didn't think we were going to play for money myself. Give him back his money." With that he takes the check from the pot saying, "I'll just destroy this, and everything will be all right." The winner may protest a bit, but he is overruled. The roper then tears the check into fine bits and burns it with a match. In reality this is not the mark's check at all, but a blank check of the same size and color which has been substituted for the mark's check by the roper. In his pocket the roper carries a number of blank checks of various colors and sizes for this purpose. The mark, having seen his check torn up before his eyes, rests easier—until he gets the statement from his bank and is surprised to see that the check has been endorsed and cashed.

This type of blow-off is known as the "tear-up" and is perhaps the most effective of short-con blow-offs because it leaves the mark completely unaware that he has been swindled. Thus the mark is not "rumbled" and does not "heat up" the train or the boat immediately—giving the con men a chance to rope and trim several other marks before they change trains. When a con man takes a check from a responsible person, he may tear up a fake check under the pretense that it is the original one after skillfully persuading the victim to get off the train and draw the money from the bank. Then the con man cashes the genuine check and thus gets double the amount. The checks taken on the tear-up are cashed immediately either through a fixed bank, or by businessmen to whom they are mailed as soon as they are taken. The businessman receives a commission.

As the grifters ride across the country, they get off the train about once a day, wait until the next flyer comes through, and get aboard, starting afresh with a new crop of victims. Sometimes they fix the conductor and then they can "rip and tear," safe in the knowledge that they will be protected. There is an old saw among con men to this effect: "What can be better than a rattler full of marks and a right kayducer?"

If the mark realizes he is swindled, or if the conductor is inclined to look with disfavor upon the fleecing of his passengers, the con men usually get off the train immediately and board another. However, Eddie Mines, one of the most famous of the huge-duke players, had a philosophy which seemed to differ from the general policy among con men. Said he, "If you rumble a mark, just ignore him. He will cool out all by himself, and sooner than you would think."

Eddie Mines, according to underworld rumor, once got a mark for the huge duke who backfired on him. He and his partner, Johnny on the Spot, were working the trains when they roped a "smart" mark. The play started and the mark appeared to be eating it up. When they put the "chill" in it was loaded with four jacks for one member of the con mob and four nines for the mark. The mark tossed in his money like hay. When they laid down their hands, the mark showed four aces. Eddie is reputed to have let out a yell that could be heard all over the train: "God damn it!" he roared. "That's not the hand I gave you!"

Con men who ride the passenger liners are not so fortunate; they cannot change ships as soon as things heat up. Hence, they are very careful about cooling their victims out because, once the heat is on, they can only retire to their staterooms and stay there, for bad news travels fast on shipboard and they are immediately ostracized.

While many con men use the huge duke, and some play that game almost exclusively, the outstanding old-timers who specialized in this swindle are Johnny on the Spot, Eddie Mines, Wildfire John, the Indiana Wonder, Scotty, Tom Tracy, Dog-Face Bradley and Crooked-Arm S——. The best of the present generation of boat-riders includes Boat-rider Bill, Big-Mitt Edgar, Stewart Donnelly, Cold-deck Charley, Ocean Liner Al and the Umbrella Kid. Recent legislation which goes into effect just as this is being written will make it increasingly difficult for these gentry to continue their depredations on passenger liners.

In the same class with the huge duke belongs the "mitt store"—now practically obsolete, but at one time a very widely used short-con game played by all sorts of confidence men. The game is practically the same as that used in the huge duke. The chief difference lies in the method of operation. The mitt store is an establishment disguised under some respectable exterior; the players wait in the store while the ropers go out on the streets and into the railway stations looking for suckers, who are moved to the store for some ostensibly harmless purpose, and are then "mitted into" the card game. The mitt store as an institution has practically disappeared, but it deserves mention here because of the large part it played in the development of big-timers for the big-con games.

6

Another short-con game which threatens to become obsolescent, but which crops up periodically with every large fair and exposition is the *money box with the con*. There are several versions, the one most used by big-con men operating as follows:

The con man approaches a mark with the old story that he needs an honest man to finance a dishonest project. The success of the game hinges entirely upon the ability of the operator to "tell the tale" to the mark, who, we must assume, is hardly endowed with a brilliant intellect. The mark is shown a little machine which was invented by a German who was murdered shortly after he completed the device; hence, it is the only one in existence. It will make money which cannot be detected as counterfeit; in reality, the money is not counterfeit, for the box contains plates stolen from the United States Printing Office. In order to make real ten-dollar bills in any quantity, all one has to have is a supply of the paper used by the government. Up to this point, even a "lop-eared" mark is inclined to be suspicious.

Then comes the "convincer." The con man takes the mark to his room and produces a small piece of "genuine" government paper, replete with silk threads which give it a very realistic appearance. There is just enough left to make two bills. The con man cuts the paper, inserts it into the machine, and presto! Two crisp new bills are turned out, the ink still wet on them. The mark examines them suspiciously, but finally confesses that he would never suspect them. The con man invites him to take them to the bank to have them changed, which he does without the slightest difficulty, for they are bona-fide bills to begin with.

By this time the larceny in the mark is thoroughly aroused. He can visualize an unlimited income from this little machine. But there is one hitch. There is no more paper. The con man knows where he can get more paper from a government employee who will steal it for him. But this man must be paid in advance. For $1,500 enough paper can be procured to make $10,000 worth of money.

Then he proposes that the mark put up the $1,500—if the mark has not already offered to do so himself. There will be no risk involved for the mark, because they rent a safety-deposit box in the bank, place the machine therein, and give the key into the mark's hands as security. Then the mark produces the $1,500 and turns it over to the con man, who takes it to Washington to purchase the supply of paper. But when the mark has waited for some time and his partner does not return, he opens the safety-deposit box and finds that he has only a worthless gadget to show for his $1,500.

This game, like many short-con games, requires some ability at sleight-of-hand in order that the operator may appear to turn out the real money from the machine, although he only creates an illusion by substituting the real bills for the blank paper which he puts into the machine. Several days may be required to take off a score with this game and for that reason it is not very popular with big-con men, who prefer short-con games like the smack, games which strip the mark immediately and allow the operator to be on his way. Foreigners make especially good marks for this swindle, of which there are several well-known variants. Lee Reil, Count Victor Lustig and the High Ass Kid (in his younger days) were specialists at this game and used it with great success.

## 7

A very popular short-con game worked with great success by American con men abroad is the *hot-seat.* Victims are often well-to-do American tourists; Roman Catholics are especially susceptible.

The roper picks up a mark and "feels him out" in much the same manner as he would for the big con. If he decides that the mark can be played, he signals his partner, the insideman, who plants himself near the roper and the mark until the two of them find a rosary. They pick it up and speculate on what to do with it. It is a handsome and expensive rosary, evidently highly prized by someone. While they are examining it, the insideman approaches. He is hunting a rosary. They return it to him and he is overjoyed, for it is a relic which he could not replace; it belonged to his mother, and has been blessed by the Pope.

It develops that the stranger who has lost the rosary is a wealthy Irishman. He tries to reward the roper and the mark for finding the rosary, but they refuse. He professes a great liking and admiration for them. He reveals that he is about to give a large sum of money to charity, and proposes that the mark and the roper be appointed to distribute this money, as he is too busy to attend to it properly. Some con men here introduce a minor variation in that the wealthy Irishman is about to take a large sum of money to the Pope, but cannot go personally and wants the mark and the roper to be his representatives. But the outcome is all the same.

The roper suggests that the Irishman does not know them, and that he has no way of knowing that they are reliable and can be trusted. It is then proposed that the two of them put up a sum of money, say $5,000 apiece, as a sort of bond to guarantee their good faith in the deal. The Irishman takes them to his hotel suite and produces a tin box. He goes to the bank and withdraws a large sum of cash which he places in the box. The roper gets his "bond" and the mark produces his. To cement the pact and establish their good faith in one another, they put all the money into the tin box. Then an ingenious little conversation about trusting one another is begun. The upshot is that to show how firmly he trusts the mark and the roper, the insideman gives them the tin box and suggests that they walk around the block with it. This they do, and return. Then, in order to make the test of faith all the way round, the mark and the insideman take the box and walk around the block, returning to the roper. The last test of faith requires that the roper and the insideman walk around with the box, and return to the waiting mark—who waits and waits, from which situation the game takes its name.

The American version of this game, called *the wipe,* is very seldom used by present-day big-con men, though many of them have used it at some time in the past. While the hot-seat is at present used in Europe by such masters of their profession as Pretty Sid, Snowy T——, Kangaroo John, Melbourne Murray, Devil's Island Eddie, Slab B——, and others, the wipe in America has degenerated to a rather low reputation among professionals. It is now used mainly by Negroes, low-class Italians and Gypsies.

The American version goes like this: the operator visits the mark with the story that he is looking for an honest, trustworthy man to guard a large sum of money which he is going to give the Church; he tells the mark that he has inquired into his reputation and finds it is all he could desire. The mark agrees to act as guardian, so the stranger counts out $500 in cash and they tie it up in a handkerchief. They then shake hands over the matter and the mark agrees to hold the money until the stranger is ready to turn it over to the priest.

Then, as a matter of establishing good faith, the mark is persuaded to put up $500 in cash. He goes to the bank and draws out the money. They open the handkerchief again, count the money, find everything intact, and tie it up again. The stranger takes the $500, puts it in the handkerchief, and instructs the mark to take the handkerchief full of money home, hide it under the mattress, and under no circumstances to open it until they are both together. The mark takes it home and holds it until his curiosity or his cupidity, or both, get the better of him and opens the handkerchief—only to discover that the $1,000 has mysteriously been converted into newspaper clippings cut the same size as bills. The game takes its name from the argot word for the handkerchief used in the swindle, and the crucial point in the game is the "switch" by which the money is exchanged for the clippings, a sleight-of-hand trick which must be done with great dexterity. The mark, presumably an ignorant person, may be persuaded to yield up quite a sum in cash—often the savings of a lifetime. In many instances, superstition plays a large part in this game. Hardly a week passes that our American newspapers do not report a touch of this type somewhere in the country.

8

Three-card monte, too well known to occupy much space here, was once widely used by con men, many of whom got their start in the con rackets playing this very effective game. Since the present generation of big-timers do not use it, like the three-shell game, it has sunk to a rather low estate. One now sees it played only on the backstretch of large race-tracks, at fairs, in New York City down along the Battery (sometimes played on a little boy's back), and on trains carrying large holiday crowds. It is usually played "on the sneak"—that is, without protection.

The game itself is very simple, the important points being skilled manipulation of the cards and the cross-fire which goes with the play. The mob consists of an insideman, one or more outsidemen, and several shills or sticks who are local men and not a regular part of the mob; they are given money to play with and win or lose at the will of the insideman, who manipulates three cards on a little board, picking them up deftly and throwing them face down on the board in any order he chooses. He invites the crowd to watch and offers to bet that no one can pick out the queen. The sticks come into play, making it look easy to do. The outsideman singles out a mark and whispers to him that they can beat this man at his own game; he offers to "crimp" or "put an ear" on the queen so that the mark cannot mistake the card he is betting on. So, under the pretense of examining the cards, the outsideman crimps the queen, winks at the mark, and the play goes on.

The mark does not see the insideman very cleverly remove the crimp which the outsideman put on the queen, then put a similar one on another card, an operation which cannot be detected with the eye; he bets on what he takes to be a sure-thing, only to find when the cards are turned up that he has lost. Of course, he has no recourse, for he lost while he was trying to fleece the insideman. Sometimes if he is good for an elaborate play, he is given quite a build-up, and then is allowed to win some small bets by this method before he is fleeced. Scores run from ten to fifty dollars, but pickings from the monte players these days are slim. When all circuses carried the grift, monte was played with the send and this arrangement was called the *big-joint.* In the old days when men like Canada Bill and Farmer Brown were operating monte stores very similar to the mitt stores, the game was a very lucrative one; there is still a saying among grifters, "He put a crimp in that card that Canada Bill couldn't take out." In Chicago alone Farmer Brown took off touches amounting to hundreds of thousands of dollars, taken largely from farmers and ranchers who came to Chicago. And there were scores of monte stores going full blast in all cities in the West, Midwest, and South until the World War, after which the game seemed to lose much of its popularity.

Many other games might be described, but they would hardly bear upon this account, for they are seldom if ever used by the big-con men. For a brief account of these short-con games, see the Glossary in the last chapter. It should be added that new short-con games are being invented every day and the best ones will doubtless be ultimately included in the repertoire of the big-con men. Perhaps here we should include one other—the "single-hand con."

This is a simple and easy method for a competent professional to get a little cash if he is in need of it. He picks up an elderly man traveling alone, gets his confidence thoroughly, explains his embarrassed condition, and gets the old man to advance him some funds on a personal check. This is the only game used by big-con men in which the mark may be quite innocent of any cupidity. "Whenever I'm chicane," comments one slick rascal, "I just step into the shed and borrow some nice old pappy's bank roll on the single-hand con."

# 9

# The Con Man and His Lingo

It is a peculiar fact that every professional criminal group has its own language. This is true not only of the modern criminals who have streamlined crime and put it on a big-time basis, but also of professional criminals in all times and in all countries. Denizens of the Roman underworld seem to have had their argot. With the growth of cities in Europe, crime became a profession; by the time of the Renaissance, professional criminals appeared in hordes in all Continental cities. England had her share of them and from that time to the present the language of thieves and cut-purses (thieves' language has been suggested as the origin of the word "slang") has constituted an ever-vital source from which the literary language is enriched and freshened. But only an infinitesimal portion of the criminal argot of any age survives as a part of the literary language, for most of it perishes before it is written down.

Criminal argots are really artificial languages used by professionals for communication among themselves. The professional criminal speaks one or more argots *in addition* to colloquial English. Each profession has its own argot, based on one or more of the several large systems of argot-formation which are at work in the American underworld. Intimately related professions usually have argots which are closely related; unrelated professions speak less similar argots. But all professional criminals speak at least one argot or lingo fluently—the argot of their own profession. It is a mark of professional affiliation, a union card, so to speak, which requires several years to acquire and which is difficult to counterfeit. Most criminals understand several argots other than their own and some, those with wide and varied experience, old-timers who have grown up with the rackets, speak and understand most of the professional argots.

Why do criminals speak a lingo? There are several reasons, perhaps the most widely accepted of which is that criminals must have a secret language in order to conceal their plans from their victims or from the police. In some instances it is undoubtedly used for this purpose—for instance, flat-jointers, three-card monte men, and other short-con workers sometimes use it to confuse or deceive their victims. But most professional criminals speak argot only among themselves; they are amused at the idea that crooks are supposed to deceive people with their lingo, for the mere fact that they speak argot in public would mark them as underworld characters whether or not they were understood. It is a fact that argots are unintelligible to the layman, but I think that we should not assume that this is a deliberate protective device invented by criminals; we might as well conclude that, because the professional lingo of railroaders, doctors, sailors or tobacco auctioneers is not readily understood by outsiders, it was created to deceive the public. The argot is inherent to the profession; secrecy is a very minor motive for its formation and use.

There are other much more important factors which govern the creation and use of argots. Criminal groups or *mobs* work outside the law and consequently count very little upon it for protection. There is a very strong sense of camaraderie among criminals, a highly developed group-solidarity, which is further increased by internal "organization" and by external pressures from both the upperworld and the predatory underworld. A common language helps to bind these groups together and gives expression to the strong fraternal spirit which prevails among them. This is true of the entire underworld, with the partial exception of prostitutes. On the other hand, each specific trade or profession develops a feeling of mutual exclusiveness among its members; this feeling springs from the fact that they are all criminals, that they have a commonalty of life-experience, that their training and backgrounds are somewhat similar, that they face identical mechanical problems which must be solved with somewhat similar tools and techniques, and that certain professional attitudes or "ethics" must be recognized if the mob is to prosper. Professional crime is in reality nothing more than a great variety of highly specialized trades; hence it is only natural that many of the same factors which operate among legitimate craftsmen should affect criminal speech. Especially in criminal professions, elements exist for which there are no words in the legitimate vocabulary; it is quite natural that criminals should coin or adapt words to meet these needs. It is, I think, significant, that the occasional criminal or the lone-wolf professional, however skillful he may be, usually has no knowledge of criminal argots unless he has at some time or other been connected with organized professional mobs.

Perhaps we have oversimplified in an attempt to generalize. Different attitudes toward argots prevail among different individuals and are markedly apparent among different criminal groups. Pickpockets, for instance, are generally very talkative among themselves and like to use their argot in private; peter-gees (safe-blowers) are usually silent boys who have a very well-developed professional argot which they appear to dust off and use only on very special occasions; because the profession is dwindling, that argot seems on the road to extinction. Criminal narcotic addicts, in general shunned by other criminal groups, are extremely clannish and when they are together talk or *jive* incessantly in their own argot about the one subject which obsesses them—dope. Prostitutes have almost no argot of their own, but borrow freely from other professions. Grifters, and especially confidence men, like to talk and tell merry tales among themselves; in private they compensate for the fact that they must speak a conventional language while they are working by indulging in the excessive use of an argot which is very highly developed. In general all professionals share certain attitudes toward the lingo of their profession; they recognize it as an artificial language to be assumed or dropped at will; they have a certain professional pride in a fluent command of the lingo; they frequently judge strangers or outsiders by their use of the professional jargon; they restrict its use to their own group or to friends whom they trust.

Of all criminals, confidence men probably have the most extensive and colorful argot. They not only number among their ranks some of the most brilliant of professional criminals, but the minds of confidence men have a peculiar nimbleness which makes them particularly adept at coining and using argot. They derive a pleasure which is genuinely creative from toying with language. They love to talk and they have markedly original minds, minds which are singularly agile and which see and express rather grotesque relationships in terms of the flickering, vastly connotative metaphor which characterizes their argot.

The lingo of confidence men is one of the most extensive in the underworld. The large number of technical situations which arise in the course of confidence games make for a very complete technical vocabulary which covers many different types of game, the nature of the victims, standard situations within the games, etc. Con men are continually studying to improve their games, all of which make for a rapid enlargement of the technical vocabulary. Furthermore, the fact that con men are recruited largely from other branches of the grift means that they bring with them methods, techniques, and attitudes which require argot for expression; this fact also links the argot of con men closely with the general argot of the grift.

But con men, as contrasted to other professional criminals, have creative imagination. Their proclivity for coining and using argot extends much beyond the necessary technical vocabulary. They like to express all life-situations in argot, to give their sense of humor free play, to revolt against conventional language. Thus they have a large stock of words and idioms for expressing ideas connected with travel, love-making, the creature-comforts including food, drink, clothing, etc., recreation, money, people, the law, social relationships, etc. In fact, if con men find it necessary or convenient to discuss any topic for long, they will soon have an argot vocabulary pertaining to that particular subject. And one may rest assured that they will use good rich, roistering, ribald words which will radiate connotations for the initiate.

Closely related to the phenomenon of argot-formation—in fact, one aspect of it—is the use of *monickers,* many of which have already been used in referring to individual confidence men. Relatively few criminals are known in the underworld by their real names; in many cases their closest friends know little of their family connections. Often professionals abandon their original family names and assume others. All of them work under numerous aliases and many have no criminal records under the names by which they are commonly known in the underworld. These underworld nicknames (known as monickers) usually stick to a professional criminal throughout life; they are genuine and cannot be shaken off like a mere name. However, not all con men bear monickers; those who do often carry them over from some other criminal occupation which they followed before becoming con men.

The monicker, like the names used by primitive peoples, is vastly connotative and becomes even more suggestive when one knows the circumstances which lead to its acquisition. Sometimes it reflects some striking physical characteristic of the bearer, as, for instance, the Bow Legged Lip who had the misfortune to be both bow-legged and harelipped, the High Ass Kid, who was quite long-legged, the Square Faced Kid, Nigger Mike of swarthy complexion, and Crooked Arm S—— whose crippled arm resulted from jumping through a window in his early thieving days. The Narrow Gage Kid's height was just the distance between the rails of a narrow-gage railway.

Some monickers commemorate a personal exploit or recall some personal idiosyncrasy or former occupation. The Yenshee Kid chewed yenshee (gum opium); the Postal Kid was once a messenger boy; the Brass Kid peddled cheap jewelry; the Yellow Kid sold cheap watches with a story that they were stolen property; Brickyard Jimmy was once assigned to work in a prison brickyard during a brief reprieve from grifting.

Other monickers only designate the home town of a con man or the city in which he was turned out, as, for example, the Ripley Kid, the Harmony Kid, the Honey Grove Kid, the Big and Little Alabama Kids, the Indiana Wonder, Gloucester Jack, Kid Niles and many others.

The con men who have monickers have often acquired them in other branches of the grift and carry them over into the big con which, incidentally, is not so rich in colorful monickers as are many other rackets. I should like to include here such pungent monickers as the Collars and Cuffs Kid, Proud of his Tail, the Narrow Minded Kid, the Money from Home Kid, Slew Foot W——, the Squirrel Toothed Kid, the Harum Scarum Kid, the Gash Kid, the Seldom Seen Kid, the Molasses Face Kid, and many others, but the talents of these gentry lie in other fields.

By whatever manner the monicker is acquired, it fits the personality of the bearer well and is often the only permanent name a grifter has; once it is applied and accepted, it becomes one of his few permanent possessions. It is tagged to him for life.

In the Glossary, no attempt has been made to present a complete list of con-argot; a sizable volume would result if that were attempted. Rather, a representative section of con-argot has been selected in order to clarify the argot which it has been necessary to use in the previous chapters, and at the same time to give the reader some idea of the general nature of confidence argots. Both big-con and short-con argots are represented, for it is impossible to separate them; short-con workers may not know any big-con argot, but most of the outstanding big-con workers know and use some short-con argot along with the big-con lingo.

## GLOSSARY

*Addict.* A mark who believes so firmly in a sure-thing investment that he comes back again and again. See to *knock (a mark).*

*Apple.* **1.** See *mark.* **2.** Any person.

The *autograph.* A short-con game in which the mark is induced to sign his autograph to a piece of paper which is later converted into a negotiable check.

*Bank.* A faro-bank game.

To *bankroll*. **1.** For the insideman to finance an outside man with expense-money. **2.** See *faro-bank* 2.

The *bat*. See the *gold brick*.

*Bates, Mr. Bates* or *John Bates*. See *mark*.

To *beat the donicker*. For two confidence men to ride the trains on one ticket by keeping one concealed in the washroom while tickets are being collected. Also to *play the run-around*.

To *beef*. For a mark to complain to the police.

To *beef gun*. For a victim to complain that his pockets have been picked.

*Behind the six*. See *chick*.

The *best of it*. **1.** A prearranged method of cheating which will ostensibly allow the mark to profit by dishonest means. "All marks crave the best of it." **2.** A cinch; a sure-thing.

*Big con*. Any big-time confidence game in which a mark is put on the send for his money, as contrasted to the short con where the touch is limited to the amount the mark has with him. There are three recognized big-con games: the wire, the pay-off and the rag. However, competent confidence men often put the send into short-con games, especially the smack and the tip, with very good results. Touches on the big con range from $10,000 up. Cf. *short con*.

The *big block*. The second touch taken from a mark. Restricted to the rag. Cf. the *little block*.

The *big mitt*. A short-con game played against a store with insidemen and ropers. The victim is enticed into the store, drawn into a crooked poker game, and is cold-decked on his own deal. See the *tear-up, big store, huge duke*.

The *big store*. An establishment against which big-con men play their victims. For the wire and the pay-off, it is set up like a poolroom which takes race bets. For the rag, it is set up to resemble a broker's office. Stores are set up with a careful attention to detail which makes them seem bona fide. After each play, the store is taken down and all equipment stored away in charge of the manager. Also *store* 1.

The *bilk*. A short-con swindle worked on a brothel-madam. Similar to *laying the flue*.

To *bill (them) in*. For swindlers to induce marks to enter a swindling establishment. (Short con.)

*Block game*. The three-shell game played with small hollow boxes, weighted on the top. Also the *blocks*, the *boxes*, the *dinks*, the *hinks*, the *nuts*, the *peeks*, the *shells*.

To *blow*. **1.** tr. To allow a mark to win some money in a confidence game. "Blow a fin on the run-around." (Short con.) **2.** tr. To lose. "I blew my okus." **3.** tr. To realize. "The mark never blowed it was a gaff." **4.** intr. To leave. "Let's blow." **5.** or *blow off*. tr. To separate the mark from the insideman or get him out of the big store after he has been fleeced. See the *cackle-bladder*.

*Blute*. A newspaper, especially fake clippings from a newspaper which are used in big-con games.

*Board-marker*. The clerk in a big store who marks up the fake stock quotations or fake race results.

*Boarding-house deceiver*. A cheap suitcase which is often left empty in a hotel when the grifter leaves without paying his bill.

*Boat-rider*. A professional gambler who rides the ocean liners and frequently ropes for confidence games. Also *deep-sea gambler*.

To *bobble*. To excite a mark's suspicions, especially while short-changing him. (Short con.)

*Boodle*. **1.** A bank roll made up to resemble the mark's money. (Short con.) **2.** On the big con, a fake bank roll of small bills made up to pass for, say $100,000. Also *B.R.*

*Bookmaker.* The manager of a pay-off store. See *manager.*
The *boost.* The shills used in big-con games.
The *boxes.* See the *block game.*
*Brace* (or *braced*) *game.* A crooked gambling game.
The *breakdown.* The stage in big-con games where the operators find out exactly how much money the mark can raise.
*Broad.* **1.** A railroad ticket. **2.** A playing card.
The *broads.* Three-card monte. "Little Chappie Lohr used to steer against the broads for Farmer Brown." See *open monte, closed monte.*
*Brush one's tail off.* To avoid or lose someone who is following.
*Bum rap.* A conviction on a trumped-up charge.
*Bumblebee.* A one-dollar bill. Also *push-note, case-note.* (*The hype.*)
The *button.* **1.** One method of blowing a mark off after he has been fleeced. A fake detective raids the con men and arrests them. The mark is allowed to talk his way out. Cf. the *cackle-bladder,* the *tear-up.* **2.** A type of short-con swindle in which the mark and the roper are accused by the insideman posing as a detective of passing counterfeit money. The insideman pretends suspicion and takes their money to "headquarters" for examination. Cf. the *shake with the button.*
C or *the c.* **1.** The con, or confidence games. "He's on the C now." **2.** The mark's confidence. "The insideman always has the mark's C."
*C-gee.* A confidence man. (Big con.)
*C-note.* A $100 bill.
The *cackle-bladder.* A method of blowing off recalcitrant or dangerous marks after they have been fleeced. The insideman shoots the roper with blank cartridges on the pretense that the roper has ruined both the mark and the insideman. He then hands the mark the gun,

while the roper spurts blood on the mark from a rubber bladder he holds in his mouth. The mark flees, thinking he is an accessory to murder. The insideman keeps in touch with him for some time and sends him to various cities on the pretext of avoiding arrest. (Big con.) Cf. to *cool a mark out.*

*Cannon.* A pickpocket. Also *gun, whizz, dip,* etc.

*Cap.* Expenses connected with roping and fleecing a mark, especially the roper's expenses while he is on the road. See to *cut up the score.* Also the *nut.*

The *Carrie Watson.* The best; anything or anyone of high quality or high attainments. From the old Carrie Watson House in Chicago.

*Chick* or *chicane.* Short of money. Also *behind the six.*

To *chill.* **1.** For a mark to lose interest in a con game. **2.** To refuse to recognize someone. **3.** To stack a deck of cards. (Gambling and short-con games.)

*Chump.* See *mark.*

To *clean.* To strip, as to strip the equipment out of the store.

To *clear the book.* For the police to attempt to pin several unsolved crimes on a known criminal.

*Closed monte.* A monte game played in a store, with ropers and an insideman. Now obsolescent. See *three-card monte.*

*Coarse ones.* Large bills used to impress the mark in a big store. (Big con.)

The *cold-poke.* A mock-con game played on gun-molls for a joke. A young grifter points out an old grifter as a wealthy old gentleman and connives with the girl to steal his wallet. Meanwhile, the old man has substituted for his full wallet one filled with paper and often garnished with ribald verses. Just as the girl slips out of the night club with the wallet, the old man "beefs gun" and a hue and cry is raised after the girl. Cf. the *engineer's daughter,* the *tish.*

To *come hot.* To take a con-touch when the victim realizes he is swindled. See the *pay-off against the wall.*

*Come-on.* **1.** See *mark.* **2.** A mark who has been put on the send and is returning to be fleeced.

*Come-through.* A fleeced mark who refuses to be blown off and follows confidence men or attempts to have them arrested.

*Confidence game* or *con game.* Any type of swindle in which the mark is allowed to profit by dishonest means, then is induced to make a large investment and is fleeced.

*Con mob.* **1.** On the big con, the personnel of the big store, strictly speaking, the insideman, the manager or bookmaker, and the staff of ropers and shills. **2.** On the short con, an insideman, his ropers and handlers. Also *mob.*

*Consideration.* A straight fee paid the boost in stores where they do not work on a percentage basis.

*Convincer.* The cash which the mark is permitted to win before he is given the big play.

To *cool (a mark) out.* To pacify a mark after he has been fleeced. Most marks are kept under perfect control by the insideman. Cf. the *cackle-bladder,* the *button,* to *blow* 5, the *tear-up.*

To *cop.* **1.** v. To take money from a mark, in contrast to To *blow.* 1. **2.** v. To take, as to cop a peek, etc. **3.** n. The money which a mark is allowed to win.

To *cop a heel.* To run away. Also to *light a rag,* to *take a powder.* Cf. to *cop.*

*Copper on and copper off.* A crooked system for beating the faro-bank from the outside, worked by a mob of four—one of whom keeps the cases. The case-keeper, by means of a hair and a swivel attachment, removes the copper from a bet which he sees is going to win, thus keeping the mob from losing its money.

To *cop the short.* For a railroad conductor to accept half-fare from grifters, few of whom ever pay full fare on any transportation system. "A kinky kayducer will always cop the short."

The *count and read*. A short-con swindle in which a mark's money is examined, presumably for counterfeit bills or for premium notes, and he is fleeced by the *slide*. (q.v.)

The *countess*. Mrs. Maurer. Also the *Raggle*.

To *be coupled in the betting*. For con men to work together. Also to run as an entry.

To *crack out of turn*. **1.** For one member of a con to miss his cue and speak his lines in the wrong place. Big-con games are rehearsed like plays and each man must know his part perfectly. See to *rank a joint*. **2.** To butt in, or offer unwanted advice.

The *cross*. A short-con game in which the mark loses his money betting on the roper's ability to beat a third man at dice. Five square dice are used and the mark is played for in a saloon which is right.

*Cross-fire*. **1.** In short-con games, a conversation in argot between the insideman and the outsideman to deceive the mark and any by-standers. **2.** In big-con games, where no argot is used, conversation between the insideman and the other members of the mob for the mark's benefit. "It's really the cross-fire that beats the mark." When secret signals must be given in big-con games, they are made in the form of *offices*. (q.v.)

*Crow*. Fake or cheap. Also *snider*.

To *curdle*. For anything, especially the fix, to go wrong.

*Cush*. Money. For other specific terms relating to money, see *ridge, meg, deemer, cose, push-note, fin, sawbuck, double saw, C-note, half a C., G-note, coarse ones, soft ones*.

*Cushions*. **1.** A passenger train. **2.** The day coaches as contrasted to Pullman coaches. **3.** Reserved seats at a circus. (Short con.)

To *cut in*. **1.** intr. To break into a conversation; to accost a mark. **2.** tr. To share the profit of a con game with an outsider, as for instance someone who furnishes the names of lucrative marks.

To *cut up the score*. To divide the profits of a con game. In big-con games the lay is usually as follows: The insideman takes fifty-five per cent of the score, out of which he pays the manager ten per cent of the total, gives each of the ten or twelve shills one per cent of the total, pays the bank at least five per cent and takes care of the fix. The outsideman takes forty-five per cent of the total out of which he pays all expenses incidental to roping.

To *cut up the old scores*. To gather together and talk over old times. Also to *punch the guff*.

*Deemer*. A ten-cent piece.

*Deep-sea gamblers*. See *boat-rider*.

*Dinks*. See *block game*.

*Dip*. A pickpocket. This word, still used by old-timers, is not much used by younger pickpockets.

*Dollar store*. An early form of the present-day big-store originated by Ben Marks at Cheyenne, Wyoming, during the building of the Union Pacific Railway. The dollar store displayed valuable articles priced at one dollar in order to bring in marks, who were played for with short-con games.

The *Double-trays*. A short-con game in which the mark is roped and agrees to help fleece a gambling house with mis-spotted dice (double-trays). However, a pair of loaded *and* mis-spotted dice is slipped in to replace the originals, and the mark is fleeced.

The *ducats*. A short-con game played with five business cards. The roper connives with the mark to put a pencil mark on one card which will enable him to draw the right one and beat the insideman. But the cards are turned end for end and a duplicate pencil mark on a non-winning card misleads the mark. Also the *tickets*.

The *duke* or *huge duke*. A form of the big mitt played on railroad trains without a store. A mob of three collects marks and fleeces them one at a time in a compartment or stateroom. Probably coined by Eddie Mines, noted duke-player and big-con roper. See the *big mitt*.

*Drop-in*. Something which is easy; easy money. So-called because a fat mark may sometimes "drop in" to a confidence game without being steered.

*Ear-wigger*. Anyone who tries to overhear a conversation. Also *wiggin's*.

The *electric bar*. A swindle worked at a saloon bar with a magnetized plate and dice with metal spots so arranged as to turn up the desired numbers when the current is on.

*End*. **1**. A share of the score which is due each grifter who participates. **2**. A portion of the score taken as a bribe by the law. See to *have (someone) right*.

*The engineer's daughter*. A mock-con game played by con men for a conceited grifter. A grifter's wife or girl poses as the "engineer's daughter." The point-out is played for the victim, who finally manages to get on intimate terms with the engineer's daughter. Another con man dressed as an engineer bursts into the apartment, brandishing a pistol. The victim collects what clothing he can and rushes out into the street, where he is welcomed by all the grifters who happen to be in town. Peculiar to resort cities like Hot Springs, Arkansas. Cf. the *cold-poke*, the *tish*.

*Excess baggage*. A grifter who is incapable of discharging his duties with the mob.

*Expensing*. The process of getting payments from a mark

who believed he was hiring telegraph operators to tap wires and get race results in advance for him. Obsolete except among old-timers. (Short con.)

The *fake.* **1.** A short-con game practiced by news-butchers on trains. The prospective customer buys a cheap book for two dollars because he thinks he sees a five-dollar bill protruding from it. **2.** Also *fakus* or *Mr. Fakus.* Any cheating mechanism used in short-con games, especially on gambling devices and flat-joints.

To *fall.* To be indicted and convicted of a criminal offense.

*Faro-bank.* **1.** n. A gambling game much used by con men in which the players bet on the order in which the cards will be drawn from a dealing box. See the *last turn.* **2.** v. To take a mark's money by allowing him to win and lose, always losing more than he wins. Also to *bankroll.*

*Fight store.* An early form of the modern big store in which the roper connived with the mark to beat the insideman through betting on a fixed prize fight. Similar swindles were worked through the foot-race and wrestle stores.

*Fin.* A five-dollar bill.

To *find the leather.* See the *poke.*

*Finger-egg.* See to *put the finger on.*

*Fink.* See *mark.*

The *first count.* The total score from a con touch, the implication being that the insideman has cheated the other members of the mob. "The first count is always the best."

*Fish.* See *push-note* 1.

To *fit the mitt.* To bribe an official. See to *have (someone) right.*

*Fitted event.* The "fixed race" upon which the mark is induced to bet. See the *pay-off.*

*Fitted mitt.* A bribed official.

The *fix*. Co-operation bought from the police by a fixer. "The fix is in." See to *have (someone) right*.

*Fixer*. A local man employed by grifters to fix the law.

*Flat-joint*. A form of short-con swindle with many variations. Used extensively with circuses, fairs, etc.

*Fly-gee*. An outsider who understands confidence games, or who thinks he does.

*Flyer*. A warrant for arrest sent out simultaneously in all large cities.

The *flop*. A short-con racket sometimes worked by con men when they are short of money. Also the *hype*, the *sting*. Not to be confused with the *slide*, the *push* and the *boodle*, which work on a different principle and are restricted largely to short-con workers and circus grifters.

The *foot race*. A pay-off game now obsolete which preceded the modern big-con games. The outside man posed as the disgruntled secretary of a millionaire (the insideman) who fancied runners and bet heavily on them. The secretary offered to double-cross his employer, fix the race, and share the profits with the mark. The racer who was "fixed" to win collapsed, a "doctor" pronounced him dead, and the mark lost heavily.

*Forty-some-odd*. A pistol. Also the *odds*. See the *cackle-bladder*.

To *frame (the gaff or the joint)*. To set up the big store.

*G-note*. A $1,000 bill, used in making up the boodle. (Big con.)

*Gaff*. See *joint*.

To *get a hard-on*. To reach for a pistol.

The *give-away*. See the *high-pitch*.

To *go round the horn*. For an arrested suspect to be transferred rapidly from one police station to another to prevent his attorney from serving a habeas corpus writ.

The *gold brick*. An obsolescent con game in which a

sucker bought what appeared to be a genuine gold brick from a farmer or Indian. Also the *bat*.

*Green-goods racket*. See the *spud*.

*Grift*. **1.** n. A racket or criminal profession. Often used where grifter would not be used in a strict sense. "I've been on the grift all my life." **2.** n. A group of criminal professions which employ skill rather than violence. "All those boys were on the grift." **3.** v. To work any profession included in the grift. See *grifter*.

*Grifter*. In the strict sense, one who lives by his wits as contrasted to the heavy-men who use violence. For the professionals recognized as true grifters, see the chapter *Birds of a Feather*.

To *guide*. See to *rope*.

*Gun moll*. A thief-girl, especially a female pickpocket. The term has no connection with guns or with killings—as is sometimes suggested in the newspapers—but comes from Yiddish *gonif*, thief.

*Half a C*. A fifty-dollar bill.

*Handler*. The accomplice in a short-con game who directs the betting of the shills. (Short con.) Roughly comparable to the *manager* in the big con.

To *have smallpox*. To be wanted on a warrant; "smallpox" is said to be "catching" because anyone in the company of a wanted man may be arrested also.

To *have (someone) right*. To buy protection from an official. "The Postal Kid had the chief right for years." Also used of cities, banks, etc.: "The Yellow Kid had Rochester, Minnesota, right at that time." Also to *fix*, to *fit the mitt*, to *take*.

The *head of the joint* or *top of the joint*. The total amount taken in a single confidence touch. "Sometimes the nut comes off the head of the joint." Also the *top of the score*.

*Heat*. Trouble, especially pressure from the law or tension created by a beefing mark.

*Heavy-gee.* A professional on the heavy-rackets, usually a safeblower.

*Heavy-rackets.* Those rackets involving violence or threat of violence as contrasted to the grift. See *grift.*

*Heel-grifter.* A cheap, small-time grifter. See *grifter.*

The *high-pitch.* A short-con game involving the sale of cheap merchandise, the price of which is refunded by the operators, who then sell worthless goods at a high price and drive away. Also the *give-away.*

*The hipe* or *hype.* See the *flop.*

*Home guard.* **1.** A victim who lives in the city where the store is located. **2.** A local grifter as contrasted to an itinerant one.

To *hopscotch.* To go on the road with a confidence game. (Largely short con.)

The *hot-seat.* A British version of the American wipe in which the victim is convinced that he has been commissioned to deliver a large sum of money to the Pope. In reality he takes a parcel of newspaper, while the money he has posted as security is kept by the swindlers.

Insideman. **1.** (Big con) The member of a con mob who stays near the big store and receives the mark whom the roper brings. Insidemen are highly specialized workers; they must have a superb knowledge of psychology to keep the mark under perfect control during the days or weeks while he is being fleeced. See to *cut up the score.* **2.** (Short con) The one who operates the game by which the marks are fleeced, as the three-shell game.

*Jacket.* **1.** An entry in the police records which may stand against a criminal if he is picked up on another charge, so called from the folder or "jacket" in which the entry is filed. **2.** A tip-off, or a witness to a crime who may testify later. "We got a jacket on that one."

*Joe Hep* or *Hep.* Smart, or "wise" to what is happening. Probably ironically so called from one Joe Hep, the proprietor of a saloon in Chicago where grifters had their headquarters.

To *join out the odds.* To turn pimp.

*Joint.* **1.** A place of business (Legitimate.) **2.** A gambling house, big store, or other establishment where marks are trimmed. Also *gaff.* See *big store.* **3.** The score from a confidence game. See the *head of the joint.*

*Jug* or *jay.* A bank.

*Kicking hand.* The member of a mitt-mob who has a set line of cross-fire, grumbling and protesting because he loses. See *big mitt.*

*Kip* or *kipper.* **1.** A room, especially a hotel room; the place one lives. **2.** A bed.

To *knock (a mark).* To convince a mark that he is being swindled. "There's a mark born every minute, and five to trim him and five to knock him." Usually the term is used ironically, for all con men know that a good mark literally cannot be knocked. "That fink craved the tat and you couldn't knock him." See *mark.*

*Lagged.* Sent to prison.

*Lamster.* One who is wanted by the law.

*Larceny.* A tendency to steal; "thieves' blood."

The *last turn.* A faro-bank con game in which the dealer agrees to tip off the mark to the last turn, on which the betting is very heavy. The mark loses steadily during the early part of the game, and thus finds it impossible to recoup on the last turn. "After the mob finished with G—— R——, they turned him over to us and we gave him the last turn for $50,000." See *faro-bank* 1 and 2.

To *lay the flue.* To work a short-con swindle in which money is put into an envelope (flue) in the victim's presence, then removed through a slit. Another version swindles a merchant who changes a twenty-dollar bill and retains an envelope which he believes to contain twenty dollars. See the switch. Cf. the *bilk,* the *cold poke,* the *poke* 2, the *tish.*

To *light a rag.* See to *cop a heel.*

The *little block.* The first touch taken from a mark. Restricted to the rag. Cf. the *big block.*

*Lookout.* A member of the con mob who serves as doorman for the big store.

*Lop-eared.* Stupid. Used in reference to a victim so stupid that he cannot see his own advantage in a con game, sometimes so stupid that he cannot be trimmed. See *mark.* Cf. to *knock a mark.*

*Lugger.* See *outsideman.*

To *lug.* To steer a mark for a confidence game.

To *make.* To see or recognize.

To *make a man on his merits.* Theoretically, for a detective to be able to pick up a grifter even though he does not know him; to recognize that he is a grifter from his manners and general appearance. "Camera Eye McCarthy is the only dick in the country who can really make a man on his merits." Actually, there probably are no such detectives.

The *manager.* The member of a con mob who has charge of the big store. See *bookmaker.* (Big con only.) Cf. *handler.*

*Mark.* **1.** A victim, or intended victim. Also *apple, Bates, egg, fink, John Bates, Mr. Bates, savage, winchell, chump.* **2.** A term of disdain and opprobrium, applied to anyone. For specialized meanings see *addict, come-on, come-through, lop-eared.*

*Meg.* A one-cent piece, used in the smack.

*Mickey Finn.* Confidence men use the term to denote a very fast physic given by the bartender to cocky grifters after the toilet doors have been locked.

*Mill's lock.* A sure-thing.

To *mitt a man in.* To get a mark to bet a stack of checks

placed before him, or to bet them for him, to get him into a mitt-game. (Short con.) See *big mitt.*

*Mob.* See *con mob.*

The *money box.* A swindle in which the mark is induced to purchase a machine which he thinks will make genuine paper money. (Short con.)

*Monicker.* An underworld nickname.

*Mudkicker.* A prostitute.

*Mugged.* Photographed for the rogues' gallery.

The *mush.* A short-con game played at the ball parks. The operator poses as a bookmaker, takes money for bets, then raises his umbrella (the mush) and disappears into the maze of umbrellas in the bleachers.

*Nut.* See *cap,* to *cut up the score.*

The *nuts.* See *block game.*

The *odds.* **1.** See *forty-some-odd.* **2.** A woman, especially one who does or will support her man through prostitution.

The *office.* **1.** On the big con, a cluck with the tongue or velar fricative used as a signal among members of the mob while the mark is being played. Also, a similar sound made on the street when a con man does not want other grifters to recognize him. **2.** Any private signal, as with the eyes, or hands. For details see Section 5 of the chapter *The Mob.*

*Open monte.* Three-card monte played outside, as contrasted to closed monte. See *three-card monte.*

*Outsideman.* The member of the con mob who locates the mark, brings him to the store and assists in fleecing him. Also *lugger, roper.*

*Pack it in* or *pack the racket in.* To leave the grift for some legitimate form of business.

To *pad the cap* or *pad the nut.* For a roper to falsify his expense account. (Big con.) See to *cut up the score.*

*Panel store.* A brothel where marks are robbed.

*Paper.* A check or other negotiable document.

*Pay-off.* A big-con man.
The *pay-off.* The most lucrative of all big-con games, with touches running from $10,000 up, with those of $100,000 being common. It operates on the principle that a wealthy mark is induced to believe that he has been taken into a deal whereby a large racing syndicate is to be swindled. At first he plays with money furnished him by the confidence men, then is put on the send for all the cash he can raise, fleeced, and blown off. The pay-off (invented in 1906) evolved from the short-pay at the *track* (q.v.) and was fully developed by 1910, when the big stores appeared in many of the larger cities. See *big con.* For details see page 63.
The *pay-off against the wall.* A type of the pay-off which is played without a store, boosters, props, etc. Good confidence men can take off a touch this way, but it always comes *hot* (q.v.) and facilities for cooling the mark out are lacking.
The *peeks.* See *block game.*
*Peter.* A safe.
*Pick-up guy.* A "wise" outsider who hangs around a monte or shell game hoping to beat the operators at their own game. (Short con.) Cf. *fly-gee.*
The *pigeon.* See the *short-deck.*
*To play the C.* **1.** To get a mark's confidence. "I'll play the C for that old pappy." **2.** To operate a confidence game.
To *play the chill.* To ignore someone. "We'll play the chill for him."
To *play the hinge* or *work the hinge.* To look behind. "Don't play the hinge or you may get sneezed for it."
To *play the run-around.* See to *beat the donicker.*
*Plinger.* A street beggar.
*Pogy O'Brien.* A grifter who will not pay his debts.
*Point-out.* **1.** A method of tying up a mark for the big-con games. The outsideman points out the insideman as a

former acquaintance who has very good connections in racing or investments. **2.** An agent who locates prospective marks for a roper on a percentage basis.

The *poke.* **1.** A method of tying up the mark for the payoff or the rag. The outsideman and the mark find a pocketbook containing a large amount of money, a code-cipher, newspaper clippings describing the owner's phenomenal success in either gambling or races or in stock-market investments, and race tickets or stock receipts. (Big con.) Also to *find the leather.* **2.** A short-con game in which the mark and the outsideman find a wallet full of money. The mark is induced to raise a fund equal to the amount in the wallet to show his good faith. When he gets the pocketbook, it contains only scraps of newspaper. Now played mainly by Negroes, Gypsies and Italians.

The *prat-out.* See the *shut-out.*

To *punch the guff.* See to *cut up the old scores.*

*Push-note.* **1.** A one-dollar bill. Also *bumblebee, case-note, seed, fish.* **2.** A person who resembles someone else. "He was a push-note for John W. Gates." Also *stand-in.* Cf. to *put (someone) away.*

To *put (one's) hump up.* To stall for a pickpocket mob; that is, to use the hips to jockey the victim into position and distract his attention while his pockets are picked. Also to *stall,* to *prat (a mark) in.*

To *put (someone) away.* For a confidence man to pose as some prominent person whom he resembles, or to point out an accomplice as some prominent person.

To *put the bite on.* To try to borrow money.

To *put the finger on.* For a roper to locate a good prospective mark, especially in line at a railroad ticket office. Some ropers (especially for the tip) have agents who put up marks for them in advance and are paid a commission.

To *put the mug on (a mark).* To put a strangle-hold on a mark who grows obstreperous after he has been fleeced. Cf. the *cackle-bladder.*

To *put the shiv in the touch.* See to *cut up the score.*

The *quill.* Genuine. Cf. *crow.*

The *rag.* An intricate big-con game very similar to the pay-off, except that stocks are used instead of races. The insideman poses as an agent for a broker's syndicate which is trying to break the bucket-shops. The mark profits on several investments, is sent for a large sum of money, and is fleeced. See *big-con.*

*Raggle.* An attractive young girl.

*Rags.* Clothing.

To *raise.* To signal by raising the hat.

To *raise a mark.* To force a mark in a confidence game to raise his price by bluffing as in poker. "I was playing the hinks and I raised a mark that had a C-note in his seams. He blowed it on the run-around."

To *rank a joint.* For a grifter to make a mistake while a mark is being played for, thus revealing that the confidence game is crooked. If the mark sees the mistake and realizes what is happening, the store is then ranked. See to *crack out of turn.*

*Rat.* See *stool pigeon.*

*Ribbing hand.* The member of a mitt-mob who has a set line of humorous talk which he keeps going while the mark is being fleeced. He distracts the mark's attention from the still hand, who holds the winning cards. The ribbing hand is usually a large man, the still hand a small man. See the *big mitt.*

To *ride in (a mark).* To rope a mark and bring him to the store. See to *steer against the store.*

*Ridge.* Metal money.

*Right.* 1. As in right territory, territory protected by the fix. 2. As in right copper, one who will accept a bribe.

**3.** As in right guy, one who is trustworthy, especially one who is in sympathy with criminals. Cf. *wrong*.

To *rip and tear*. To grift without restriction in a protected or "air-tight" area.

The *rocks*. A short-con diamond swindle in which the mark is shown "stolen" diamonds and invited to have a jeweller evaluate them. The ones submitted are good, the rest are paste.

To *roll*. To rob someone, especially a drunk. Largely used of prostitutes.

To *rope*. To secure a mark for a confidence game. Also to *lug*, to *steer*, to *guide*.

*Roper*. See *outsideman*.

To *rumble*. To excite a mark's suspicions. Cf. to *knock*.

*Savage*. See *mark*.

*Sawbuck* or *saw*. A ten-dollar bill.

*Scat*. Whisky.

*Scatter*. A saloon.

*The score*. See *touch*.

*Seed*. See *push-note* 1.

The *send*. The stage in big-con games at which the mark is sent home for a large amount of money.

*Send store*. Any type of store which plays for a mark and sends him home for his money. (Short con and circus grift.) Not to be confused with big store.

To *sew a man up*. **1.** To caution a mark, who has just been beaten with a short-change racket (but doesn't know it), against pickpockets, then sew his wallet in his pocket with needle and thread carried for the purpose. (Short con.) **2.** To make any arrangements necessary to prevent the mark from causing trouble after he has been fleeced. (Big con.) See to *cool a mark out*.

The *shake*. **1.** A shakedown; extortion of money from criminals by officers. **2.** See the *shake with the button*.

The *shake with the button*. A short-con swindle in which

the mark and the operators are arrested for gambling on the street and "shaken down" by a fake officer.

*Shed.* **1.** The railroad station. **2.** Loosely, any terminal, as a bus station.

*Sheet writer.* A minor employee in a big store—usually the clerk who takes the bets.

*Shill* or *shillaber.* An accomplice who plays a confidence game so that the mark sees him win. Many con games use shills, but in the big con the shills are frequently professional confidence men who dress and act the parts of men high in the financial world.

The *shiv.* A short-con game played with a knife, the blades of which can be locked at will. Cf. the *slough.*

*Short con.* As contrasted to the big con, those games which generally operate without the send. Also *little con.*

The *short-deck.* A short-con game operated by a man who drops one card out of a deck he has offered to sell a mark very cheaply. They argue over whether or not it is a full deck, then bet. The mark thinks the deck is short one card, but the operator produces a full deck. Also the *pigeon.*

The *short pay at the track.* A crude, short-con version of the pay-off, played by race-track touts without a store, etc. See the *pay-off.*

*Short rider.* A mark who lives close to the city in which a big store is located. Big-con men usually agree with the fixer to avoid fleecing all local residents and short riders.

The *shut-out.* One stage in playing for a mark in a big store. For instance, in the pay-off, the mark goes to the window to make a bet, but is "shut out" by members of the boost who are all betting huge sums of money. By the time the mark gets to the window, the announcer says, "They're off," and betting is closed. The mark hears the race called precisely as the con men had predicted, and resolves to get his bet down on the next race at all costs. (Big con.) Also the *prat-out*.

The *single-hand con*. A short-con game played by one man who picks up an old gentleman on a train, shows him a large check, gets his confidence, borrows a sum of money with the check as security, and leaves the victim to watch the baggage.

To *sit in (with a mark)*. For a roper to feel a mark out with regard to a con game, then signal his partner to come in on the deal. (Short con.)

The *slick box*. A controlled dice game played with a roper and shills. The mark is fleeced by a skilled manipulator who controls the dice by means of a box shellacked inside. (Short con.)

The *slough*. A short-con game similar to the shiv, except that a small padlock is used.

To *slough*. To lock.

The *smack*. An intricate short-con game based on matching pennies. Big-con men often apply the principles of big-con work to it and take off scores of several thousands of dollars. See *big-con*.

*Sneezed*. Arrested.

*Soap game*. A short-con game in which the grifter appears to wrap up a twenty-dollar bill with each cake of soap he is selling. It is worked with shills and cross-fire. Said to have been invented by the notorious Soapy Smith.

*Soft ones*. Old bills used by a short-change artist to make up his boodle. (Short con.)

To *spiel the nuts*. To play the shell-game under cover of a brisk cross-fire.

The *spud*. A swindle in which the con men convince the mark that he can buy real money from a man who has stolen plates from the government. Also the *green-goods racket*.

*Square paper*. An honest person, usually a legitimate person.

*Squeeze.* A dishonest device for controlling a mechanical gambling game. (Short con.)

*Stand-in.* See *push-note* 2.

To *stand a rap for (someone).* To resemble someone closely. Cf. to *put (someone) away.*

*Starter.* A crooked dealer in a gambling house.

To *stash.* To hide something.

To *steer against a store.* To rope marks for any con game using a store.

*Stick.* A shill, especially one used in a short-con game. See *shill,* the *boost.*

To *stick up.* For detectives to question a grifter, then release him.

*Still hand.* The member of a mitt-mob who holds the winning hand. See *ribbing hand, big mitt.*

To *sting.* To take a mark's money. "We'll sting coming into St. Louis."

The *sting.* **1.** See the *hipe.* **2.** The point in a confidence game where a mark's money is taken.

*Stir.* Prison.

*Stool pigeon.* A police informer. Also *rat, fink, long-tailed rat, mouse,* and many other uncomplimentary names.

*Store.* **1.** See *big store.* **2.** Any establishment against which short-con games like the mitt or monte are played. Cf. the *big store.*

The *strap.* A short-con game played with a coiled strap, one coil of which the mark tries to catch with a pencil.

To *street.* To get a mark out of a store.

*Subway dealer.* A card-player who deals from the bottom of the deck.

*Sucker-broad.* A woman who is dishonest and unreliable, but who is not of the underworld. Cf. *gun-moll.*

*Sucker feel-out.* The constant questioning to which the mark subjects the outsideman while he is tied up. "He's got me waxy with that sucker feel-out."

*Sucker gambling house.* A gambling house not run by professionals. Sucker is used for anything not strictly professional. See *sucker-word.*

*Sucker-word.* An argot word used or misused by outsiders, and hence not generally used by professionals. For example, *stool pigeon* or *plugger* used for shill.

The *switch.* The sleight of hand by which one object is substituted for another, used in the wipe, the poke 2 and other short-con games.

To *switch.* To transfer a mark's confidence from the roper to the insideman.

To *tab.* To make note of.

*Tailer.* The armed grifter who keeps tab on the mark while he is not with the con men. See *con mob.*

To *take a powder.* See to *cop a heel.*

To *take* or *take his end.* To accept bribe money. Applied to anyone who is fixed. See to *have (someone) right.*

The *tale.* A British swindle played at the race track. An Englishman pays the con man for a lost bet, even though he did not instruct the con man to make it. Cannot be played in America owing to the difference in sporting ethics.

The *tat.* **1.** A crooked dice swindle worked by grifters in night clubs. The mark is allowed to find a die (sometimes made from a sugar cube) and is inveigled into a betting game. The tat is substituted for the square die when the operator throws and the mark is fleeced. Also *up and down Broadway.* **2.** A crooked die made with fives and sixes on all sides. It is otherwise a duplicate of the one which the mark finds.

*Taw.* A bank roll.

*T.B.* Literally, total blank; no score. "That savage from Omaha was a T.B." Also 28.

The *tear-up.* A method of blowing a mark, especially with the mitt and the duke. The roper tears up the check covering the victim's losses, saying that the man did not understand the play. This check is a duplicate and when the victim returns home he discovers that the original check has been cashed.

To *tear (someone) off.* To cheat one's partner of part of his share of a touch.

*Tell-box.* A faro dealer's crooked dealing box.

To *tell the tale.* **1.** For the insideman to tell the mark the story of his illicit dealings. (The big con.) **2.** To tell any story to a prospective victim. (Short con.)

*Three-card monte.* The well-known card swindle, worked with insideman, outsideman and shills. (Short con.) Cf. *closed monte, open monte.*

The *tickets.* See the *ducats.*

*Tie-up.* **1.** The process of keeping the outsideman constantly with the mark while he is being played. (Big con.) **2.** A mark who is being played. (Big con.)

*Tiger.* A faro-bank. To "twist the tiger's tail," to play the faro-bank.

To *tighten up (a mark).* For the insideman to give the mark a convincing talk just before he is sent home for his money. (Big con.)

*Tin-mittens.* A fixer. By implication, one who likes to hear the coin clank in his hand.

*Tip.* A crowd of people.

The *tip.* A short-con game sometimes worked by big-con men. The roper offers to help the mark fleece the insideman by tipping off his hand in a poker game. He is allowed to win a convincer, and is then faro-banked out of his money. See *big con.*

The *tish.* A mock-con game used with women. A con man puts a large bill in a woman's stocking with an admonition that she will be sorry if she takes it out before morning. She takes it out at the earliest opportunity, only to find that it has turned to tissue paper. Cf. the *engineer's daughter*, the *cold poke*, the *switch*.

*Tool*. The member of a pickpocket mob who does the actual stealing. Also the *wire*.

*Top of the joint* or *top of the score*. See *head of the joint*.

*Touch*. The money taken from a mark. Also *score*.

*Transpire*. A short-con game in which the mark is led to bet on the meaning of the word *transpire*, which the outsideman uses to mean *perspire*.

To *turn out*. **1**. tr. To train a grifter in some special line of work. "Old John Russell turned out the Yenshee Kid when he was only fifteen." **2**. intr. For a grifter to start on the rackets.

*Twist*. A woman or girl, usually one in the rackets or connected with the underworld. From the Australian twist and twirl.

To *whip*. To walk.

*Wiggin's*. See *ear-wigger*.

*Winchell*. A mark. Also used in such combinations as *willing winchell*, *winning winchell*, etc.

The *wipe*. A short-con game worked largely with Negroes, Italians or Gypsies. The victim is induced to put a large sum of money into a handkerchief, which is tied up and put away. The switch is put in and the mark finds that his money has turned into newspaper cuttings. Cf. the *poke*. 2. See the *switch*.

*Wire*. See *tool*.

The *wire*. A big-con game in which the insideman (passing as a Western Union official) convinces the mark that he can delay the race results going to the bookmakers long enough for the mark to place a bet after the race is run. The roper makes a mistake and the mark loses. Cf. the *rag*, the *pay-off*.

*Wire-tapping*. An obsolete short-con game from which the *wire* developed.

*Wrestle store.* See *fight store.*

*Wrong.* **1.** As in wrong town, one not protected by the fix. **2.** As in wrong copper, one who cannot be bribed. **3.** As in wrong guy, one who is untrustworthy, especially a stool pigeon. Cf. *right.*

*Yellow.* A telegram, especially a fake telegram used in the pay-off and the rag.

# 10

# Looking Toward the Future

Before we leave the confidence man to his work, it might be well to look into the future for a moment. No one can say with any accuracy what will happen in the days to come; we can only speculate on the basis of past events. Many different forces, some of them perhaps entirely new, will probably leave their mark on the big-time confidence games.

The present European War is already affecting international stores. First, it has practically eliminated tourist traffic in Europe and also is hampering the free movement of con men abroad. Since the international con man preys, for the most part, on wealthy tourists, his only recourse is to follow the tourist trade to safer waters—namely, South America, the West Indies or Mexico. The problem of the fix is also becoming more difficult in the face of increasing military control over civilian life. This situation will probably force many confidence men to seek other hunting grounds for the duration of the War.

War profits are already finding their way into the pockets of certain European citizens who may be depended upon to make excellent marks. It is probably only a matter of time until something very similar occurs here. Thus the second World War may produce another crop of "war babies" with corresponding profits for the confidence man.

Changes in the mode of travel seem to have little effect upon the success of modern ropers, who travel by plane, by train, by private car or by steamship and pick their victims where they find them. Once they secure a mark's confidence, it matters little how they meet him or how they transport him to the store. The faster the better, so far as the con men are concerned.

Recent federal legislation against securing passports under false names will probably seriously hamper the activities of confidence men and deep-sea gamblers who rope for the big con. For, once they reveal their true identity, they run the very grave danger of arrest by federal officials on an old charge or social ostracism on shipboard, for no con man can work effectively if a whole shipload of passengers is pointing him out as the notorious so-and-so. Neither of these obstacles is insurmountable, however; con men have overcome many more serious ones in the past.

The increasing interest of federal authorities in the activities of confidence men is undoubtedly making itself felt. The Post Office Department has built up a reputation for deadliness whenever con men infringe upon the mails-to-defraud laws. In addition to this, federal operatives now have other effective weapons with which to attack the problem, not the least of which is a booming campaign of propaganda designed to rob the criminal of the sympathetic public opinion he has for so long enjoyed. In some localities where the local fix has been secure for years the unsuspecting fixer has been hustled off to federal prison for simple income-tax evasion. For this reason con men have grown rather wary of local fixing whenever there is a conflict between local and federal authorities. Thus many cities which have been reliably "right" for years have suddenly become inhospitable. This is not really a new problem facing confidence mobs, for the same thing has happened sporadically in the past. The con mobs survived the purge of Council Bluffs, Colorado Springs, Reno and Denver. Other cities were simply "righted up," headquarters were moved, and the big store went on. It remains to be seen what effect federal pressure applied simultaneously to all the important American centers for confidence men might have.

There is at present a determined movement on the part of the Federal Government to cut off the wire service from race-tracks to legitimate bookmakers. Should this move succeed, confidence men, specifically those operating the pay-off, might be somewhat inconvenienced for a time. They could rest assured, however, that very shortly illicit or "bootleg" service would be common enough that the mark would not be suspicious of a big store set up with what appeared to be illegal service. It is even possible that the outlawing of legitimate track-service might work in favor of the pay-off men.

Confidence games are cyclic phenomena. They appear, rise to a peak of effectiveness, then drop into obscurity. But they have yet to disappear altogether. Sooner or later they are revived, refurbished to fit the times, and used to trim some sucker who has never heard of them. In the past, short-con games—literally hundreds of them—have gone through this cycle, some several times over. Just as it appears that the gold-brick game is a chestnut and worthless, some operators in Texas revamp it and take $300,000 from a group of financiers and bankers; just when the wipe appears to be effective only for small touches among ignorant Negroes and immigrants, a sharp short-con worker polishes it up a bit and takes $1,500 from a sophisticated movie star. Just as this is being written, a pair of con men in Mexico City are trying to revive the old *Spanish prisoner* con game on a wholesale basis, using *Who's Who* as their sucker list. The big-con games are probably here to stay for some time, though, like the fight and foot-race games, they may ultimately be superseded by others more effective. The wire, not much used at present, may be at any time revived by con men with new ideas and made into a first-rate swindling device. However, the pay-off and the rag are still king among con games; they are being constantly improved and perfected; they show no tendency to fall into disuse. The principles on which they operate are so sound and the results they produce are so satisfactory that it is probable that, until another Ben Marks or Buck Boatwright appears with some effective innovation, they or games very much like them will dominate the big-con field exclusively.

Confidence men trade upon certain weaknesses in human nature. Hence until human nature changes perceptibly there is little possibility that there will be a shortage of marks for con games. So long as there are marks with money, the law will find great difficulty in suppressing confidence games, even assuming that local enforcement officers are sincerely interested. Increased legal obstacles have, in the past, had little ultimate effect upon confidence men, except perhaps to make them more wary and to force them to develop their technique to a very high level of perfection. As long as the political boss, whether he be local, state or national, fosters a machine wherein graft and bribery are looked upon as a normal phase of government, as long as juries, judges and law enforcement officers can be had for a price, the confidence man will live and thrive in our society.

DAVID W. MAURER was a professor of Linguistics at the University of Louisville until his death in 1981. His other books included *Whiz Mob* and *Kentucky Moonshine*.

LUC SANTE is the author of *Low Life*, an acclaimed account of New York's underworld; the memoir *The Factory of Facts*; and *Evidence*. He lives in Brooklyn, New York.